Also by Gene Wojciechowski:

Pond Scum and Other Vultures: America's Sportswriters Talk About Their Glamorous Profession

Nothing but Net
(with Bill Walton)

It Takes Balls to Make It in This League
(with Pam Postema)

I Love Being the Enemy

A Season on the Court
with the NBA's Best Shooter
and Sharpest Tongue

———

Reggie Miller

with **Gene Wojciechowski**

Simon & Schuster
New York London Toronto Sydney Tokyo Singapore

SIMON & SCHUSTER
Rockefeller Center
1230 Avenue of the Americas
New York, NY 10020

First Simon & Schuster paperback edition 1999

SIMON & SCHUSTER and colophon are
registered trademarks of Simon & Schuster Inc.

Designed by Meryl Levavi/Levavi & Levavi

Manufactured in the United States of America

10 9 8 7 6 5 4 3 2 1

Library of Congress Cataloging-in-Publication Data is available.

ISBN 13: 978-0-6848-7039-7 (pbk)

To my family: Saul Sr., Carrie, Saul Jr., Darrell, Cheryl,
and Tammy; to my teammates; but most of all,
with love and passion, to my wife, Marita.
—R. M.

To Cheryl
—G. W.

Acknowledgments

The authors would like to thank Spike Lee; Arn Tellem; the amazing Gail D'Agostino; Jeff Neuman, who is the M. J. of editors; Art Kaminsky; Janet Pawson, who earned a letter sweater for contract law; Scott Waxman; Famer Cheryl Miller; Indiana Pacers Community Relations Director Kathryn Jordan, who deserves a raise; Pacers Media Relations Director David Benner, the only NBA P.R. guy with a bodyguard; Larry Brown, who, on being informed about the book project, told the coauthor, "If there's anything I can help you with, let me know," and, "Reggie, huh? You've got yourself a character"; Donnie Walsh; T. L. Mann; Dan Dunkin; Steve Brunner; Scott Howard-Cooper; Mark Heisler; Rick Majerus; Billy Crystal; Joe Wojciechowski; Frank Scatoni; Bill Benner; Ivan Maisel; Ian O'Connor; Jan Hubbard; Peter Vecsey; and, of course, to Knicks fans everywhere—thanks for booing.

Foreword: Reggie & Me

It all began so innocently: Game one, the New York Knicks vs. the Indiana Pacers, Madison Square Garden. I had seen Reggie a couple of times when they came into town. We had said, "What's up?" and that's about it. This guy from a news station in town wanted us to do an interview together, a live remote for the six o'clock news. At the end of it, we agreed to a bet: If the Pacers won, I would put Reggie's wife in my new film, *Clockers.* If the Knicks won, Reggie would have to visit Mike Tyson in prison.

Fast forward to game five. The Knicks and the Pacers are tied two games apiece. The Knicks are ahead, but Reggie starts to go berserk. He's throwing up threes left and right. Starks, Hubert Davis, and Derek Harper are all trying to defend Reggie, but it doesn't matter. And while he's doing this, Reggie is also raining profanities upon my ears. He's calling me everything but a child of God. He gives me the choke sign with his hand and grabs his crotch with his other hand. And to be honest, I didn't do anything to provoke him, but I wasn't going to sit like a bump on a log, so I began to yell back. Regardless, the Pacers won, dealing the Knicks a crushing defeat. The Pacers now led the series 3–2 and were going home to the crazed Market Square Arena. I was vilified in the New York dailies and blasted on the sports radio station, WFAN. Of course, Reggie fanned this by saying I had a big mouth and I ought to be quiet sometimes. I thought, *Me* be quiet? Reggie talks more trash than anybody!

I fly to Indianapolis and when I get off the plane, six local television crews are waiting for me. One idiot asks me where I am staying. I said, "The Governor's Mansion." He replied, "Which wing?" I snapped, "In the slave quarters." From the airport, I went to the prison and spent several hours visiting Mike Tyson. We both got jeered by prison guards and inmates. They were saying the Knicks' season would be over after tonight.

The newspapers called my office and wanted my comments on the fact that my face would be given out on sixty-thousand masks. I calmly responded that I didn't want anyone to lose their membership in the Klan by putting a black mask in front of their face. Needless to say, it was a highly charged atmosphere.

Throughout the game, I was constantly being heckled by the Pacers' fans. I didn't care, and I was on Reggie the whole game. Nobody expected the Knicks to come back to New York tied for game seven, but we did. With police escort, I was led from my front row courtside seat with arms raised triumphantly. I looked for Reggie but he was avoiding me at all costs.

Game seven, we prevailed: Reggie committed a key turnover, Patrick dunked a Starks miss over the heads of the entire team, and it was over. Reggie and I hugged at midcourt. We both apologized for getting caught up. He went to the losers' locker room, and the Knicks went on to lose to Houston in the Finals.

Fast forward to the 1994–95 playoffs: Knicks and Pacers, game one.

We got this one in the bag; it's gonna be a breeze. Then lightning—I mean Reggie Miller—strikes. Threes from everywhere. Reggie steals, knocks people down for balls, and gets no calls (of course). How in the hell could we lose with under two minutes and an eight-point lead? REGGIE MILLER! The horn sounds, bedlam erupts, and Reggie is running straight toward me like a rabid dog. Again he's cursing me out, and is finally held back by the Pacers' strength coach. I'm in shock, so are nineteen-thousand-plus in the Garden. Reggie runs off the court yelling, "Choke, choke, choke." I'm thinking, "This is getting out of hand."

Fast forward to game seven. Reggie, as usual, is lighting the Knicks up. We come back. We get the ball, seconds left: Patrick gets an inbounds pass, he moves, spins, puts up a layup, and the ball rolls off the rim. Pacers beat the Knicks. I go out and congratulate Reggie and Larry Brown. They won it. They deserved to win. Reggie Miller finally beats the Knicks.

I enjoy his playing, I respect his game . . . his mouth, well, people say I got a big mouth also. It's funny, wherever I go all over the country people ask me, "Where is Reggie Miller?" People might be asking him the same about me, who knows? We're linked together, basketball player and fan.

—Spike Lee
Brooklyn, NY
Summer, 1995

I
Love
Being
the
Enemy

September 1994

Friday, September 11
Indianapolis

It should have been us, not the New York Knicks, in the NBA Finals. It should have been us against the Houston Rockets for the world championship. It should have been us playing for the ring.

Should have been . . .

Could have been . . .

Instead, we got beat by New York in the '94 Eastern Conference Finals. And the year before that we got beat by New York in the first round of the playoffs.

I'm telling you right now, I hate the Knicks. Absolutely hate those kids.

I'm not saying we would have won the world title, but we should have been there to find out. Instead, we lost to the same team for the second straight year. Three games to one in '93, four games to three this past June.

I cried in the locker room after the game seven loss in New York, and it still hurts to think about both of those series. I guess every team has its demons. The Knicks are ours.

I never used to hate the Knicks. But then came the '93 play-off series against them, and all that changed. Now I can't stand that team.

They beat us in that best-of-five series, but not before John Starks made a complete ass of himself—which, if you think about it, isn't unusual. I had never had any problems with Starks before that series. He had always played hard, tough basketball, and I respected that. But on the first play of the first game, I drove to the hoop and he gave me a shot in the back.

"Whoa, John, what's up?" I said.

"It's going to be like that all the goddamn series," he said.

Hey, I figure, it's the playoffs, so I let it go.

On the second play of the game, I got to the top of the key, made a move to the hoop, and he fouled me again, giving me an elbow to the throat. Two plays, two fouls.

I looked at him, and he said, "Bitch, it's going to be like that all series. I'm just going to let you know that right now."

Well, first of all, you don't ever call me "bitch." I call *you* that. That's *my* game, my house. I'm listening to Starks and I'm thinking, "This guy don't know who he's dealing with."

Those two fouls changed my whole way of thinking about those guys. I went into that series not knowing if we could beat the Knicks, but those first couple of plays changed my whole attitude. They beat us, but their intimidation tactics didn't make the difference. They were the New York Knicks, and we were the small-market Pacers, but once the series started it was just basketball, and that stuff didn't give them any edge. That gave us confidence, and that series was the last time I ever questioned myself and our team. It was also the last time Starks was stupid enough to call me "bitch."

Game one of that series was the beginning of the ongoing Starks-Reggie confrontation. I didn't start it, he did, but damn if I was going to let him get the last word. From then on I tried to make life hell for the Knicks—especially Starks.

I scored 36 in a three-point loss in game one. It wasn't just the points, though; I was in a zone just talking shit. I don't

think about what I say. It just comes out. It's best when I don't
have any set things to say, it's just natural.

In that first game when I started to get on a roll and I was
scoring point after point, I'd look at the scoreboard and say to
Starks, "Miller 26, John Starks 5. You ever gonna score tonight?"

That would piss me off if someone said that to me. And I
know it pissed off Starks. But I wasn't about to let up, so I told
him, "You should have never touched me in the first place. In
fact, I think you kind of like me."

Oh, man, you could see him steaming. And every time I said
something to him, I made sure I turned and acted like I was
talking to the referee. That way if he decided to try something,
the referee would see him do it. Hey, it's a war out there. You
play every angle you can.

We lost game two, too. One more defeat and we were out.
We went back to Indianapolis for game three, and it was close.
One time there was a loose ball, and Starks stuck his feet out
to trip me. I jumped over his feet because I knew what he was
trying to do. I fell, and as I was rolling I made sure I kicked him
in the face. I just wanted him to know that I was on to his
cheap shit.

He got up all upset, but the referee didn't see the kick because I was sliding on the ground. But I'll admit it: I was purposely trying to kick him in the face, but only because he tried
to knock me over with that move of his.

A couple of plays later he came down the lane—this was in
the third quarter, and the game was close—and made a very
nice move and then a nice shot over me. I thought, "That's
kind of sweet." I kind of elbowed him on the play as we were
running down the court, and, well, he snapped.

If you look at the videotape, you'll see him running at me,
pointing at me like some psycho man. It was hilarious. The
whole time I was thinking, "This is going to be the perfect opportunity to bait this bitch into something."

So I walked up to him like I was going to confront him. Then

I put my hands up real quick like I wanted no part of him. Jimmy Clark, one of the refs, was looking at me. All of a sudden, John head-butts me. Starks's little hollow head didn't hurt, but I didn't want Clark to know that, so I do some Academy Award–level acting and fall out of bounds from the supposed force of Starks's mighty pop. It was a great fake fall. You would have thought I'd been shot in battle, that I'd suffered a concussion, that I needed a CAT scan.

Of course, Clark teed Starks up with a flagrant foul and then kicked him out of the game. Our crowd went nuts, and so did Patrick Ewing and Charles Oakley. They were pushing Starks and saying, "How dumb can you be, you dumbass?" That's because the score was tied at the time. After that, they were dead.

Rolando Blackman came in, and I knew he had no chance of guarding me. Too old. Then they sent in Hubert Davis, who was a rookie at the time. Too young. I scored 36, and we won, 116–93.

That was one of those games where I felt I couldn't miss a shot. It also was the first time I ever felt in a shooting zone at home. I've always shot well on the road, gotten into one of those zones, but never at home. I don't know why. That's really wild, isn't it, to play much better on the road?

I was making everything that game—an absolute shooting frenzy. I remember getting the ball right in front of the Knicks' bench at the "short three." (Before they changed the three-point line, the "short three" was the shortest distance, twenty-two feet, to the hoop.) I could hear the crowd and the fans yelling, "Three!" Then I heard Charles Oakley on the bench yelling, "Reggie! Reggie!"

I took the shot, and soon as the ball left my hands—and remember, the ball hadn't even gone through the net yet—I turned around and said to Oakley and the rest of them, "Take this, you bitches. You bitches aren't as tough as you say you are."

Well, the ball was still in the air. I just stood there talking shit to them. Pat Riley was standing right there, and I was telling his team, "You bitches aren't as tough as everybody says you are." Fans behind the bench were going crazy, and Oakley was busting up laughing at me. I must have cried when I saw the tape of that. But the ball went right through—all net. I must have looked like a madman, but when I step on the court I become a different person. Always have been that way.

That's how it was in our seven-game series against the Knicks in June. People say it was the best series of the entire playoffs that year, and I think they're right. I just wish I could have changed one thing: the ending.

The Pacer losses in games one and two were definitely my fault. Going into the series, I tried to be Mr. Nice Guy. After what happened the year before—the trash talking, the head-butting incident with Starks, getting Starks ejected—I said to myself, "We're in the Eastern Conference Finals now. I'm going to show New York that I can play a straight-up game. I'm not going to talk shit. I'm not going to do those antics. I'm just going to play basketball. I'm going to see how that is. I'm just going to beat them with my basketball talent."

The year before I didn't do that. Yeah, I scored some points and got Starks thrown out, but we lost the series, so none of that meant a thing. Face it: The Knicks are dirty players. Let me take that back. They're not dirty players, but when things aren't going New York's way, they're going to do whatever it takes to win. And if that means hurting someone, then they'll do it. That's what makes them the Knicks. I'm not going to say that's dirty, but sometimes they take it to the extreme. But I was determined not to let any of that bother me. I kept telling myself: Just play basketball. I was going to play the game and prove that I didn't need any of that other stuff.

Dumb move. In game one, I had 16 points. We lost by 11.

In game two, I had 20 points. We lost by 11.

I was scoring okay, but I wasn't playing Reggie Miller–type basketball. From Gar Heard to Billy King to George Irvine, who are our assistant coaches, to some of my teammates, guys like Vern Fleming and Sam Mitchell, everyone was telling me, "You need to play the way you know how to play. You just can't be going through the motions and not getting on us and not talking shit to them. You need to play like Reggie Miller."

I was listening to them, saying, "Yeah, yeah," but I already had my mind made up.

But the thing that really got to me was when my sister Cheryl called. It was the first time she ever called to jump all over me. Usually she just calls to give me tips: "Reggie, you're falling away on your shot." That sort of thing. But this was different. This time she was disgusted with the way I was playing. She said I had always been a man's man, but now I was being too nice. I was helping the Knicks out. I wasn't taking the ball to the basket. I wasn't shooting enough. She said the only reason I was out there was that they needed five Pacers on the floor. She said I was doing exactly what the Knicks wanted me to do.

Then she really criticized me.

"What in the hell are you doing?" she said. "Don't you know you're in the Eastern Conference Finals, that you're playing the New York Knicks? You think you can just go through the motions with them? What in the hell have the New York Knicks won? Did they win the championship last year?"

"No," I said.

"Did they win the championship the year before that?" she said.

"No."

"Did they win the championship the year before that? I mean, what the hell have they won? When's the last time they won anything?"

I was listening to this and *bam,* it hit home. "Damn . . . yeah, you've got a point there. If I need to go out there and cuss somebody out, then I'm gonna cuss somebody out."

So we went back to Indiana for game three, and that's when

the series really started. I got into foul trouble in game three and ended up with 15 points; still, we held them to 68 points and won by 20. Then in game four I had 34 points, and I knew then that everything was going to be okay. The series was tied, 2–2, and we were headed back to New York for another game.

It was crazy. We were staying at the Plaza Hotel, and when we got off the buses, there were photographers and fans everywhere. People were screaming things at me, but I loved it. Oh, my God, I wanted to play the game right then. I was in New York, the media capital of the world. The Knicks fans were yelling things like, "Starks is gonna shut you down! You ain't nothing!" I just soaked it in.

I knew something weird was going to happen in game five, because that day everything went wrong for me, from room service to being late for the shootaround to all the media asking all the wrong questions. Everything was just going bad that day. I was wondering what else could go wrong.

Then I got on the court, and everything seemed perfect. Going into the fourth quarter I was 6 of 16 from the field, but it was a good 6 of 16. Every shot I took looked good and felt good. I actually thought I was scoring better than I was.

We were down by 12 going into the last period, so I said to myself, "You've got to do something to spark this team. You're either going to shoot us in or you're going to shoot us out, but you've got to take the fall, whichever which way."

At the beginning of the fourth quarter, with the score 70–58, I ducked behind a screen set by Kenny Williams and hit my first three-pointer of the quarter. Starks, who was supposed to be guarding me, couldn't get through in time.

When I hit the first one, Spike Lee, who sits at courtside and considers himself the Knicks' number one fan, was yelling at me, "That's luck, man." I just looked at him and started smiling. We had a bet: If we won the series, my wife Marita would get a role in his next movie. If the Knicks won, I'd have to visit Mike Tyson in prison in Indiana.

Then, with Hubert Davis in for Starks, I hit a second three, and I gave Spike a look like, "We're starting to come back." He said, "Aw, y'all ain't gonna do nothing."

About a minute later I noticed Greg Anthony was on me. I drove right, pulled up, and hit from about fifteen feet out. I have five or six inches on Anthony, so it was no problem getting a shot off over him.

Then I hit a wide-open twenty-footer. Then a twenty-seven-footer from up top, which put us ahead, 75–72. That's when the famous choke sign made an appearance. I grabbed my neck with both hands and looked at the crowd, telling it that New York was gagging, that it had no balls.

After that third three went in, I could have tried a hook shot from half-court and it would have gone in. It didn't matter who was trying to guard me—Starks, Derek Harper, Anthony, Davis—I didn't care. It felt as if everything was in slow motion, like I was lifted above the court and I could see plays before they actually happened: a back door, a cut, anything. It was weird.

I finished with a playoff career high of 39 points, 25 of them in the fourth period, 5 of them three-pointers, and we won the game 93–86. When it was over, I slammed the ball down really hard. Bill Murray was there, and I said to him, "I swear, this is like another *Groundhog Day*." He busted up laughing. Remember that movie? Things kept happening over and over and over again. That's how it was in the fourth quarter. I just kept making those shots.

Afterward, when we were on the team bus and then on the plane, people kept saying, "Man, I can't believe the things you were saying out there." But I couldn't remember anything I said. I had a terrible migraine headache after the game. People were saying, "Man, you were in a zone." Well, if that's how the zone is, then I hate the after-zone, because my head was killing me.

We were up, 3–2, in the series, but then we relaxed. We

went home to Indiana and lost by 7. Then we went back to New York and got beat by 4. End of season.

I flew back with the team to Indianapolis and then the next day flew to New York to do the Letterman show. That was a strange experience.

Letterman was talking to me during the interview, and out of nowhere he started asking me about Spike Lee. Well, I was getting ready to rip Spike when I saw David looking over my shoulder. All the time he was saying, "You know, the quarrel between you and Spike. . . . What's that about?" I was thinking, "What the hell is he looking at?"

I turned around and there was Spike coming out, and he was holding a Starks jersey. I was saying, "Oh, God. How funny is this?"

The New York papers and fans really ripped into Spike for inspiring me into that game five performance. But that's ridiculous. Sure, he was talking some shit to me—still does—but that's fine. I wish more teams had fans like Spike Lee. He pays his money, and he's there night after night. You can't fault him because he's the Knicks' number one fan. He got a lot of flak about talking shit to me and then having me go for 39. They were ready to lynch him. It was front-page news. Even today I kid him: "Man, your movie *Crooklyn* was sagging at the box office until I started going off on you. If it hadn't been for me, that movie would never have gotten over the hump."

And if it weren't for the Knicks, we would have gotten over the playoff hump. But we didn't. Maybe we weren't ready. Maybe we were scared to win. I don't know the answer. I do know that this is going to be our year. I'm going to make sure of it—Knicks or no Knicks.

October 1994

Wednesday, October 5
Indianapolis

Where's Michael when you really need him? Here it is, the beginning of my eighth season with the Pacers, and there's no Michael Jordan. No one to look up to.

He retired in 1993, but I say he was forced out by the media and all the pressure of just being Michael. For instance, if you and I were to go to Atlantic City during the Eastern Conference Finals, which is what Michael did one time, nobody would care. I mean, he is a night owl anyway, but because it's Michael Jordan, it's front-page news in all the newspapers and the top item on every sportscast. Then his father dies and the first thing that comes out, the first thing anybody says or thinks, is that the death was gambling related. Nothing but allegations.

That is so cold, so inconsiderate of a person who has created such a mystique, such a legacy in the NBA. This kid made basketball the number one sport in the country, and that's how you treat your number one player? You'd think common decency would keep people from asking that question first. But it didn't. The whole thing was ridiculous.

There are a lot of great two-guards—shooting guards, as opposed to point guards—in this league, but nobody, absolutely nobody, pumped me up like Michael. I wish he had never retired. He was my man. I loved playing against him. I scored 42 and then 44 points against him, and that's when I knew I could play against anybody in the league.

Now he's playing minor-league baseball or out on some golf course working on his short game, and I'm without my favorite measuring stick. I mean, John Starks? Puh-leeaaassse. You measure yourself against Michael, nobody else.

I still spend part of every summer hanging with Michael. I watch him shoot commercials, play cards, whatever. I wish he'd come back. I was thinking of Michael because tomorrow I leave for training camp. We're going to the University of North Carolina, where Michael played.

Has it been eight seasons for me already? I still remember the day I went to Indiana to sign my first contract. I had been working out at UCLA, playing against the pros at the daily jam sessions. UCLA kept the same team, and the pros came in and played us. You'd have all the Lakers and some other guys, too, like Isiah Thomas, Kiki Vandeweghe, and Mark Aguirre. Everybody lived in Los Angeles during the summer, so we'd all meet at UCLA at three o'clock and practice from three to five. Still goes on today. The UCLA team stays together, and you have two sets of pro teams. Winners' court and losers' court.

From the time I was a freshman at UCLA, Byron Scott, Michael Cooper, and Magic Johnson took me under their wings and told me if I wanted to be successful, what I had to do was test my game against the best. I thought, "Man, these guys play on the Los Angeles Lakers, the team of the '80s. Just listen to them and learn."

They had won NBA championships, and they really knew

what they were talking about. The day before I left, Coop came and said he wanted to talk to me. So we got in his car, and he said, "Well, you're getting ready to make your big step."

He sounded like my father.

"Yeah," I said. "I'm scared, I'm nervous."

"Don't be nervous, because the players in the NBA already perceive you one way. They already think you have an attitude."

Basically what he was saying was, "They already think you're a dick." That's good, I guess.

He said, "So when you get there, don't change. You got good players there, like Herb Williams, Chuck Person. Listen to those guys, learn from those guys, but don't back down."

I wasn't about to back down, especially after the way some of the fans in Indiana reacted after the Pacers drafted me in 1987. They booed.

I was at my parents' Riverside, California, house, and we had a live hookup with the TV people. My sister Cheryl, myself, and my mom and dad were on the living room couch. Cheryl and I had the live hookup—you know, with the ear wire, so we could hear people talking back and forth. They got to the tenth selection, and I heard one of the announcers say to the director, "Oh, we're going to go to them? He's number eleven?"

So Cheryl and I knew the Pacers were going to pick me with the eleventh pick, but the people watching the draft on TV didn't know. Cheryl looked at me and said, "Just act surprised when they call your name." So they said, "The number eleven pick, Reggie Miller. Indiana Pacers."

Well, I was all excited. Yeah, great, and all that. I did the TV interview, and then the next day I flew to Indianapolis, got off the airplane, grabbed a local paper, and saw the stories about the draft: "Miller Booed" and "Walsh Criticized." Donnie Walsh is the team president.

Now you have to remember this was the same year Indiana

University won the national championship, so everybody in the state wanted the Pacers to pick Steve Alford, who was Mr. Basketball in Indiana and the Hoosiers' hot shooting guard.

To tell you the truth, I had no idea the Pacers were serious about drafting me. I went to visit Indiana, and they barely talked to me. I really thought I was going to Philadelphia with the sixteenth pick. Philly was my last visit, and I was sure I was going to play there. I was so sure that I started thinking, "I'm going to be playing with Charles Barkley. I can't wait."

Kevin Johnson and I had been traveling together to the different teams, and we got invited to the NBA pre-draft camp in Waikiki. We were on the West team, and I knew I had to prove to the scouts there that I could play two-guard. They wanted to know if I could put the ball on the floor because they knew I wasn't big enough (six feet seven, 185 pounds) to play small forward in the pros as I had in college.

Sure, my numbers were good coming out of UCLA. (At the time I was second on the school's all-time scoring list, behind Kareem Abdul-Jabbar—officially, Lew Alcindor back then.) I averaged 25.9 points as a junior, 22.3 as a senior, and led the team in scoring three consecutive seasons. But I still had to show the pro scouts I could do more than shoot jumpers.

Well, I dominated that camp. I wanted to make a big enough impression so I'd move up to lottery territory, but the chances of that weren't good because those things are usually etched in stone. The Clippers had the third pick, and they took Reggie Williams, who was a big bust. They could have had me. In fact, I visited them, Dallas, Philly, and Indiana.

Back then you'd give blood each time and then work out for all those teams. You were giving blood, working out, and trying not to faint. It isn't like today when you give one blood test and they give the results to all the teams.

Through it all, Indiana never acted as if they were interested in me. So when they picked me, I didn't know how to react. Don't get me wrong. I was excited to go to Indiana, especially when you jump from number sixteen to number eleven in the draft. That's a big jump. I was pumped.

Then it hit me.

Holy shit . . . Indiana. Except for going to South Bend to play Notre Dame, I'd never seen much of Indiana. I kept saying, "If it's anything like South Bend, I'm in trouble." I mean, there isn't anything to do in South Bend except wear Notre Dame plaid and wave to Touchdown Jesus. The place is in the middle of nowhere. But Indianapolis was nice. Compared to South Bend, anyplace was nice.

Anyway, I got there for my press conference, and was looking at the newspapers and watching the TV news. Everybody was saying the same thing: "What do we need Reggie Miller for? We need a shooting guard, not a small forward." They were like killing me. They wanted Steve Alford, the home state hero.

But I loved it. I loved the controversy. Chuck Person knew about me. He was telling the Pacers, "Get Reggie. Get Reggie."

I went to the press conference, and I was all excited. I said all the right things. They asked me about Alford, and I said that it was Alford's problem, not mine. That was in June.

At the time, the Pan Am Games were about to start in Indianapolis. My UCLA teammate Pooh Richardson was on that USA team, and they were traveling around playing against the pros to get ready for the games. One of those exhibitions was at Market Square Arena in Indianapolis, and I really wanted to play in it. I didn't have a contract at the time, but Donnie Walsh called me up and said, "It's no big deal; if you want to play in the game, you can. Do what you want to do."

I was thinking, "I have to play in this game. I've got to show the Hoosiers I can play this game."

My dad said, "What are you thinking? You don't have a contract."

Arn Tellem, my agent, said, "Hell, no. Why would you want to do that? This is going to make your value go down."

I said, "Look, guys, this is something I have to do. Right or wrong, I've got to go there and play."

So I went and played. It was a sold-out arena. Isiah was playing, which meant another familiar face. I went up to him before the game and said, "Zeke, man, I'm real nervous." And he said, "Look, it's a little too late to be nervous now. It's showtime. Just tune everybody else out and play the game like you know how to play."

They introduced the players, and when they got to me, I'd say it was about 75 percent cheers and 25 percent boos.

I went out and hit my first shot. As soon as I did that, everybody went crazy. I played well. Played maybe fifteen minutes or so. I remember saying, "What a relief." And then Donnie said, "That took a lot of balls."

I could have held out like a lot of rookies do, try to get mine before I've shown them anything. But I thought it was important to show that I wasn't like those other guys. I wasn't a spoiled rookie. I wasn't Steve Alford, either. I was Reggie. Take it or leave it.

Not long after I got to Indianapolis, I heard that Washington was going to trade Jeff Malone, who was playing for them at the time, to Denver for Fat Lever, and then they were going to pick me. I was never going to make it to Philly anyway. I would have been their two-guard, but Indiana picked me. To tell you the truth, I was glad Indiana picked me, because it gave me a chance to play, but not so fast that I'd have the pressure of carrying a team. I played every game my rookie year, though I think I started only one game when John Long got hurt. I played in eighty-two games, and I learned a lot about the game under him. Most rookies go in and have to produce instantly, and when they don't, they're considered a bust.

Rookies today get paid way too much money. They need to spread some of that out to the veterans who made sure there was money there for them. There's way too much money for those rookies. I'm not saying some of them don't deserve it, but there's no way a rookie who hasn't played a minute in a game yet should make the most money on the team like some of these guys do. That's nuts.

I was lucky. I got a chance to learn about the system and about different players. Then the second year I started. But I've played for six different coaches. That's not so lucky. There was Jack Ramsay for a season, then Mel Daniels for two games, then George Irvine for half a season, then Dick Versace for a year and a half, then Bob Hill for two-plus years, then Larry Brown.

Jack Ramsay was probably the best basketball technician. He really knew the game, but a lot of people felt his techniques were really old. I know he won a championship in Portland back in the '70s, but by the time he got to Indiana, many of his teachings were outdated. As far as knowing the game and knowing the players, he was probably one of the best, but his coaching methods needed some updating.

Versace . . . he was, uh . . . well, he probably had the best vocabulary of all of them. Some people think he conned his way into getting the Pacers job. He was in Detroit with Chuck Daly and Ron Rothstein when the Bad Boys were in power. I know lots of guys didn't like him.

Then there's Larry. Larry believes in team basketball. He believes everyone on the floor should know everybody else's position. It's like a quarterback knowing what a halfback should do on a play or what an offensive lineman should do. If Dale Davis, our power forward, gets isolated on the wing, he should be able to take his man off the dribble. At least that's the theory. Or if I'm down on the post and the ball is thrown down to me on the post, I should be able to post up. Larry wants us to be able to adjust and react to any situation on the court. The more we know about another guy's position, the better we can do that.

Larry is a perfectionist and good at motivating players. And X's and O's? Probably the best I've ever had. Right now, if you took all the coaches in the game, Larry has to rank in the top two or three. He's that good.

Thursday, October 6
Chapel Hill, North Carolina

First day of training camp.

We're here at North Carolina because this is where Larry and Donnie went to school back when the players wore those little game shorts with belts. Nice place, though, this Dean Dome. Nicer than some NBA arenas.

I know this is going to be a tough training camp, mostly because of our own expectations and because I know Larry. By the way, Larry is feeling pretty good these days. He signed his new five-year contract on the plane down here this afternoon.

Just about every one of the preseason basketball magazines is picking us to win the Central Division and challenge for the Eastern Conference title. One of the preseason guides even has us in the NBA Finals. We should have been there last year. Have I mentioned I hate the Knicks?

So here we are. To tell you the truth, it seems as though the season was just over a few days ago. After reaching the conference finals and then going directly to Dream Team II and the World Championship of Basketball, well, I'm not going to lie, I'm anxious, but I'm also very fatigued. I've been going nonstop for nearly a year, and I need time to recharge my battery.

I've already talked to Larry and Donnie about my concerns. I told them I didn't think my body could handle too grueling a training camp. They knew what I meant—I don't want to leave camp a physical wreck. So we compromised. We have two-a-day practices for the next seven days, so I'll probably practice in the morning, do the warmup drills for the evening session, and then sit out the rest of the workout. At least that's the plan.

I know there are going to be times when I'll feel good and want to keep working. I just have to pace myself.

Sunday, October 9
Chapel Hill

Every day the same schedule. Morning practice from 9 to 11:30. Evening practice from 5:45 to 8.

We're having a great training camp. That's what happens when everybody's on the same page and making the same commitment. Everybody is pumped up.

We've had a taste of what it's like to advance through the playoffs. We came within a victory—hell, within thirty seconds—of reaching the NBA Finals. Now we think we have a chance to take the next step.

We've added a few new faces: Mark Jackson, whom I've known since high school, came here from the Clippers. I played against him when I was at UCLA and he was with St. John's, and then again when he was with the Knicks and then with the Clippers. The guy's a fierce competitor, and it's good to have him on our side. Larry loves his game, which is why he traded Pooh Richardson, Malik Sealy, and the draft rights to Eric Piatkowski to the Clippers for him. Now we get a shot to show our magic together. We also get to show our hatred of the Knicks together.

If any player hates the Knicks more than I do, it's Mark Jackson. I know, win or lose, that the Knicks are going to be in for a dogfight whenever we play them because of Mark's attitude. What he went through, what he survived . . . man, I wouldn't wish it on my worst enemy. He was booed. He was benched for no reason. He had all sorts of troubles with Al Bianchi, who was the general manager when he was there. Listening to those stories, we'd tell him, "Kid, we got your back."

Having Mark will really help our backcourt. We have Mark, Vern Fleming, and Haywoode Workman at point guard, and

Byron Scott and myself at shooting guard. I think that gives us one of the best five-man backcourt rotations in the league. I don't think the critics think so, but we think so and that's all that really matters.

Vern is one of my heroes. He's been with the Pacers since 1984 when he was drafted in the first round. Eleven seasons with one team. You don't see that much anymore. Vern is the team's all-time leader in games played, minutes played, assists, and steals. And never once has he been teed up for a technical foul. Everybody respects Vern. He's a pro's pro.

Haywoode started fifty-two games for us last year, and this guy just wants to win. He plays great defense and actually asked the team to send him to Orlando during the off-season so he could work with a shooting coach. That's Haywoode's only weakness, his shooting.

Duane Ferrell came from Atlanta as a free agent. He's a forward and another fierce competitor. He's a veteran who knows how to win, and he's been around a winning atmosphere with Lenny Wilkins. He could have signed with New York or Cleveland for more money, but he said he wanted to play where he felt most comfortable and where he had the best chance to win a championship. I like that kind of thinking.

We also got John Williams. I know you're going to laugh at this, but I think John Williams is going to help us win. He's had a lot of problems; everyone calls him "Hot Plate" because he weighs more than 300 pounds, but he knows how to play the game. He really does. Once he loses some weight, he's really going to help us out. Larry says if he'd get down to 270, he'd be one of the ten best players in the league.

People can laugh and joke all they want about John, but the guy knows how to play basketball. The bottom line is that he can help us win. I think signing him to a non-guaranteed contract was a steal for us. As much as Coach Brown is going to be riding him in practice and as much as his teammates are going to be riding him, he's going to help us out. I guarantee it.

The rest of our roster is virtually written in stone. Antonio Davis, Dale Davis, Derrick McKey, and Sam Mitchell are our other forwards. Rik Smits, LaSalle Thompson, and Scott Haskin are our centers.

We have a good mix of veterans, guys who really want to win and know what it takes to do it. Antonio and Dale are bruisers, Derrick can do just about anything, and Sam is always tough. Tank Thompson, who has been in the league since 1983, has played great during camp.

The guy I really have a good feeling about is Rik. You can just see that every part of his game has improved. This kid has really come a long way. He was drafted number two overall in 1988, and that's a lot of pressure—even more so for a seven-foot-four guy from Holland who went to Marist College, a small school in Poughkeepsie, New York. It was like, "Who is this guy, and where the hell is Marist College?" Everybody was on his case: fans, media, even some of the players and coaches. People were brutal to him.

I first saw him when I was watching that Eddie Murphy movie *Coming to America*. There's a scene where they go to Madison Square Garden for a college game, and it turns out that Marist was one of the teams and you could see Rik playing in the background.

I knew he was a seven-four guy with a shooting touch, but that was about it. Marist was never on national TV, so it was hard to know a whole lot about him.

In that draft we definitely needed a big man. Steve Stipanovich was hurt and was getting ready to retire, so we had to get somebody. The way it turned out, it was between Rik and Syracuse's Rony Seikaly for that number two pick. Everyone on our team was thinking we'd go with Rony because he was from the Big East Conference and had a bigger reputation, but now that I look back at it, I'm glad we went with Rik.

At first, Chuck Person and Detlef Schrempf weren't happy with Rik because they thought he slowed down the offense, but part of the problem was that the coaches kept telling Rik to gain weight to get stronger. He got up to 296 and couldn't move. He scored okay, but he couldn't really defend or rebound.

One of the first things Larry did when he came was ask Rik to drop some weight. Rik lost about twenty to twenty-five pounds, and it's made a big difference. He's moving better, and it's really helped his offensive game. He also isn't prone to so many injuries. If Rik keeps improving, that's going to help us a lot. Having a force inside makes all the difference.

Our first-round draft pick, Greg Minor of Louisville, isn't even in camp. He played in the rookie camp and in the summer leagues, but Donnie and Larry don't think he has much chance to help us immediately. They're trying to trade him, which is probably best for the kid.

Damon Bailey, our second-round draft pick, is also on the roster. Damon played for Bobby Knight at Indiana, and it's been good to get a chance to talk to him about the whole experience. You have to remember that Knight was hyping up Damon when the kid was in eighth grade. That's a lot of pressure, especially in Indiana where basketball is like a religion.

When I came to this state, I knew what I was getting into. People are obsessed with basketball in Indiana. I see kids, three, four years old, shooting hoops when I'm driving to Market Square Arena. The commitment to basketball is amazing all over the state. It's always been that way.

I saw the movie *Hoosiers,* and that typifies Indiana basketball. When the state playoffs are going on, the whole state shuts down. It's pretty much like the movie, and that's great. I mean, there's nothing like Indiana as a place for basketball. Nothing compares with the heartland.

Sometimes I swear Bobby Knight runs the state. Everybody thinks "Go Big Red" first and then thinks about us and Purdue and some of the high school teams next.

As far as Bobby Knight's record goes, you can't really criticize the guy. He's won NCAA championships, he doesn't cheat, he gets some of the top high school players, and he does a good job of teaching them the game. But some of the things he does I don't agree with. He tries to break down players to build them back up. Sometimes players don't need to be broken down. Damon has great respect for Bobby Knight, but I don't think Damon—if he had the chance to do it all over again—would go back to IU. That's just my opinion.

I also don't think Knight could coach in the NBA. There's more give and take between the players and coaches in the NBA than there is in the college ranks. I don't think a lot of the college players understand the game, which is why the coach is so important. Even on good teams, probably one or two players on the roster truly understand the game. In the pros, twelve guys on a team know the game, really know how to play. I don't think Bobby Knight could criticize and get in guys' faces like he does at IU and get away with it in the pros.

You hear all sorts of stories about Bobby Knight. The best one I heard supposedly happened on the first day of fall practice in 1990. I guess Indiana hadn't had an Indiana-type season the year before, and when the players showed up for the first day of workouts, there was a closed pizza box at the center of half-court. Everyone was looking at the pizza box, not knowing what the hell was going on, when Knight walked over, nudged it open with his foot, and there was a pile of shit.

Knight said, "Last year, you guys played like shit. Now you're going to play in shit."

So they did. They started practicing with a box of shit in the middle of the court.

Now don't get me wrong. I think Bobby Knight is a great coach, but I don't think his style would have been for me. Anyway, he has his following, and we have ours.

I think with the recent success of the team, we're now running side by side with IU. We've built a following even on the road. You even see some Indiana Pacers stuff on the road. Winning solves everything.

Monday, October 10
Chapel Hill

Derrick McKey turned twenty-eight today. After practice we brought a cake out and sang "Happy Birthday" to him. I don't think that ever happened to him when he played for Seattle, which isn't exactly Team Harmony.

Wednesday, October 12
Chapel Hill

Not much to report. Spencer Dunkley, a second-year player out of Delaware, and Sam Mitchell almost got into a fight Monday night. That's about it for excitement.

Every day it's a college coaches' Who's Who at our practices. Lou Campanelli, who was forced out at Cal a few years ago, is helping our assistant coaches Billy King, George Irvine, and Gar Heard on a volunteer basis. He wants to get into the NBA on some level and figured this would be a good way to get some experience and exposure.

Everybody comes to see Larry coach. Dean Smith has been here a few times. So has Utah's Rick Majerus, who was an assistant on Dream Team II. I've seen Lefty Driesell, Dick Hunsaker, and a bunch of assistant coaches. Larry lets them all in. He isn't afraid to share what he knows.

Had to jump on my man Mark Jackson tonight. We beat his team again in a mini-scrimmage, and it was time to chirp a little bit.

"You gonna win one game?" I said. "Just win one time. I'll

tell you what. Tomorrow, I'll take Billy for defense, because that's all he's known for. I'll take George. I'll take Gar, because if I need a last-second shot, he can do like he did against Boston in '76 and send it into triple overtime with that little floater of his. I'll take Larry, but only if he promises not to coach while he's out there. And I'll take Dean. He can come off the bench shooting threes."

Dean Smith was sitting across the court from us, so I yelled, "Run to the corner and spot up. Dean, I've got you."

Coach Smith, who played at Kansas way back when, pretended like he was going to shoot one of those old-fashioned two-hand set shots.

Thursday, October 13
Chapel Hill

Larry and Donnie weren't at the practices today because they flew to Columbia, South Carolina, for the funeral of Frank McGuire. McGuire was their coach at North Carolina in the late 1950s and early 1960s. Donnie later worked for McGuire at South Carolina. Larry and Donnie had a lot of respect for McGuire. Donnie always talked about him as a second father.

I guess McGuire is a legend in these parts. He's the one who turned North Carolina into a college basketball powerhouse. He's also the one who recruited a lot of players from New York, guys like Larry and Doug Moe and Billy Cunningham. He also hired Dean Smith, which turned out to be pretty smart, don't you think?

Saturday, October 15
Indianapolis

I know it's sort of unusual, but Larry and Donnie are going to let me miss a couple of exhibition games to take care of some business commitments. These aren't your regular kind of commitments.

Someone called from Billy Crystal's production company—Billy is good friends with Larry and Donnie—and said they were doing a movie and wanted to know if I could be in it. The movie is about an NBA ref (Billy Crystal) who falls in love with a woman (Debra Winger) while he's visiting France. Stuff like that. Anyway, he needed me, Sean Elliott, David Robinson, Kevin Johnson, Charles Barkley, Shawn Kemp, Spud Webb, Kareem Abdul-Jabbar, Chris Mullin, Tim Hardaway, and a couple of other guys for the basketball scenes.

I met Billy when I was playing at UCLA. I was always a big fan of his, and he's a big fan of basketball. You see him at Clippers games all the time. He asked if I'd be interested in being in the movie, and what guy wouldn't jump at that chance? So I asked Donnie and Larry, and they were nice enough to let me miss a few days for filming.

Sunday, October 23
Los Angeles

Heard that the crowd at our exhibition game in Moline, Illinois, was pissed when they found out I wasn't there tonight. Heard that they booed when the announcement was made before the game. I feel bad about that. A lot of good people paid good money to see us—and, I guess, me—play. I'm here for a few days to do that Billy Crystal movie, and I did have the permission of the Pacers. But I don't blame those people in Moline for getting mad. Hey, Moline, it was nothing personal.

Monday, October 24
Los Angeles

I've done commercials before, but a movie is totally different. They had a live audience to fill the stands at the L.A. Sports Arena. It was wild.

It took about two hours for my scene because they had to keep changing camera angles, that sort of thing. I kept adding little things, mostly because Billy wanted our input to make the scene more realistic. Billy wanted to know the things I would say and do during an actual game. He listened and we made the changes.

I screwed up only once. Flubbed my line.

Billy, who was directing the movie, said, "Reg, you fucked up."

"Yeah, I did, huh."

After you did a scene, you'd go huddle around a monitor screen to see how it looked. I'm telling you, that stuff is going to be funny. It's going to be hilarious. Joe Mantegna is in it and so is Julie Kavner. You know, now that I think of it, Billy's done pretty well for himself with his movie love interests. Winger in this movie; Meg Ryan in *When Harry Met Sally.* Not bad for a little guy.

I've come a long way with this stuff. I remember the first commercial I ever did—McQuick Lube in Indianapolis. It's like a Midas muffler place. They had this little bunny rabbit logo, and I was playing Pictionary with the bunny. My first shoe endorsement: Spotbilt. Still have a poster of it. Man . . .

Then there was the Super Dave Nike commercial. That was five or six years ago. He called me Roger instead of Reggie. He's hilarious, that guy.

I was lucky to get Nike. They have so many players, especially a lot of guys from the big-market cities. But if you ask me, they should use more players from Cleveland and Milwaukee and Sacramento and Indiana, places like that. But since those teams aren't in very big media markets, they sometimes don't get the endorsements.

Grant Hill, the Detroit rookie from Duke, already has this huge following—GMC truck commercials, Fila. Some of this stuff goes worldwide. He has a lot of talent, from what I've heard and seen on TV. Nice guy, too. But he hasn't even played an NBA game yet, and already they've anointed him the next great star. I'm not saying it won't happen, but that's a hell of a thing to put on someone this early in his career.

The off-court stuff is fun for me. Mabye it's my L.A. background, but I get a real kick out of doing movies and TV. I've done a number of commercials, and I got to do a guest spot on "Hangin' with Mr. Cooper," which is on ABC. Fortunately, I had Cheryl, who was on "Living Single," to talk me through it.

Then last month I went to New York and did the "Live with Regis and Kathie Lee" show. Regis Philbin is crazy, I'm telling you. We were supposed to have a little competition on the street corner, him and me shooting baskets, with the crowd and the cameras right there. Not long before the show started, he came into the green room and said, "I want a piece of you!"

"You and everybody else in New York," I said.

He said, "The basket's all ready: Regis versus Reggie."

I wore a sweater that day so I could shoot. I told him so, too. "Didn't want to give you an edge because you're the host."

"Just don't do to me what you did to the Knicks," he said.

"I may not be able to help myself."

New York does that to me.

Mike Lupica, who is a sports columnist for New York's *Newsday* and a writer for *Esquire,* can confirm the whole thing. He was there, taking notes for an article.

I brought roses for Kathie Lee Gifford and a Pacers jersey

for Regis. We had a real good time. Regis hit one, I hit three of nine. Hey, it was a windy day out there on the street corner.

I know my playoff series against the Knicks in '94 had a lot to do with getting some of these endorsements, but I also think I've worked hard at doing things the right way. I play the game hard. I have a reputation for talking trash, but that's overrated. Yeah, I talk, but it's never anything malicious or personal. Well, not personal, anyway. I respect the game and the players in it.

For instance, I would never, ever cross the boundary and talk about somebody's family. I would never talk trash to, say, Scottie Pippen about something personal in his life. I would never cross that line. I might give you some serious shit about your jumper or about your team, but I would never bring your mother into it or your wife or something like that.

Anyway, Shaquille O'Neal has a big global appeal as well, but Grant, Michael, and myself are very clean-cut. And black or white doesn't enter into it.

I think basketball—and especially the NBA—is the most color blind of the sports. You have Isiah Thomas going to Toronto to run that team. You have Elgin Baylor with the Clippers and M. L. Carr with the Celtics.

I wish there were more black coaches, but we have more than major league baseball and a whole lot more than football. I just think we relate better to the general public because the game is so integrated. Also, I think the game itself is so pure; the game is the important thing, not necessarily the players playing it.

Still, I think it's going to be tough for Grant this year. He's just a rookie, and already there's so much expected of him. People will want him to raise the level of his game and to raise the team's level. I don't envy him.

Wednesday, October 26
Indianapolis

Came back from Los Angeles and scored 18 points in twenty-four minutes of our exhibition game against Charlotte. Banged up my left knee (nothing real serious), but I was excited to be playing again.

Conrad Brunner, who covers us for the *Indianapolis News*, asked Larry about the Billy Crystal movie. Billy wanted Larry in the movie, too, but Larry couldn't do it. Conrad wanted to know if Larry had ever seen an NBA referee with someone as good-looking as Debra Winger.

"No," said Larry, "but I know they all try."

Conrad and the other beat reporter, Dan Dunkin of the *Indianapolis Star*, cover us all the time: all the home games, all the road games. The columnists and beat guys in Indianapolis know the game. They report the game, they're honest, and they're fair, which is all you can ask of the media. You get a lot of beat writers out there who want to add their two cents' worth, who want to put themselves in the story, but these guys write what they see. They have to know the game, coming from Indiana, or else the fans, who really love hoops, would rip the hell out of them.

Monday, October 31
Indianapolis

I don't think the team missed me too much. We were 7–1 in the exhibition season, the best in franchise history.

I'll say it right now: I hate the new three-point line. They moved it in from the farthest point—twenty-three feet nine inches—to twenty-two feet all the way around, and it's too damn close. Larry Bird calls it the "kiddie line" because everybody can make that shot. Even Antonio, who had only one three all last year, is sticking that shot. It's embarrassing.

The way the old three-point line was set up, it came out in a straight line from the baseline at around twenty-two feet and then became an arc once it got out to twenty-three feet nine inches. The shortest three was made from the corners; we called it a "cupcake." Then there was the "titty" shot, which is where the twenty-two-foot mark met the 23-9. I don't know who came up with these names, but that's what everybody called them.

Now it's cupcakes everywhere.

You don't need to be a genius to figure out why the NBA changed the three-point line. They cut the distance to twenty-two feet so they'd get more scoring. Now you have to go out there and guard guys. It also opens up the low post.

I'll give you another likely reason why they did this: the Knicks. Because of the Knicks, the NBA got rid of the 23-9 line and outlawed handchecking. The league saw how slow and dull the finals were between the Knicks and the Rockets, and said enough was enough.

The thing is, if the league had just changed the three-point line to twenty-two feet but not outlawed handchecking, the Knicks would be the best team in the league. Starks and Harper can hit threes, and nobody plays better team defense than New York. If they could handcheck this year, there is no way they could be stopped. They'd win it all. They'd be able to do all their rough stuff and get away with it, plus they'd have a better chance at making their threes. But the league put those two changes together. I guess I'm not the only one who doesn't like those guys.

November 1994

Friday, November 4
Atlanta

The season starts tonight. Even after seven years in this league, I still get tingles. Maybe that's because I was never supposed to be in the NBA in the first place.

My mother cried when I was born. I came out with my legs and hips all contorted and twisted, like somebody had tried to tie me in a knot. The doctors said I might not ever walk. And don't even think about playing sports, they said. That was August 24, 1965.

Almost thirty years later, I'm walking the walk and talking the talk. That's one thing my mom never had to worry about, me talking.

I wore steel braces on my legs until I was four years old. I'd sit in the kitchen with my mom and watch everyone else play basketball in the driveway. I was like the ultimate momma's boy, but there wasn't much I could do about it. I couldn't run. I couldn't jump. I just had to lurch around in those braces looking like a little Forrest Gump.

My mom would see me looking out the window and say, "Don't worry, honey. You'll be out there soon. Your legs just got to get stronger, that's all."

That's how my mom and dad have always been with me. Never anything negative, always positive. They always told me I'd walk, that I'd run, that I'd even play basketball. Damn if they weren't right.

My dad played at Hamilton High School in Memphis. He went to college at Southern Illinois, joined the Air Force, and met my mom at a jazz club in Memphis. He was playing the sax with Phineas Newborn Jr.'s band at the time.

I had the best childhood a kid could want. There was my dad, who was a chief master sergeant, and my mom, who was a nurse, and my four brothers and sisters. I'm second youngest in the family. Saul Jr. is nine years older, Darrell is eight years older, Cheryl is one year older, and Tammy is four years younger.

It was crazy around our house. My dad would leave for work at 8 A.M., and we'd all race to the breakfast table so we could hang around Saul Jr. and Darrell.

My dad and mom had rules, and you obeyed them—or else. We ate dinner every night at 5:30. Everyone had to be at the dinner table, or we wouldn't eat. You look at today's families and nobody eats together, but we always did.

We went to church every Sunday. Baptists through and through. My dad being a military man, there weren't any Afros in our family, either. You said, "Yes, sir," and "No, sir." It was strict, but I think that's good. We learned the difference between right and wrong, which is missing in today's society, I think. Kids sometimes don't see a difference between the two.

Everybody played sports in our family. Cheryl was a basketball All-American in high school and at USC, and played on the 1984 U.S. Olympic gold medal–winning team. She's the coach at USC now. If you ask me, she was the female version of Michael Jordan, Larry Bird, and Magic Johnson. She could do anything. She's the best woman player past, present, or future. Watching Cheryl play was an entertainment show. She was fantastic. In fact, there's no doubt in my mind that in her prime she could have played some minutes in the NBA. Easily. She was that talented.

Tammy played volleyball at Cal State–Fullerton. Darrell played baseball and football, and spent five seasons as a catcher with the California Angels before moving to the front office as a scout. I played baseball and basketball.

To tell you the truth, baseball was my first love, too. I wanted to be the next Roberto Clemente or Rod Carew. We played corkball all the time. You'd get a broom handle and use it as a bat, and then get a cork from a wine bottle and wrap it in white tape. You could make that cork curve or sink, and it was a bitch to try to hit it. Kids still play that game in Riverside.

I thought I loved baseball so much that I played it my freshman year at Riverside Polytechnic High. I had had a lot of success in Little League and Pony League, and I figured I'd do the same in high school. But I was standing in the outfield one day, and it was cold. The wind was whistling, and nobody was hitting the ball to me. That's when I decided I needed something nonstop. I needed that excitement, that adrenaline to get me going. After that freshman year, I decided I was going to concentrate on basketball, where you have the cheerleaders, the band—it's always going crazy.

Basketball was the constant at our house. We had a hoop over the garage door at our first house in Riverside and then put one in when we moved to our second house when I was in eighth grade. The driveway was too small, so my dad put the hoop in the backyard.

Everyone in our family took turns kicking my butt in basketball. It wasn't difficult at first. I was only five feet nine and 140 pounds by the time I was a freshman in high school. I couldn't beat anybody, especially Cheryl who was a star, one of the best in the country by then. That became my goal in life: beat Cheryl. I wasn't jealous of her success; I just wanted to win. That's how it was at our house. I wanted to win at basketball, cards, checkers, corkball . . . everything. I never cheated, but I was willing to do just about anything to win, no matter the cost.

My dad's the one who taught me how to shoot, how to hold my release and keep it there after the ball left my hands. I practiced every day. When people ask me, "How do you get better?" I say, "Practice." They go, "No, really, how?" I say, "Practice."

I used to shoot five hundred, six hundred, seven hundred shots a day. Not all at once, but over the course of an afternoon. I tried to master every shot from every corner of that backyard court. I'd go from the baseline to the outer reaches of the concrete. I'd work on bank shots and every other kind of shot. I'd just shoot and shoot and shoot.

I spent so much time out there that my dad had to extend the court four or five more feet. By then I had ruined parts of my mom's garden. I'd always want to shoot from a little farther out, and she'd say, "Get out of my rosebushes, boy."

It wasn't until my sophomore year that I developed a real jump shot. Before that I used to heave the ball up with a one-handed set shot that started down at my hip. I had grown two inches over the summer but was still the first or second forward off the bench. Of course, my dad kept telling me to stay ready, but I could see I was stuck behind those other guys.

Then one day we were on the road, getting dressed in the visitors' locker room. One of the starters pulled out a home uniform instead of the required away uniform. He couldn't play—league rules. So the coach looked at me and said, "Well, Reg, I guess you have to start this game." He wasn't very enthusiastic about my chances, if you know what I mean.

I started the game but messed up the first couple of plays. I mean, after all, this was my first real game, my first real competition. But then—and I still don't know how it happened—a light went on. I ended up with 35 points, and was thinking, "This is cool. This is nice." Best of all, I knew he couldn't take me out of the lineup.

Sure enough, he told me, "I'm going to start you again, Reg." I scored 45 points, was player of the week, and started the rest of the season. To this day whenever I talk to kids about playing basketball, I tell them, "Always be ready to play." The strangest thing about it is: What if that kid had brought the right uniform that day?

But the points didn't mean a thing until I took care of business at home. I had to beat Cheryl. One of the reasons I practiced shooting from the outside was that Cheryl used to block my shots when I drove to the hoop. It's a bad feeling when your sister is knocking your best stuff into the rosebushes. But that's how it was. She was always better than I was. She'd beat me one-on-one. She'd beat me easy. But she could beat everybody on the block. She was the best player in Riverside, bar none. Before long she was the best female player in the country.

I couldn't dunk until I was a sophomore in high school. I was so skinny and frail that I'd eat and drink milk all the time. I wanted to grow so bad, but I finally realized that it's not necessarily how big you are but how strong you are, both mentally and physically.

Even in high school I knew that I was quicker than the other guys. And mentally they were terrible: No toughness. No discipline. No focus.

I'd never let anyone know I was tired. If they got tired, I'd always make sure to give that little extra effort, to try to break them mentally. If I got hurt, I'd never let them see me in pain. I'm still that way. Shaquille O'Neal knocked me to the floor one time, and I just got up and started yelling, "Harder! Hit me harder!" I want the guy I'm playing against to look at me and say, "God, what makes this guy go? I'm doing everything I can against him, and he's not tired, he's not hurt, he's not thirsty."

I know I'm not the most talented player in the NBA. I don't have the classic shooting motion. I'm skinny. I mean, UCLA didn't even recruit me until three other guys turned down scholarship offers. I was like their fourth choice. But I'm here.

You might not like me on the court, but you have to respect me. I'm not there to win friends, I'm there to win games.

I've spent my whole life overcoming obstacles: the steel braces, my size, the shadow of Cheryl. In fact, people still chant, "Cher-yl, Cher-yl," when we're playing on the road. Hey, that just adds fuel to my fire. Their sole purpose is to mess with me, to try to affect the way I play. If only they knew. They're concentrating so much on me, screaming at me, rooting against me, and I *love* it. I love the attention. I love playing on the road. If it was quiet on the road, I'd die.

I don't take anything for granted. When I was in high school, my dad told me after a game that I hadn't played worth fifty cents. From then on I taped two quarters under my left wristband to remind me to play hard all the time.

So I am who I am because I never gave up. I am where I am because my parents and brothers and sisters wouldn't let me give up.

Well, one down, eighty-one regular season games to go.

We opened up on the road at Atlanta, the same team we knocked out of the playoffs last year in six games. Danny Manning is gone—he signed with Phoenix—and the Hawks signed Tyrone Corbin and Ken Norman to fill in at small forward.

We knew they were losing a lot of their firepower, but they're still a dangerous team. Mookie Blaylock and Stacey Augmon are one of the better duos in the backcourt in the league. Plus, it was opening night on their home turf.

We beat them, 94–92, but it shouldn't have been so hard. Maybe that's the difference between this season and last year: We expect more.

Antonio hit some clutch free throws in the last four seconds to win it, but geezus, we made a lot of mistakes. Twenty turnovers. Shot 42.1 percent from the field.

Mark had a good debut, though. Scored 21 points and hit 9 of 13. He also had 4 rebounds and 3 assists. We need him. He's the thirteenth point guard during Donnie's nine years at Indiana, and it's hard to have that kind of turnover and expect to challenge for a championship.

Damon, Scott Haskin, and John Williams started the season on the injury list. Damon has those bad knees. Scott isn't ready because of a pinched nerve that affects his right calf muscles. And John is too heavy.

I've been lucky when it comes to injuries, but I've also worked hard to prevent them. I missed three games during the 1994 season (bad ankle), but I played in every game the previous four years. I take a lot of pride in that, in playing even when I'm nicked up.

I stretch and work out during the summer. At the end of this season I'm probably going to start doing some type of yoga, too. And massages. Massages will help.

When the season is over a lot of guys say, "Fuck it. I'm out of here." Then when training camp comes around, they try to get in shape in a month. You can't do that. There are too many guys out there who want your job, who are working their asses off every day.

Sure, everyone has to take some time off, let their bodies recuperate from a season's worth of wear and tear. But you also have to work your way back into it. You can't wait until the last minute.

I know I look skinny and frail, but I think I'm durable. The most my body fat has ever been is 6.5. Right now it's probably 4 or 5. The average for the league is around 10.

I hired a trainer the last two years. The weight training really helps. Byron Scott, who really hits the weights hard, got us all involved.

But a lot of people don't do it. They get to the NBA and they relax. They take it for granted. They figure they've already got women, cars, money. They think they can go to the clubs and party all the time. But that's not what it's all about. This is your job. This is your profession. You've got to remember what got you here.

When I came out of UCLA, I was a great shooter, but I couldn't take it off the floor. When I first came into the league, my first thirty ballgames I had a 15-point average. I was thinking, "Whoa, this is easy." But that's because none of the opponents had any videotape of me yet. That is what's so big in this game, people taking away your first two or three moves.

It didn't take long before I hit the wall as a rookie. I struggled from game thirty-five to about game fifty-five. I couldn't make a jumper. I couldn't make anything. By then, everybody in the league knew my pet moves.

Then there was the travel, the hotel food, the stress. I was constantly tired.

Eventually, I picked up my scoring near the end of the season, but the book on me early was, "Get to him; he can't take the ball off the dribble."

So during the off-season I started working on doing more with the ball. I came up with some other dribble step-back shots and a few other moves. I was constantly trying to improve my game. I didn't want to be predictable. Being predictable in the NBA is death.

Practice is the key. People think you were born a great shooter, but that's not always the case. You might be born with natural talent, but you have to develop it, enhance it. I went in my backyard as a kid and shot until I could master a ten-foot shot. Then I stepped back and shot until I could master a twelve-foot shot. Then it was a fifteen-footer. Then a twenty-footer. And I mean *master*; I was out there shooting by myself from different spots until it became second nature.

Over a period of time you get into a routine. You train yourself to become a shooter. The same thing goes for hitting big shots. Once you hit your first big shot, people start to label you a clutch shooter. You start to want the ball in clutch situations. With me, it started in high school. I've always loved being the go-to guy. The way I look at it, you have a fifty-fifty chance: You can be the hero or the goat. But with me, considering the amount of work I've put into my shot, I tell myself, "You've got a seventy-thirty chance of making the shot." I'll take those odds any day.

But you've got to work at it. I have a routine. I'll start at the baseline and keep moving across the court. If I miss one shot, I'll do a layup and start over again.

I always tell kids it's better to work out on your own. I think that's the best way to develop concentration and self-discipline. Anybody can work out with a buddy, but it's harder to do it by yourself. Cheryl and I would play, but a lot of times I just practiced by myself. I just made up games for myself.

I've always been able to shoot off the screens—that's the easiest thing to do. But learning to take the ball off the dribble, getting fouled, and going to the free throw line, that's when you end up with the big boys. You can get to the foul line in college, but this is a different game here. Taking the ball off the dribble is what separates the shooters from the players. There are a lot of shooters—such as Dale Ellis; he's a great shooter, but he can't do much with his dribble. But if you give him an inch to shoot, he's going to kill you. I like to think I can do both now.

I know I don't have the classic shooting form. Guys such as Ellis and Jeff Hornacek have a much more classic shooting motion than I do, but the results are the same. And when you're at the very top of your game, there's almost nothing better than knowing any shot you take is going to have at least a 50 percent chance of going in. It's the best feeling in the game.

With me and my shot, I'm almost where Michael Jordan

must be when he's driving to the hoop and knows he can jump over everybody and dunk on them. If I'm coming down on the break and I'm spotting up in the corner, and Mark or Vern sees me, it's like everything is in slow motion. I can see the rotation on the ball, and I can visualize myself knocking the three down before it happens.

The big shots are what get me going more than anything else. I love making those. I might miss early on, but when the game is on the line or I'm coming back or we need a big shot, that gives me more gratification than anything else.

One shot can make such a big difference. One shot can affect my opponent, my teammates, the fans, the coaching, the strat-egy—everything. I like to make the opposing team use their timeouts. When you're making a run, you want them to call a timeout and have to adjust to you and your team. The best-case scenario is when they're calling timeouts and they still can't adjust to what you're doing. That's when you've really disrupted them.

Big shots are the absolute best. There's no better feeling than coming off the break in a playoff game, with the crowd going crazy, and hitting the game-winning three. There's no feeling like it. People can't understand the fan noise. It's indescribable the way the applause lifts you up. That's why I feel so lucky to be a part of this game. I get to experience things that other peo-ple dream about.

I'll never take the game for granted. I used to have a local TV show in Indianapolis, and Larry Bird was a guest one time. Someone from the studio audience asked him how tough it was to be a player in the NBA.

He said, "We practice for two hours. We play a game. That's our job. Other people get up at the crack of dawn and work all day."

He's right. We've really got it made. But a lot of people take it for granted. I've seen players who should have been really good in the pros but for whatever reason they don't make it. Look at Walter Berry from St. John's. He was the college player of the year. Why didn't he make it? Was it because he was a tweener, someone between a guard and forward? Was it because he didn't make all the sacrifices? Only he knows for sure.

Look at Christian Laettner of the Minnesota Timberwolves. I know he plays for a suck-ass team, but he causes more of his problems than the team causes for him. If he asked me for advice, I'd tell him to shut up and play. He has a game. If you put him on our team, he would look great. You put him with the Knicks, Phoenix, Orlando, he would be fantastic. But he has to learn to make the most of his situation.

People don't remember that I've seen both sides. I've been on Pacer teams that have done okay, but not great. That's why I can relate to what Christian's going through. My first year here we won thirty-eight games and didn't make the playoffs. We won only twenty-eight the next year. It wasn't until my third season that we climbed over .500 and reached the playoffs. And then we got ripped by Detroit, 3–0.

But a guy like Orlando's Penny Hardaway, he's going to be blessed his whole career. I doubt if he'll ever have a losing season. He'll never see both sides.

What a bitch of an early schedule. Of our first thirty-three games, twenty-one of them are on the road. Somebody in the NBA office doesn't like us.

Saturday, November 5
Indianapolis

Uh-oh. We're 2–0 after beating the new-look Celtics, 112–103, but Larry was upset with the way we played. We're a little lethargic, and it shows.

You know what they say: What goes around comes around.

Until the 1993–94 season, the Celtics kicked our butts for as long as I can remember. When I was a rookie in 1987–88, we played the Celtics five times and lost to them five times. Things started to even up when Bird retired and Kevin McHale and Robert Parish got older. But you know what? A lot of teams started to even the score with the Celtics after Bird retired and McHale and Parish got older.

This was our twelfth straight win against Boston here and our sixth overall. So much for all that shamrock stuff. We've got our own tradition working now.

Strange to see Dominique Wilkins in Celtic green. He signed with them during the off-season when the Clippers let him go as a free agent. I got to know 'Nique on Dream Team II. I've been a fan of his ever since he was known as "The Human Highlight Film."

But 'Nique was showing his age a little bit during the World Championship. I know if I was dragging going into the training camp, his old legs must really have been tired. Even some of the younger players on the other national teams were trying to take advantage of him; we started calling him "Antique" instead of Dominique. I'm telling you, though, he can still put up numbers with the best of them.

Seeing 'Nique brought back some good memories. Even though I didn't have much of an off-season, I wouldn't trade the Dream Team II experience for anything. I wasn't one of the original players chosen for the team a year earlier; when they added me to the roster, I was just excited to be part of it.

Golden State's Don Nelson was the coach. I know he and Chris Webber have had all sorts of problems, but Nellie was fair with me. Demanding but fair.

You have to remember, I play for Larry Brown. Larry is very direct, very loud, very discipline-oriented, but he's also very fair. I'm used to that style of coaching. I don't have any problems with it.

Some guys didn't want to play on the Dream Team II because they weren't willing to give up their summers. That's cool, but I think anytime you can represent your country, you should do it. And if I get lucky enough to be selected to the 1996 USA Olympic team, I'll say yes in a heartbeat. I mean, you don't get many chances, if any, to play for a gold medal. I wasn't good enough to be on Dream Team I, and I wasn't old enough for the other Olympics. In fact, the more I think about it, the more I think some of those NBA players are crazy for saying they wouldn't want to compete for an Olympic gold medal. That's something you have to do, for yourself and for your country. It's not an obligation, it's a duty.

I tried to use Dream Team II as a learning experience. I usually ate breakfast with the coaches—Nellie, the Detroit Pistons' Don Chaney, Providence's Pete Gillen, Utah's Rick Majerus—just so I could pick their minds about the game.

I remember one evening when I saw Majerus at the team hotel. I was wearing a suit, and Majerus gave me one of those "So, what time will you be staggering in?" looks. Then he said, "Where you going tonight, Reggie?"

I told him the truth: "I'm taking my mother-in-law to dinner."

"Oh," he said. I guess he figured if it was a lie, at least it was one he hadn't heard yet.

Those coaches were kind of funny sometimes. They called a video session one time, but there was one problem: None of them knew how to work the VCR. Four coaches, and not one of them knew how to turn it on. They were so used to having their assistant coaches take care of the video stuff that they didn't know how to operate the equipment.

Nellie was swearing, Chaney was shaking his head, Majerus was all nervous, like we'd all walk out of the film session if something didn't happen soon. So Majerus tried to fix the thing, which must have had a hundred buttons on it. Finally, I got up and said, "Here, give me that." Some big problem: I turned the power switch on.

People are always asking who was better, Dream Team I or II. That's a tough one. They had some of the greatest players ever on Dream Team I: Larry Bird, Magic Johnson, Michael Jordan. But I thought Dream Team II was one of the best ever assembled, too.

Look at it this way: We both accomplished our goals. Dream Team I went to Barcelona to win the gold medal for the United States, and they did it. We went to Toronto to win the gold medal for the United States, and we did it. But everybody still tries to compare us to Dream Team I. That game will never happen. It would be nice, though.

I think if it was one game, winner take all, and everyone was in shape . . . I would have to go with Dream Team I. To tell you the truth, I think they would beat the shit out of us.

But in a seven-game series—and that's how things are decided in our league—you never know. We had young legs.

I had never been on a championship team on any level until Dream Team II. I knew we would beat teams by 30 points every game, but I wanted to see what made these guys so great. Were they committed to winning? Did they prepare the same way I did? Did they take it seriously? Did they get ready the same way every game?

Shaq was a guy I really wanted to watch. He might not be the best player in our league, but he's one of the top five. I was curious to see if he was going to come with his real stuff. And sure enough, every night, every practice, he brought it.

I think some of the guys on the team were resentful of Shaq's fame, of the attention, of the money. They thought it had been given to him on a silver platter. But I have to give him credit: He's under a lot of pressure for someone twenty-three or twenty-four. He's dealt with it. He took everyone on and survived. He'll dunk on you in a heartbeat and rap on you on the other end. A real character.

Then there's Mark Price, who thinks rap is something you do on a door. He's a great point guard who can take it off the dribble, and a great three-point shooter who knows how to use the pick and roll. A fierce competitor.

Kevin Johnson was also on that team. I've known him since high school. He's another player who's great taking it off the dribble and running the pick and roll.

Joe Dumars was the unsung MVP of Dream Team II. He played great defense on the other team's shooting guards and still was able to get his own shots off. He's just a true professional on and off the floor.

Dan Majerle is a great three-point shooter, a good pool shooter, and an even better Ping-Pong player. We had some huge Ping-Pong battles in the game room, but he couldn't beat me.

I feel sorry for those guys who don't get right on Dan on defense, who dare him to shoot. You can't leave Dan open. If you do, he'll shoot from anywhere. He might have the most range in the league. He'll shoot from half-court and get mad if he doesn't make it. You want Dan to drive on you, not square up for jumpers.

Steve Smith was on the team, but he didn't get a lot of playing time. I think he had some knee problems. But playing against him in previous games, he's kind of like a point forward. He got traded to Atlanta, and he'll help them out.

Then there was Derrick Coleman, who's probably the best power forward in the NBA. He can do it all. He can shoot from outside, power it up on the inside, run the floor, and he is long. He's a big six feet ten and very tough to stop. People give him grief about his attitude, but I'd take him.

Shawn Kemp. That man is probably the most athletic and most fun-to-watch power forward—hell, the most fun-to watch player—in our league. Give him the ball on the open floor and it's lights out. Rain Man is going to deliver for you.

I have a soft spot for Alonzo Mourning. I love this guy's demeanor. He's mean all the time. All he wants to do is win. Whenever you have a big man on your team who can block shots from the floor, shoot from the outside, and play hard every second, man, you want guys like that on your team.

Larry Johnson was a tri-captain, along with Joe and me. He was hurt with a back injury for most of 1993–94, and he didn't have the spring in his legs that everyone was used to seeing. Everyone was saying, "What's wrong with Larry?"

But I think Larry was just getting back into basketball shape. I think he was having fun, but a lot of media people and fans were trying to figure out what was wrong with him. He knew he wasn't one hundred percent healthy, but he was there busting his ass, playing hard for his country. You have to respect that.

About the only regret we had on that team was that we wanted to play the Croatians real bad, but they screwed it up by losing to Russia. Everyone wanted to go against Toni Kukoc. He had just signed this big deal with the Chicago Bulls, and there was this whole controversy with him and Scottie Pippen. Everyone was kind of getting geeked to go against him and Dino Radja. But when Russia beat them, we had to face Russia twice in a row. NBC wanted us to play Croatia. It was disappointing because we wanted to shut down Toni and kind of go at him a little bit, show him what he would face in the NBA.

And by the way, I hope NBA Commissioner David Stern doesn't hold a grudge. One day at the hotel I was bored stiff, so I went down to the USA Basketball hospitality room. Some of the USA team workers were there, and they had a list of phone numbers.

"What are these numbers for?" I asked.

"Oh, those are the beeper numers for Commissioner Stern, Rod Thorn, and Horace Balmer."

I had hit the prank jackpot. Stern, the commissioner; Thorn, the NBA vice president of operations; Balmer, NBA director of security—and I had their numbers. So I started calling their beepers. They didn't know what was going on until later.

The guy I got the best was Balmer. I got his hotel room number and called him one day. In fact, I think I woke him up because he sounded kind of groggy.

"Horace," I said, disguising my voice, "we have a problem."

"What is it?"

"One of the players just got into a fight in one of the clubs. There were blows thrown. I think one of the players was hurt. There were arrests."

"Oh, my God. Where? And who is this?"

"I'm a reporter for the *Toronto Sun-Times.*"

"Oh, my God. All right, who was the player?"

I couldn't keep a straight face any longer.

"Horace, c'mon, I'm just kidding. It's me, Reginald."

He must have cussed me out for five minutes straight. "I swear, if it's the last thing I do, I'm going to get you."

So far, so good. Horace hasn't gotten me back—yet.

Wednesday, November 9
Indianapolis

The Houston Rockets, the defending NBA champions, came in tonight, and in the back of everyone's mind we were wondering what would have happened if we had beaten New York and played them in the NBA Finals.

You have to give Houston credit. They find ways to win around the big fella. Hakeem Olajuwon is the best center in the league, no question about it. Now he's finally getting the recognition he deserves. He has a championship ring. I want that ring, too.

They got off to a big lead. We came back, but it wasn't enough. We lost, 109–104, and I thought we got screwed by the referees. I wasn't the only one who thought so. The crowd starting getting on this crew (Paul Mihalak, Blaine Reichelt, and Tim Donaghy) early in the game, especially when the refs called two illegal defenses on us in the first period and tossed Larry in the same quarter.

By the end of the game, we had five technicals called against us. I finished with 25 points, but I also got tossed with 30.3 seconds left in the game. Hakeem was his usual self, scoring 43 points, but Rik was 1 of 11 for three points in eighteen minutes. He also picked up 5 fouls, which is another reason the crowd started getting nasty. At the end of the game, the fans actually started throwing stuff on the floor.

Darrell Garretson, who's the supervisor of the NBA officials, was at the game and you could tell, too—the refs were really nervous and tight. That's what got Larry his first T: He told Paul Mihalik that Garretson must be there. Mihalik thought Larry was trying to show him up, so he gave him the T.

But you can't bitch forever about the referees. They're going to do what they've got to do and tonight they did a lot.

I know this is going to sound bad, but I kind of liked the way our fans trashed the place after we lost. They went a little overboard by throwing coins and pretty much anything they had in their pockets, but at least they cared. I've ridden them so hard over the years about getting more vocal, and during the last two years they've responded and given us the home court advantage. You need that in this league.

Let me tell you about refs.

First of all, they want you to call them by their first names. And like anything, some are better than others.

A top player in college can really influence a referee. In the pros that doesn't happen. Yes, veteran players might get the benefit of a call, but you can never strong-arm a ref. They don't care. They don't give a damn. It's like Hollywood: You've got to sell yourself to them and the fans.

The ones you tend to have a problem with are the guys who've been doing it for three, four, five, six years. They don't think their shit stinks. They're working for the NBA. They're just like players in that regard; it's like, they've made it through their rookie year, so they don't have to carry any more bags or wash any more cars for the veterans.

When I was a rookie, a veteran would kick the ball into the stands, and I'd have to go get it. I'd have to arrange wake-up calls. I'd have to get newspapers. I'd have to get coffee and doughnuts. And that was the minimum. Refs are the same way. Once they think they've paid their dues, watch out.

These refs think they're successful, but some of them have a chip on their shoulder. Steve Javie . . . he threw out a mascot. But he sees a good game. You can talk to him, but then again sometimes you can't.

You can really talk to Jess Kersey and Jake O'Donnell, and you can talk to Eddie T. Rush up to a point, but with these guys you're not going to get anywhere, because they've seen it all and heard it all. You can talk to Javie, and then he gets pissed off. Joey Crawford gets agitated so quick, and it gets tough. You find yourself telling him, "C'mon, just relax, you know."

Some nights it feels like you're playing another team. You're playing the team on the schedule and also the refs. But I've got to admit that they don't discriminate. I used to think in the back of my mind that they knew who they wanted to win anyway, but this year and 1994 really changed my mind. I used to think the league offices wanted New York or Orlando in the finals, so the refs would do everything they could to make sure it happened. But when we eliminated Orlando in the 1994 playoffs, the refs called every game solid. No discriminating. They didn't care that we were Indiana. I'd figured, with two games in Orlando, we were dead; Shaq was going to get 50 every game, and they were going to let him do whatever he wanted. But that wasn't the case. They let the players decide the game.

I'll say this, though: Rookies do get screwed. When we were playing Boston my rookie season, something happened and I said, "Aw, man, c'mon."

Eddie T. looked at me and said, "Don't say shit to me, rookie."

I said, "You know what, you're right. I'm sorry."

They have to learn your game, your strengths and weaknesses. They have to see everything you've got. And generally speaking, they'll let the players decide the outcome in the last five minutes of the game.

Thursday, November 10
Detroit

I have no idea how we lost this game. We were up by 17 late in the third quarter, and then we blew it, 112–110. Like I told the media after the game, we've got 78 games left. There are going to be worse games than this—but geezus, I hope not many.

Grant Hill had 23 points and looked good doing it. Smooth kid.

Saturday, November 12
Cleveland

Someone told me that Conrad Brunner wrote in the *News* that our killer instinct ranks somewhere between Tiny Tim and Aunt Bea. Very funny.

Hey, Conrad, Tiny-Tim this: We beat Cleveland tonight, 93–86, and had a big lead until the final seconds. About time.

Tuesday, November 15
Milwaukee

How did we lose to those guys? They had us by 26 points in the second quarter before we made a comeback. They missed

15 straight shots and scored only 8 points in the fourth, and we still lost to them, 82–81.

Larry came into the locker room after the game and said, "Training camp is over. I don't want any excuses about not playing together long enough. We've had six games. That's enough."

I got my first look at Glenn Robinson, the first pick in the draft. "Big Dog" got 18 points in twenty-three minutes, but you could tell he was rusty from missing training camp.

Thursday, November 17
Indianapolis

Routines and superstitions. Every player has them.

I have two routines, depending on whether my wife's home. When she is home and the team has a shootaround at 9:45, I'll get up at 8:15 and leave by 8:45 for the shootaround. On my way back I'll call ahead, and she'll cook breakfast: grits, eggs. Then I'll take a nap from 12:00 to 3:30. Then I'll take my vitamins, get my legs going, and see what she's doing.

If my wife isn't in town, I'll go to Waffle House or Morning Cafe and have breakfast after the shootaround. Then I'll go home and get up at the same time. I do have to put my own clothes out when she's not around, which is pretty tough. But, hey, that's what Garanimals are for.

If we're on the road, I'll go to breakfast with Byron, LaSalle, Mark, and sometimes Derrick. We'll read the paper, talk about what's going on. Then we'll go to shootaround and try to kill time before the game starts that night.

When I come back from practice, I try to get a little sleep. Some guys go to the mall, but I need my nap.

Before we leave the hotel, I'll go up to David Craig's room (he's our trainer) and get my legs and feet worked on. Sometimes I'll get a rubdown or have him work on my lower back—

whatever is hurting at the time. Then I'll order room service and have it delivered to his room. I'll eat, then go back and wait for the bus to leave.

If we're playing at home, I leave my house by 4:15, get to the arena by 4:45, get my ticket situation straight, dress, get my ankles and feet taken care of, and get a rubdown. Then I'll get taped and go back into the locker room and watch tapes of the other team. I'm always the first one in the locker room and the last one to leave after the game. It's always been like that.

I'm on the court by 6:05 to do my shooting with Billy King. I do a thing with a TV station at 6:20 and go back to shooting at 6:25 or 6:30. Then I'll sign autographs for the kids on the way down the tunnel. I go in by 6:45; we're supposed to be in by 6:50.

Once I'm inside, I get my regular game bottoms on, get some water, stretch a little bit, look at some of the video of the previous game of our opponent. I'll watch my man, watch what he wants to accomplish on the offensive and defensive ends. I'll see how the other guy defended the man I'm guarding that night, how I can get myself free, and how they're doubling down, because that's going to mean a lot for me. When they double down on Rik and Derrick, I have to know where to go to get the best shots and be available so these guys can see where I am. That's because ten out of ten times it's not my man doubling down; they never leave me open for an open shot. I have to find an opening to be available for the shot.

To me, basketball is like a chess game. You've got to be able to read the pieces—reading where the screens are, reading where you can slip screens. It only takes that much for me to get my shot. Do you want a seventeen-footer as opposed to a nineteen-footer as opposed to a twenty-two-footer, which is a three-pointer now? What does the team need? You missed your last five shots, why don't you try to take this all the way to the hole so you can get your rhythm back? That is what's going through my mind out there.

As a player you have to know where you are on the court all the time. That's wild, because when I look at other sports— football, hockey, baseball—I see a Wayne Gretzky out there, and I'll say, "How did he know to pass that off?" Or when I watch John Stockton or Magic dishing it off, I think, "How did he know that guy was behind him?" But that kind of court sense is the secret of great basketball.

That was the one thing that was great for me on the Dream Team II: I got to pick all those guys' minds. I wanted to work on my pick-and-roll game this year, so I asked K. J., who I think is one of the best pick-and-roll players in the league, "What do you look at when you're coming off pick and rolls? What do you focus on? How do you get so open?"

Or I'd ask Joe Dumars, who's maybe the best defender in the league, "When you're playing me, you're always forcing me to do these certain things. Why do you do that? And what's the best way to play Latrell Sprewell and Mitch Richmond and those kinds of guys?"

Joe told me he always likes to take a player's strength away from him. With me, that's coming off screens, just shooting, going right. He takes those away. Whenever I come off screens, he's right there. He's not going to let me go right. What he's saying is, "You've got to beat me going left." When Bill Laimbeer was playing, Joe would dare you to go the other way and have Laimbeer hit you upside the head.

Now, most of the time, I just go left; he made me learn how to do that. Still, during the course of the game I'll get an elbow to the back of the neck, to the ribs, or bump knees about a dozen times. That's the price you pay for working off screens, setting screens down low and trying to get open for a shot. You've got to work so hard just to get a shot in this league; people who say I don't take enough shots don't realize what it takes out of you.

I asked Majerle, who shoots farther out than anybody, why he takes those shots, and he said, "Hey, look, if they're going to give me that shot, I'm going to take it." I can appreciate that sentiment; they don't give you much in this league.

Back to routines and superstitions.

As soon as the national anthem starts, I pray. I close my eyes and say, "Lord, please watch over me in this game. Without you, I know none of us would be here. Please bless everyone in Indiana [and if I'm on the road, I'll ask the Lord to bless the people in whatever city we're at]. We know that your son died on the cross for everybody here. Please bless my family, my mother and father, Saul and Anna, Darrell, Kelly, and D. K. Jr., Cheryl and Katrina, myself and Marita—wherever Marita is at—Tammy and George, and please watch all of our dogs, at home or in the kennel. I can do all things through Christ, who strengthens me. Please watch over me. In Jesus Christ, we pray. Amen."

Then I'll finish singing the national anthem.

Usually, before an 8 P.M. game, like a network TV game, we line up facing one another. So if it's New York, I'll want to find their guards—Harper, Davis, and Starks—and look at their eyes. It's like a gunfight. I want to look in their eyes and see if they're prepared, too.

As soon as the anthem ends, I'll tell one of the ball boys, "Give me a ball," and then I'll make a layup. Haywoode is always right behind me. That's the only time I do that—if it's a TNT or an NBC game. It has to be a nationally televised game for that routine. If it's a regular game, I've got to be the last one to put a layup in. Then I hit Mark Jackson's hand and then give dap to all the coaches and players. Dap—handshakes, fist handshakes. Mark and I are the last ones in line.

Haywoode and I do a dance before every game. Last year it was Janet Jackson and a little Michael Jackson. This year it depends on how the team is going at the time, and on who's hot and what we see on video. We do something every single game.

Not too long ago, Byron's little son Thomas was at a practice, and I asked him, "You gonna give us a little something to do?" I wanted him to give us a dance step, but he was all shy. Later, though, we saw him and he had something. So before the next game we did his little move, and we won, so I'm sure we'll use that one again. But if we lose two in a row, we'll change it.

Superstition is a lot in this game.

Friday, November 18
Indianapolis

Everybody was picking Seattle to win the Western Conference, but after beating them tonight, I'm not so sure about the SuperSonics. They'll get their shit together eventually, but tonight we just outhustled them.

David Letterman's mom was here tonight. She threw out the game ball. And get this: Detlef Schrempf, who used to play here before he went to the SuperSonics, has an eagle tattoo on his chest. Says it gives him inner strength. All I know is that I don't need a tattoo of an eagle flapping his wings to give me strength, I'd need strength to let somebody use those tattoo needles on me.

Saturday, November 19
Charlotte

All right, two in a row. Beat Zo and the Hornets, 102–89. It was the fourth straight time we held an opponent under 90 points, which is a big deal in this league.

I'm telling you, though, Zo is a man's man. When Alonzo Mourning came into the league as a rookie, his first game was against us here. He had held out and missed the first seven or eight games. They had TNT here, and we had Rik going against him. I was thinking, "Damn, Rik is going to eat this rook up."

But Alonzo came out like a man, like he had been informed of something, like he had gotten a scouting report on Rik. Well, I knew who had done it: Patrick Ewing and Dikembe Mutombo—two Georgetown guys helping out another Georgetown guy. Zo looked like a three-year veteran out there. He was hitting Rik. He was aggressive, growling and hitting, shooting. I thought, "Whoa, this guy's no ordinary rookie." Rik fouled him out of the game, but Zo was tough.

Ordinary rookies play timid, scared, intimidated. They'll show signs of brilliance, but they won't be able to sustain it. They hit the wall because they're not used to the eighty-two-game schedule.

My first month as a rookie I averaged about 15 points, but by the end of December and mid-January, I wasn't even sure I could make a shot. I was tired all the time. I would come home from practice, sleep during the day, and then be up all night because of the nap. You also have to deal with the constant travel and the physical punishment you take during games.

Watch Grant Hill. He'll get nicked up. He'll hit the wall. All rookies do. This NBA is no joke. You've got to be able to play every night.

If the NBA really wanted to improve the league and make it exciting for the fans, they would eliminate back-to-back games. But there's no way they'll do that. They won't give up ten or twenty games for that. But I guarantee you that more teams and players would be rested, and that would improve the quality of play. The wear and tear comes from guarding Michael Jordan for forty minutes on a Friday night and then traveling to New York and guarding John Starks for forty minutes and then hopping on a plane to Indiana for another game trying to check Joe Dumars for forty minutes. On some road trips you play Monday and Tuesday, have off Wednesday (but you're not really off; you just don't have a game), play Thursday, and then get on another plane. It's crazy.

Thank God we don't play again until Thursday, which should give us a chance to catch our breath.

Thursday, November 24
Indianapolis

I never thought I'd be so happy to play a game, even if it meant playing on Thanksgiving.

Larry was killing us in practice. Killing us. We had those four days between games, and he wanted to get back to basics. It was like a mini-camp.

It worked, though. We crushed Golden State, 123–96, and are so pumped up to play again that we even turned down Larry's offer to skip tomorrow's shootaround. With back-to-back games, Larry wanted us to be fresh for the Bucks tomorrow night. But, hey, this team isn't good enough yet to be skipping walk-throughs. We said we'd be there.

Friday, November 25
Indianapolis

I told you I had a good feeling about Rik this season. He had 28 against the Warriors and tonight had 30 in our win against the Bucks. That's four in a row for us, with our West Coast road trip coming up. I'm calling it our "Victory Tour."

Sunday, November 27
Portland

Larry's pissed again. After we lost by 10 to the Trail Blazers, Larry kicked the trainers and ball boys out of the locker room so he could rip into us for fifteen minutes. Portland kicked our asses on the boards, and we killed ourselves with twenty-four turnovers.

When the media finally came in, I told them I wasn't worried about the loss, that we have too much character on this team not to respond to the challenge.

In general, you never go at your teammates in the press. If you have a problem with a teammate, you work it out in the locker room. You never go to the press with it. You never want to betray the trust of the locker room because these are the guys on the front lines with you. Even though I might be one hundred percent right, I would never say anything to the media about a teammate. If someone does do it, it's almost like a cardinal sin.

Monday, November 28
Seattle

Another loss, another closed-door session after the game.

Larry got tossed for arguing a call on Dale Davis. Seems like all the little things are going against us right now.

And forget what I said about the SuperSonics. They've won five of their last six since we beat them in Indianapolis. I think they've figured their problems out. Now we've got to do the same.

With tonight's loss, we finished the month of November 7–5. That's not what we expected, but we had a lot of road games and we're still leading the Central Division.

Like Mark Jackson and I said, we wanted to spot the league a month. We did that. Now it's time to really go to work.

December 1994

Thursday, December 1
Los Angeles

No, sir, not us. No way were we going to be the first team to lose to the Clippers this season.

We beat them, 93–84, and those guys are 0–14 now, only three games short of tying the NBA record for the worst start ever. Hey, better them than us. We have our own problems. We needed a road win, and it didn't matter who it was against. The Clippers, Loyola Marymount, who cares?

The Clippers used to have a pretty good team until their owner, Donald Sterling, screwed things up. They had Larry Brown as their coach and guys like Danny Manning and Doc Rivers and Ken Norman and Ron Harper and Mark Jackson. They had some potential, but Sterling could never keep anybody.

Nobody wants to play for a screwed-up organization like the Clippers, so they leave. That's what happened with Harper and Dominique. They could have stayed with L.A. for more money, but what's the point if you don't have any chance of winning a championship?

When I was coming out of UCLA, I hoped the Clippers would draft me so I could stay home, but I know now how lucky I was that didn't happen. They've got to be the worst organization in the NBA.

Friday, December 3
Oakland

Guess who showed up at our practice today?

Michael.

He was in the Bay Area to see this weekend's game between the Chicaco Bears and the San Francisco 49ers. He's real good friends with Richard Dent, who used to play for the Bears but who now plays for the 49ers.

I guess Nellie invited Michael to practice with the Warriors for a couple of hours, and M. J. took him up on it. Then he stuck around for our practice, which was about an hour after the Warriors finished. He came out and said hello to everybody. I gave him a hug and some dap, and said, "What's happening?"

He said he was here for the Chicago game, and then he kind of smiled a real mischievous smile.

"What?" I said.

"I worked them out real hard today," he said, talking about the Warriors, "so they'll be real tired for you tomorrow."

I asked him how everything was going, and we talked for a couple of minutes. Then he started giving me a pep talk.

"Look," he said, "you're the best shooting two-guard in the league, but you need to be more aggressive. You need to shoot more. The team feeds off your energy. You can't appease everybody. You've got to be selfish but in a good way. Take more control."

I didn't know what to say, so I started joking with him.

"Well, I'll hold down the fort till you get back," I said.

"Shit, I ain't coming back," he said.

"Yeah, right," I said.

But you know what? He looked like the most contented person I'd ever seen. You could see the peace on his face. The media had put so much pressure on this guy when he was playing, but now he looked like he was finally at peace.

So I guess I believe him. I guess he's not coming back. But something—and I told this to a *Chicago Sun-Times* reporter not long ago—makes me think he'll return. It's just a feeling.

Antonio missed practice today so he could get an MRI done on his back. He has a bulging disk, and you can tell it's bothering him. He's made a total of only 4 shots and had 18 rebounds in the last 4 games. That isn't like him at all.

Saturday, December 3
Oakland

Maybe it was because Michael was at the game tonight, or maybe it was that pep talk he gave me yesterday, but I really tried to be more aggressive out there. I scored 33 points and took 19 shots, which is the most I've tried all season, and had 6 rebounds. I also played my ass off on defense, which you always have to do against Latrell Sprewell.

We got those Warriors, 118–107. Michael wasn't kidding—he really did wear those boys out the day before.

Tuesday, December 6
Indianapolis

Bad news. Antonio went on the injured list today. John Williams took his roster spot. We need John to step in and give us some quality minutes. No one expects him to replace Antonio, but I think he can help us.

If there is any one team that has given us trouble through the years, it's Detroit, especially when they had Zeke and Joe Dumars. That's probably the best backcourt duo in the history of the league.

Joe always gives me trouble. He's a consummate pro and plays the best man-to-man defense in the league. I always have a hard time shaking that guy.

It was a good game tonight. Grant Hill played well for them. I think the comparisons between Grant and Scottie Pippen and Michael Jordan eventually will come true. He's a great player, and once he gets comfortable with his outside shot, he's really going to be a bitch to play. He can take the ball off the dribble, he can see the floor, he's a great rebounder, and he plays great defense, which doesn't surprise me, being alongside Joe.

We won, 90–83, and we did it without Rik, who sprained his right foot, and Antonio, who got put on the injured list because of his bad back. But we did get John Williams in the lineup, and he gave us a spark. He's down to 295, which sounds like a lot until you realize what he weighed when he first showed up for training camp. He played twelve minutes and scored 7 points and had 8 rebounds. The guy isn't afraid to shoot. He had more attempts (12) in twelve minutes than I did (10) in thirty-nine minutes. But I had it tougher than John. I had Joe guarding me.

Friday, December 9
Philadelphia

Beat Philly on the road. No Rik and Antonio again, but Dale came up huge with 14 points and 18 rebounds. The win puts us up two games in the Central.

. . .

Okay, here's some stuff you can use in your next pickup game.

When you're guarding a guy, you tell him, "I'm putting handcuffs on you tonight." When I was messing around with Starks, I used to tell him, "Shackles and handcuffs, bitch." And while I said it, I had one wrist over the other.

Or you can tell a guy, "I'm putting the cork in you tonight."

And if a guy has a sweet shot, you say, "He can string it."

Tuesday, December 13
Cleveland

A lot of guys around the league think Indianapolis is boring. Hey, we're not worse off than Cleveland and Milwaukee. Those have to be the two worst cities in the world. I could never live there.

At least Indianapolis has Black Expo, City Fest—there's always something going on. We're not as boring as people think. It's not Miami or New York or Los Angeles, but I like it in Indianapolis. It's clean. It's safe. Who cares if it's not so fast-paced?

We're on our way back from Cleveland. Good game tonight . . . if you're the Cavs. They beat us, 90–83, but it was our own fault.

I knew something was wrong. I got too much rest today. Whenever I get too much rest in the afternoon, I don't play well that night. I only had 13 points on six of seventeen shooting. Not a very good night in my book. But the good thing about basketball is that there's always another game.

I take every minute of every game seriously, but I also know the difference between an exhibition game, a regular season game, and a playoff game.

Unless you're trying to make a team, the exhibition season means next to nothing. For veterans it's a way to get yourself ready for the regular season, to maybe work on a few new things, to experiment with different lineup combinations.

The regular season is too long to celebrate every win or beat yourself up after every loss. You try to find a happy medium, but sometimes that's tough. If you lose a big rivalry game or get beat on a last-second shot or get upset by a shitty team, that hurts.

The playoffs is when the season really begins. That's when everybody turns their games up a notch. That's when every possession is important. That's when I love to shine.

We set goals for ourselves before the season started. This year we don't want to settle for anything less than a Central Division championship, an Eastern Conference championship, and a trip to the NBA Finals. Reaching the conference finals last season was nice, but now we want to take the next step.

I don't think we're going to have to worry about Cleveland making it that far. They beat us, but the Cavs are playing really weird. They're slowing it down because Brad Daugherty is out with a back injury and Mark Price is struggling from the field.

They have a lot of guys who play hard, but we blew it by missing thirteen of fourteen from the three-point line. Larry told us we were mesmerized by the three-point line, that we were taking too many threes. I think he has a point, but that line *is* very tempting. I hate it because it's so close. I was one of seven and I was the only guy who made a shot, which isn't anything to be proud of. And if you can believe it, I made the three on my first shot. We went three quarters without making a three; because of that, we couldn't put any pressure on them.

Larry was definitely upset. You can tell when Larry's upset because he screams. It's one of the things he does best.

All his screams are basically the same. Sometimes you can tell when he's more pissed off than usual by his tone and by his eyes: His eyes are popping out of his head and he's looking straight at you.

He's hardest on his best players, so I guess in a strange way it's a compliment that he's hard on me.

Wednesday, December 14
Indianapolis

Okay, we came back and beat Atlanta, 81–79.

They've been playing surprisingly good, though. They got Steve Smith for Kevin Willis. Grant Long is a good player. They lost Manning to Phoenix, but I think they're going to upset some teams. They've still got Mookie Blaylock and Stacey Augmon. And Lenny Wilkens only needs a few more victories to become the all-time winningest NBA coach.

But I have to put a plug in for Larry. He won his 900th career game. Six more and he'll have 500 NBA wins.

People compare Larry to Pat Riley, but I don't see it. Yeah, they're both perfectionists, but from what I hear from other guys who played for Riley, Pat takes years off your career. He wears you down with those long, physical practices. By the end of the season you're playing on fumes.

Larry doesn't do that. He pushes us hard, but he doesn't leave our best basketball on the practice floor. And he doesn't play a lot of mind games. He's a great motivator, but he doesn't jerk you around. He gets right in your face and tells you what he expects. I respect that. And Larry likes being around players. I don't think Riley is that way.

Doc Rivers, who's one of the real nice guys in the league, said he was on a hotel elevator with Derek Harper, and at the last moment Riley got on. There wasn't anybody else on the elevator, but Riley never said a word to them. He just stared straight ahead, like they didn't exist.

Maybe Riley thinks he has to separate himself from his players. I mean, the guy does have those championship rings. But I like Larry's way better.

Larry gets on my ass a lot. You watch when we play. If I don't play good enough defense or don't take good shots or fail to be aggressive enough, Larry gets right in my face on the sidelines or in the locker room. I've got no problem with that.

That's what Chris Webber didn't understand with Don Nelson. There's a difference between two professionals and two egos. Hey, I get my shots in with Larry, too, but I do it in private—between Larry and me and my teammates. I'm not going to do or say something in public. You have to remember, it's coach and player. Those are two different titles. You've got to respect his position.

It's probably only fitting that we won tonight the Larry Brown way, which is on the defensive end of the floor, but it was ugly. We're still not playing Pacer-style basketball. We're not running as much, not getting easy baskets. We're still winning ballgames, but we're not playing well. That's encouraging in a way, but our next four ballgames are going to be a big test. We've got Charlotte back to back and Chicago back to back.

Charlotte has only won once in Market Square. But with Grandmama being healthy, with Mourning, with Hersey Hawkins, with Muggsy Bogues, they have lots of talent. A very dangerous team.

Friday, December 16
Indianapolis

Well, it went down to the final seconds.

With the score tied, Muggsy went in for a layup. We blocked it, Mark Jackson tapped it out to me, and I went in for a layup. Dell Curry grabbed me, thinking he had done it before I started my shooting motion. Six seconds left. Billy Oakes awarded me two free throws. I hit the shots, and we went up by two.

Charlotte had a final shot, and Curry almost hit a three at the buzzer. It went in and out.

After the game, Curry went after Oakes and had to be restrained. I stayed on the court to applaud the fans because they were fantastic. They really helped us get over the hump.

I don't know what Curry was so pissed about. First of all, he should have fouled me at half-court, but he didn't. Then he didn't foul me before I shot the layup. And then he went after the officials, which was stupid. If anybody on our team had done that, we would have been teed up.

Tuesday, December 20
Charlotte

The Hornets keep talking about this becoming a big rivalry. Some rivalry. We've beaten them twelve out of fifteen times. We've owned them here and back at Market Square.

Still, these are big games because Charlotte is in our division and because they're a good test for us.

We lost, 99–95.

We got off to a big lead. They came back and caught us, and it went down to the wire. Hersey hit some big plays down the stretch, which is unlike what he did at our place when he scored 2 points.

Another game we gave away. We're giving games away, and we just can't do that. About the only bright spot is that Antonio worked out before the game. He's still not ready to come off the injured list, but he might be back by next week. After getting outrebounded, 46–30, tonight, we could sure as hell use him.

We've got Chicago coming in now, a home and away series. This is just the opposite of our "rivalry" with Charlotte.

Chicago has owned us at our home building. They swept us at our place last year, and they've won the last nine times at Market Square, dating back to 1991.

During my early years in the league, when Michael was playing, I made a lot of stupid comments. I said they couldn't win without Michael Jordan, that all they had was Michael Jordan. This was before their first championship against Los Angeles. So I added fuel to a rivalry that already had some real heat. With Indiana and Chicago, it's a rivalry because of geography. We're less than four hours' driving distance. They're the big city, we're the smaller one. They had the greatest player, Michael Jordan; we had less-known players. Still, I shouldn't have said anything about them being a one-man team. That was a lot of stupidity on my part.

B. J. Armstrong and I both have the same attorney, and I talk to B. J. a lot. He's going through a transitional period right now because he doesn't know what it's like to have a bad season. He doesn't understand what it's like to struggle, which is what the Bulls have been doing this year.

When B. J. first came into the league in 1989–90, he made it to the NBA Finals. Then the Bulls won an NBA championship the next season. Then another. Then another. Three-time champs. He's never seen anything else but champagne showers and trophy presentations and victory parades and playoff checks and all the adulation. He's used to the entourage, getting off the team bus where a thousand people are waiting to see Air or Scottie. It was a road show when they had Air. Believe me, they aren't there to see Bill Wennington. So it's tough for B. J. Hell, it's tough for that whole team.

Still, in my opinion, Scottie Pippen is the most complete player in the league. He can do everything.

Scottie's under a lot of pressure. There's a big difference between being The Man, which is what Michael was, and being the man who's next to The Man. But Scottie's delivered the goods for the Bulls. I think he's the best small forward in the game. Barkley thinks Pippen is the best non-center in the world. Still, night in, night out, when you've got to deliver and all the pressure is on you, and all the microphones are in your face and not Michael's anymore, and everyone is asking you what happened, why did *you* win or or lose the game, well, that makes a huge difference.

Scottie's pissed about his contract and about all the money they paid Toni Kukoc. I guess I can't blame him in a way. If you ask me, I really do believe that Jerry Krause, their general manager, screwed up by paying Kukoc all that money. Okay, Krause screwed up, but Scottie shouldn't be mad at Krause. He shouldn't be mad at Toni. He shouldn't be mad at the Bulls. Scottie should be mad at his own damn agent. That's the guy he should fire. The agent is the guy who set up that dumbass deal, and Scottie's the one who signed it. Scottie has to look in the mirror on this one and take some blame. It was his signature, right? Nobody forged it, right?

Look, when I first came to Indiana, I had the benefit of playing with Chuck Person and Detlef Schrempf, who shouldered all the blame. When those two left, I had to take two steps forward. Everyone else is still behind you. A general has to look forward, he has to lead. You might do it wrong, but you have to lead.

Wednesday, December 21
Indianapolis

Scottie had the stomach flu for this game, and Kukoc, who I think is going to be a great player once he adapts to the NBA game, started in his place. Toni had 24 points and he played well, but our defense stepped up and we held them off, 107–99.

Byron was hurt with a hip pointer, and I hit my head on one of the cameras. Had to have three or four stitches above my right eye, so I missed some time. But Haywoode came in and did the job, which is really important in this league. He scored 19, a season high for him.

Now we go down to their place, their new United Center. Everyone is talking about how much the Bulls are struggling in their new building. They're 5–6 at the United Center, 11–12 overall, and I think this is a game we can steal. The Bulls haven't been below .500 this late in the season since 1986.

Also, this new place can't be as tough as Chicago Stadium. What a great building that was. The way I figure it, there's no way they can duplicate that kind of atmosphere, that kind of noise in the United Center.

Friday, December 23
Chicago

Well, so much for my United Center theory.

The game was on TNT, and we came out and gave a total horseshit effort. It's the worst we've played all year. The Bulls exposed everything that has been wrong with us all year. They drilled us, 116–92. What an embarrassment.

To put it real simple, the Bulls showed that our team sucks right now. We're playing individual defense instead of team defense. Our defense sucks.

Kukoc had 27, 17 of them in the third quarter. Pippen had only 13 points, but his 11 rebounds made up for it.

Larry cussed us out big-time, and we deserved it. We played terrible. Byron said afterward that we were running out there "like a chicken with its head cut off."

I was watching some highlights of the Phoenix game, and the announcers were saying, "And there's another shot from Ainge. Wow, he doesn't look thirty-five."

I was thinking, "He's thirty-five? He doesn't even seem

thirty-five. I mean, that's six more years than me. Am I gonna be playing that long, or what?"

I'm telling you, if I win a title between now and then, no, I won't be playing when I'm thirty-five. That is my one goal: to win a championship. People don't realize how hard it is to win a title. So much shit goes into winning one. There's so much pressure.

That's why I can sympathize with Michael Jordan. If I were Michael, I would have been gone after the first one. If it's anything like I went through—and we just went to the Eastern Conference Finals in 1994—can you imagine what it was like for him? He won three NBA championships. He's the greatest player of all time. How did he get through all that shit? If I won a title, I'd think about quitting in a heartbeat. A heartbeat. You have to put so much effort into it. But that's what you live for: to win the ultimate title.

Now if I were like Sam Cassell with the Houston Rockets and won it my rookie year, of course not. But I've been doing this for seven years and going out in the first round, getting beat down, head knocked. . . . It's been a long haul for me. I'm only twenty-nine, I'm still young, but it's been a long haul, so I would seriously consider it.

People don't understand. They say, "You just won a title. Don't you want to be greedy and go for two?"

People don't understand the sacrifice and hard work it took to get one. People didn't understand why Michael was retiring? Jesus Christ, give the guy a break. His dad gets killed, and the first thing they ask him is, "Do you think this has anything to do with your gambling?"

I mean, the man's dad just got killed. Ask me why Michael left and I'll tell you: The media drove the world's greatest player away. They can talk all they want about Michael, but the media drove him away from the game. The pressure. The demands.

Okay, they're playing the Knicks. He goes to Atlantic City to play blackjack. The last time I looked there was nothing illegal about that. You think they would have written all those stories if Wennington had gone there and played? Hell, no. So Michael was playing blackjack. So what? He couldn't sleep, so he went to Atlantic City. So?

Michael was there playing blackjack, and some guy who had a bet down on the Knicks-Bulls saw him and thought, "Geezus, they're playing the Knicks tomorrow, he's gonna be tired, let me see what the line is." That's not Michael's fault, that's that guy's fault.

Here's how I look at it: Michael Jordan is on a level with Michael Jackson. Those are two of the most recognizable entertainers in the field. They can't go anywhere because people will maul them. Whatever they do, it's magnified out of proprotion. People forget he's human. Just because he's doing McDonald's commercials and saying, "Off the backboard and off the moon" with Larry Bird, and doing stuff for Hanes underwear and all that, who's to say he can't have fun and go to a pool hall or Vegas or whatever? Why can't he do the same thing that Tom next door is doing if it's legal?

Okay, the man lost some serious bucks on the golf course. But you know what? Everybody gambles on the golf course. All those rich businessmen. Hey, $10,000 a hole. But because it's Michael Jordan, it becomes a story. If you have the money to back it, you have the money to back it. All those rich businessmen do it. They all chase their bets.

It all comes down to image—what looks good and what looks bad. The media thought that Michael's going to Atlantic City, betting big on golf, looked bad. What, sportswriters never go to Vegas or Atlantic City? They never bet when they play golf?

I'll tell you, there're two people whose shoes I really wouldn't want to walk a mile in: Michael Jordan's and Michael Jackson's. Those are shoes that are never going to be filled, because people are always going to expect something bigger, something better, and something more. It's hard to keep topping yourself. It's hard to keep getting 50 points. It's hard to keep selling 40 million albums.

Things change. The game changes. Music changes.

I look at my image, and sometimes I can't believe the way I'm perceived. I'm supposed to be this crazy trash-talking lunatic guy. But that's not me. Yeah, I talk some shit, but it's my game—one that I've worked very hard to develop—that does the real talking. Otherwise, none of the other stuff would mean anything.

Look at how Charles Barkley said he wasn't a role model. He took so much flak for that, but I think he was right. Your parents are role models. Teachers, principals, police are role models. I think a lot of people say, "But Charles, you are a role model. My kids look up to you so much." But your kids should be looking up to you, not Charles. Your kids should be admiring the school counselors, the principals, the teachers, and not me. I'm just the guy you're going to see play the Celtics next Thursday.

I try to act like a role model but only because the things I do in the public eye—on TV, radio, in the newspapers, at games—are seen and heard by a lot of people. I accept it. It's tough, because I bleed, too. I cry, too. I hurt, too. It's tough because you try to do things right.

People think that if you're successful and you have a lot of money that everything is peaches and roses, and everything is fine. People don't understand. Sometimes when I get home I want to punch holes in my walls. I get just as frustrated as anybody else.

Don't get me wrong. I love my life. If I had to choose between being Reggie the public figure, pro basketball player, or, let's say, working at the bank, I would be Reggie the player, the entertainer. I love doing what I do, but everything has its ups and downs. Sometimes I feel I have the weight of the whole state of Indiana on my shoulders. Basketball is so important to the people there, it's such a religion in the state. I have such high expectations for this team, and so do the fans in Indiana.

Marita and I talk about it sometimes. I tell her about the pressure, about the little kids, the men and women who are looking at you, rooting for you to do well. The state of Indiana has been picked on, dogged on for so many years. All we're known for lately is the Indianapolis 500 and putting Mike Tyson in jail. That's it. Now we're getting known for something else.

That's why I'm really scared about this season. I don't want to revert to the years when we thought winning thirty or forty games was a big deal. If we don't get back to the Eastern Conference Finals this year, the season is going to be a complete failure. We have to get to the Conference Finals, at the very least. Otherwise, this will be a complete failure in my mind and in the fans' minds.

For us to get there, we'll have to go through the Knicks. In our eyes, they're the Wicked Witch of the East.

Fans can be cruel without realizing it. One thing I'll never forget is the time we had gotten the crap beat out of us there by the Knicks in 1994, and some people were waiting for me as I went to get my car. I wasn't in the best of moods after the loss, but I was trying to be polite. People were asking for my autograph, and I kept saying, "No, thank you. Not tonight, maybe another day."

As I was walking, I was also talking to these twins who have been to every game, who have been very supportive of the team. Anyway, when I got to my car, there were all these people around it. Security police were kind of pushing them back, and I said to the people, "Thank you, maybe another game, okay?"

Well, there was this guy who was holding his son and a poster of me. The guy got mad, yelled at me, and started tearing the poster up right in front of the kid.

I was thinking, "This is some fucked-up shit."

See what I mean? Just because I didn't sign one autograph, this guy was gonna be an asshole in front of his kid. And now his kid was going to hate me because I didn't sign a jersey or a card. And this is just me. Now imagine how bad it was for Michael. He couldn't go anywere—couldn't go to a restaurant and just eat a meal.

When I'm out in public, I wear a cap and sunglasses so people won't recognize me. But that really embarrasses me. Sometimes being known has its perks. I mean, you get in a movie free, get a discount on clothes or records or tickets, or whatever. But it has its disadvantages. People say, "It would be great to be you." Nuh-uh. Don't say nothing about me until you walk a mile in my shoes.

It embarrasses me when people come up to me when I'm trying to eat a meal at a restaurant, or they scream my name in a mall. That's why I don't go to the mall on Friday, Saturday, or Sunday. I don't put myself in a position like that anymore. I learned that about three or four years ago.

My family, my wife, and my friends keep me sane. You still lose a part of yourself. Everything you do is said or read about. Everything is publicized.

I won't walk into a restaurant. I'll call ahead. Still, sometimes I'm eating, I've got a mouth full of pasta, and someone will say, "I'm so sorry to do this, I've never ever done this before, but could I have your autograph?"

I try to be nice, but what I want to say is, "If you've never done this before, don't start now."

But if you do something like that, then you've got all these people around you looking to see what your reaction will be. You're put on the spot, and then you're made out to be the bad guy. I always say to myself, "If I saw Michael Jackson or Elizabeth Taylor or Harrison Ford or some famous person, I would never go up to them and bother them."

If there's one thing that's tough to do, it's to say no to the kids. But if I say yes to one while I'm out, then I have to say yes to everybody. Then I'm not going to have fun, which sort of defeats the whole purpose for everybody.

I try to be polite about it. I sign autographs. I do things for the club. But sometimes your life has to be just that—your life.

Here's an example: I was with Randy Wittman, Vern Fleming, and Tank Thompson in Hooters about a year ago. We were in there eating when a father came up with his two kids and asked for an autograph.

"Sure," we said. "But can we finish eating and then we'll sign it?"

He kind of hestitated, all disappointed and everything, and said, "Well . . . okay." That's exactly how he said it—"Well . . . okay"—like it was our fault that we were in the middle of our meal.

We finished eating—it must have been ten minutes after the guy had asked for the autographs—and then we went looking for him in the restaurant. You have to understand that we were ready to catch a flight; we usually eat at Hooters before we leave. We went outside Union Station in Indianapolis to look for this guy, but we never found him.

We got back from the road trip two or three days later. While we were gone, this father had written and called Donnie and said we had embarrassed him in front of his sons. He was a divorced father who had the kids for the weekend, and we had embarrassed him in front of the kids and this was something they would never forget.

I couldn't believe this guy said that. We told Donnie that we had looked for the guy. But to appease him, Donnie gave him front-row seats for the Boston Celtics game and made us take pictures with him and his family. After that I said, "Never again." I tell people that I'll sign autographs at the game, but when I'm away from the arena, I will not sign.

Maybe I'm a little on the safety-first side, but I won't even go out to do a postgame radio or TV interview until I'm sure there's enough security people to help me get to and from the interview area. That's because I get a lot of potshots, a lot of threats. People think because I'm one way on the court that I'm that way off the court. They think if I talk that shit on the court, then I'm going to get in people's faces in everyday life.

It's funny, but I won't go to clubs and bars and places like that unless I'm with the guys or unless they have proper security there. That's because when people get drunk, they try to test you and try to do things. It's happened to me. So why should I put myself in that position? I don't want to be like Barkley and knock somebody out and then go to court and have all that mess. Even though Barkley was right and they acquitted him, the damage had been done. So I make sure there are witnesses.

I've had death threats. During the 1994 playoffs, people were calling saying, "If you step on the court . . . right between the eyes." I think that's kind of funny in a way, but who knows how serious the guy was? It happened in New York. In fact, that's why I changed my name on the road. Now, whenever I check into a hotel, I use a different name.

Sorry, no hints.

The first time I ever got a death threat, it gave me a chill. I remember watching the series between Chicago and Portland, I think it was, and Michael was getting death threats. I thought, "Well, that's Michael Jordan." You think that will never happen to you. I mean, why would someone want to take your life over a basketball game? It doesn't mean that much. But after the things I was saying about New York and doing to New York, especially in game five in New York in 1994, maybe it meant that much to some crazy Knicks fan.

The bottom line is that people were calling the offices and saying some crazy stuff. The Pacers management didn't tell me about the threats until after the playoffs. I laugh about it now. It's funny. People can get obsessed over a damn game. It's just a game. Granted, a lot is riding on it in terms of reaching the NBA Finals, but it's just a game.

Looking back on it, I'm glad the Pacers didn't tell me about the death threats until after the fact. I don't think I would have been able to concentrate. It would have worried me, my parents, and my wife.

And even though they didn't tell me about the specific threats, I think I had a sense something was wrong during the game, especially during the timeouts. When we got into our huddle, there were all these security people on the outer edges. I remember looking over at the Knicks huddle, and there weren't any security personnel.

After the game, those security guys were in such a hurry to surround me that they nearly ran me over. I was thinking, "What's going on here? I can handle myself."

But you never know if someone in the crowd that night had a Glok 40 loaded and ready to go.

Saturday, December 24
Indianapolis

Larry gave us Christmas Eve day off, but we asked if we could practice anyway. After last night's game, we needed it.

It turned out we couldn't even do that right. Guys showed up late, and guys came in hurt. Larry called us together and said, "You motherfuckers called this practice, and now everyone's limping in hurt, coming in late. You figure out what you want to do on your own."

He wasn't exactly in the Christmas spirit.

The coaches left, and we were all standing around kind of shocked by what happened. So I said, "Hey, y'all, we've got to get some running in and get back on the right track."

So we held a practice on our own without the coaches. We went through our plays, dummy offense, scrimmaged, and ran drills for an hour and a half.

Sometimes you need that. Players need to police themselves. Coaches shouldn't have to be getting on you all the time. I think that was a practice we needed.

I had to do some Christmas shopping. The way I have to do it is to go to the stores right before closing time and ask the manager or clerk if I can shop after hours. They're usually very accommodating.

Sunday, December 25
Indianapolis

Merry Christmas. Watched the Denver–Seattle and Chicago–New York games.

Monday, December 26
Indianapolis

Had practice before we left to go on a road trip to Denver and Utah. This was a different Larry and a different kind of practice. We had almost a three-hour workout, which is really unusual for Larry. We're just trying to get back to basics, which for us starts on the defensive end.

Anyway, I'm on the blue team with the starters. We scrimmaged five times, and we couldn't beat the white team. Nothing against our second team—I think it's one of the deepest benches in the league—but if we can't beat them, what's going to happen against Denver and Utah?

I don't think it's a lack of effort on our part. We're working hard. But last year we practiced hard and the results showed during the game. This year we practice hard, but when game time comes we don't do the same thing. That's why Larry kept us out there those three hours, trying to get us back to those basics.

. . .

More bad news: Antonio, who's already missed ten games because of that bulging disk, might have to have surgery. If that happens, he could miss at least six weeks.

He practiced with us Thursday but couldn't go Saturday or today. He's not traveling with us, either. The doctors and Donnie are supposed to get together with him today and figure out what to do next. It doesn't look good.

We flew into Denver today, thinking we were going to get off the plane, go back to the hotel, go see a movie and relax. Instead, Larry called a meeting and went off on us for two hours. He said we all had to look at the mirror and see if we were doing all we could to help the team win. I mean, wow. He was in our faces.

During that meeting, I was the one Larry was directing most of the criticism at. He's been on me all year to be more aggressive, to take more shots, to drive to the hoop more, but it's been a while since he went off on me like he did today.

I didn't take it personally. You've got to be man enough in this league to take criticism, and I don't think a lot of players in this league can do that because they're getting paid the big bucks, and they don't want to be embarrassed in front of their teammates.

But I think that's what's made this team a unique team. Larry Brown doesn't have any favorites. He doesn't look at one player as being better than another. Everyone's the same, from one through twelve. Everyone is treated the same on his totem pole. He went off on me, and we all aired out our feelings about why we weren't better than 15–8. Yeah, we're in first place, but that's not good enough because we feel we can play much better than that.

I still don't think I have to take a lot of shots for us to be successful in the regular season. I know Larry doesn't agree with that, but the way I look at it, the time for me to really step it up is during the playoffs. Also, everyone has to understand that it's harder to get some of those shots I was getting in past seasons. I'm not making excuses; it's just fact. Teams are making more of an effort to stop me, so I try to work within the framework of the offense and move the ball if I don't have the shot. I guess I could force up bad shots, but that doesn't make any sense to me.

The reality is that this year I've seen everybody step up their game against me. It's sort of what Michael must have gone through every time I went against him. If you go against Michael and have a good game, you're going to be the lead story on ESPN. Every two-guard in the league is trying to make his name off Reggie Miller this year. I have to be prepared every night. You can't take a night off just because you're tired or because it's a back-to-back or the fourth game in five nights. You have to be ready to play every night. Now some nights I get my clock cleaned, but that's how it goes.

I heard that Vern was quoted in the papers back in Indianapolis as saying that by being so unselfish I was being selfish. Hmmm. I'll have to think about that one.

We've got Denver tonight. Getting to the meat of our season.

I told you things might turn around a little bit. We came out and controlled the tempo against Denver and won, 95–91. Maybe that cussing out by Larry did help us a little bit. It sure helped Rik, who had 33 points against Dikembe, who's one of the best defenders in the league.

Now we need to continue this against Utah, which is rested. If any one team is playing well right now, it's Utah. They've won seven in a row, and this is a back-to-back for us.

The doctors recommended back surgery for Antonio. But if what they're saying is right, he might only miss three or four weeks.

Wednesday, December 28
Salt Lake City

Well, it just goes to show that when you run into a hot team, it doesn't matter what's going on.

Right now I've got to say Utah is playing the best basketball I've seen all year. We've played some good teams, but Utah just beat the crap out of us, 117–95. It wasn't even close. Man, they played great.

I don't think there's a better one-two combination in the league that John Stockton and Karl Malone. Geezus, they set one another up beautifully.

The funny thing about it is they're getting everybody in the act: Jeff Hornacek, Felton Spencer. I think a great pickup for them this year was Antoine Carr.

Friday, December 30
Indianapolis

About time we crushed somebody. We beat New Jersey by 19, and I don't care if Derrick Coleman and Kenny Anderson didn't play. We had our own Derrick tonight, and he played great. Twenty-one points, 8 rebounds, 5 assists; he missed only 2 shots.

We're 17–9 and two games behind first-place Cleveland as we head into the new year. Happy New Year.

January 1995

Tuesday, January 3
New Jersey

New Jersey again. Hard team to figure out, these Nets. Sometimes they show up, some nights they lay down for you.

Derrick Coleman and Kenny Anderson have been out with injuries, but they're supposed to be back for tonight's game. And then there's Benoit Benjamin, who had 20 against us last Friday.

One little bit of news: Larry dropped Haywoode to third team and moved Vern up to second team. Haywoode's been struggling offensively. He had those 19 points against the Bulls but then went scoreless in the next three games.

Uh-oh. The wrong New Jersey team showed up. Benoit played and had a good game, after not playing much the whole year. He got 30. Derrick Coleman and Kenny Anderson both played pretty well, and we lost, 114–103, for our fifth loss in our last six road games. Plus, Mark sprained his right ankle in the third quarter.

We keep going back and forth this season: win one, lose one, win one, lose one. For us to make a move we have to get past these teams that are middle-of-the-road. We're not showing much right now. We're capable of so much more.

Everyone's on me to shoot more. This is unbelievable. They're getting on me to shoot more, get more attempts. I always felt that this team could win without me shooting twenty, twenty-five times a game. But if they want me to put the ball up more, I'll try to be more aggressive. If that's the key, if that will help the team win, then that's what I'll do.

But that's what I did tonight. I scored 37 points, shot 22 times, hit 7 of 13 three-pointers . . . and we lost. See what I mean? It doesn't always work when I score lots of points.

Now we've got Washington coming up, then one of our longest road trips of the season: Dallas, Houston, New York, Boston, and Washington.

Wednesday, January 4
Indianapolis

We beat Washington, 94–90. Nothing really to report about that except that we nearly blew a 20-point third-quarter lead. If we don't stop doing that, it's going to be one mother of a road trip.

Thursday, January 5
Indianapolis

Antonio had surgery today to fix the bulging disk in his back. Shit.

Friday, January 6
Dallas

We just finished losing to Dallas, 103–92. I don't know how we lose to these teams.

Sometimes it's baffling in the NBA. There's so much emotion that goes into these games, it leaves you breathless. Another winnable game for us, but we came out and just went through the motions.

Larry was sick so he didn't coach. Gar Heard took the reins and did a fairly good job. He had a good game plan, but we didn't play well. I had 19 but made only 7 of 18 from the field.

I think Jason Kidd, the rookie point guard for the Mavericks, is going to be a true superstar. This kid plays hard, gets every loose ball, is fast as shit, and plays tough. He played forty minutes, had 15 points, 8 rebounds, 10 assists, and 4 steals. Once he gets an outside shot, he's really going to be unstoppable. Right now, teams are sagging on him, and he's struggling with his shot. Once he has that down, he's going to be a great one. And in that system, with Jimmy Jackson and Jamal Mashburn—two good young players coming up—and with all their draft choices, that's definitely going to be a team on the rise if they continue to play hard.

The other thing I like about Kidd is that he just plays the game and doesn't try any of this power struggle stuff with the coach.

Saw the out-of-town scores tonight. Atlanta beat Washington, which means Larry Wilkens became the all-time leader in NBA victories. Congratulations, man.

Saturday, January 7
Houston

We beat the champs down at their place! Take that, World Champion Rockets!

This was the turning point for us last year. Maybe this will be the turning point for us this year. We beat Houston down in Houston last year, and it just turned our whole season around. Now we do it again, 88–83.

This year we had a big game from everybody, with all five starters scoring in double figures. It also was Larry's 500th NBA victory.

We held Hakeem to 27 and I know that sounds like a lot, but that was tough enough. If any one player in the league is playing at his best, at the peak of his game, it would have to be Hakeem Olajuwon. You can double- or triple-team him, and this guy is unbelievable. He does some amazing stuff down low. He's the best center out there.

You can talk about Shaq all you want, or Patrick Ewing, but no one can touch Hakeem. The best. He's got ten thousand moves down low.

Hopefully we can bring the momentum to New York, which will be one of the biggest games of the year for us—the rematch from the 1994 Eastern Conference Finals. If you can't get pumped up to go to Madison Square Garden, especially after the playoffs last year, then you don't belong in this league.

I'm sure everyone's going to come out and root against us. That's okay: twelve against twenty thousand. If we can ride this crest, this little wave from the Houston win, we'll be all right. Going against Vernon Maxwell will prepare me for John Starks, because Vernon plays great defense and he's a fiery-type player like me.

Vernon catches a lot of shit, but I think we've always had mutual respect because of the way we play, the way we talk. Vernon has a reputation in the league as a feisty trash-talker, too. You know what's funny? When we get together, we never talk shit to each other. Maybe it's because we both know where we're coming from. We never have talked shit. Don't get me wrong—we've gone at each other and damn near got in fights, been at each other's throat, but there's never been any trash-talking.

I told him thanks for taking my back last year at the playoffs and beating the Knicks. He said he knew what he had to do against Starks and he did it.

Now it's our turn to go to the Garden and see what we can do against them.

Sunday, January 8
Phoenix

Filmed a McDonald's commercial today. It was an all-day shoot with Larry Bird, Shawn Kemp, Larry Johnson, and Charles Barkley. Michael's the star of the commercial, but he filmed his part back in Chicago. Mysterious, huh?

There's supposed to be lots of special effects involved, but basically I'm the Road Runner in disguise. Each one of us is a Bugs Bunny cartoon character, and we keep shedding our disguises until finally Michael the basketball player meets Michael the baseball player.

When you look at the spot and think about the timing of it—he's off playing baseball for the Chicago White Sox organization—it kind of tells you he might be coming back to hoops. Maybe I'm going overboard on the Detective Columbo thing, but maybe that's the reason he didn't film the spot with us.

Just finished watching SportsCenter on ESPN and, man, Webber was bashing Don Nelson bad. I'm telling you, Webber and Nellie were going at each other.

Then I heard about Del Harris going crazy in the locker

room at Portland. Something about Nick Van Exel saying he wasn't going to play in the second half because the Lakers were down by 30. In Seattle, Vincent Askew got suspended because he wouldn't go into a game when George Karl asked him. Dennis Rodman does his own thing in San Antonio. So do Derrick Coleman and Chris Morris in New Jersey. Butch Beard, the coach, asked Morris to tie his shoelace at a shootaround, and Morris said no. Minnesota's Isaiah Rider had a press conference so he could rip his coach. This stuff is getting out of control. Bottom line: Players should play and coaches should coach.

There's a lot of bitching going on these days. The thing is, professional athletes don't know how easy they have it. This is getting unbelievable. You've got to respect the coach. You've got to respect his leadership abilities. He might not always be right, but you have to respect that position. A lot of young players—and even some older veterans—aren't doing that. It's shocking, very shocking.

As far as that Golden State thing goes, I don't think Nellie and Webber would have ever gotten along. From what I hear, they just couldn't get along at all. I don't think Chris could take tough talk, and in this league a lot of coaches are very demanding. From the outside looking in, I think it was a great decision on Chris's part to get out of there. But I have a problem with how he did it. By taking his complaints public, I think Chris showed disrespect toward the veterans. The veterans are doing their jobs, following the rules set down by Nellie, and here comes Chris going his own way. That's one reason I think the best thing we can do in the next collective bargaining agreement is put in a rookie salary cap. Some of these rookies think just because they have a big-money contract, they can dictate policy.

A lot of these rookies are so sensitive these days. With the Pacers, we treat rookies with the standard bad stuff but nothing horrible. We'll make them sing birthday songs or maybe their college team songs. Sometimes they have to arrange everybody's wake-up calls. Other times they have to get us newspapers. And if a veteran is going to be late for the bus, we'll tell someone, "Rookie, go in there, call him, and get him up."

But we're not as bad as some teams are with rookies. We don't make them wash our cars or get our laundry. We'll never go home and call a rookie and tell him to do something. That's their off time. Once they leave the locker room, they're on their own. I don't know what Webber would have done had he played on a Moses Malone team. I hear Moses Malone used to be the worst on rookies.

You know, now that I'm thinking about it, that damn Chuck Person made me get up one morning, drive over to his house, and wash his car in the middle of winter.

I was looking at the standings this morning, and you can't help but notice Orlando's quick start. The Magic added Brian Shaw and Horace Grant to that lineup, and it's going to help them out a lot.

But my question is this: How long can they hold on to that lead? You watch, come playoff time there's going to be a lot of expectations on that team to win. I think they'll win lots of regular season games, but I don't think they'll be coming out of the Eastern Conference. Too much pressure on Shaq and Penny. I think we'll be coming out of the East.

Can you believe it? The Clippers are 0–16. Damn, that's an awful team.

Mark Jackson used to play for them. He's always telling us stories about that team and its owner, Donald Sterling, the millionaire real estate developer. Brutal stuff, but nothing I can repeat without hearing from Sterling's lawyer.

I'll give them this much, though: They play hard, and Bill Fitch has done a pretty good job with them. But still, they're a horseshit team. There's no other way to say it. I think if Sterling would let a general manager run that team instead of trying to make all the decisions, that would help a lot. I know Sterling says he doesn't meddle, but Elgin Baylor couldn't make all those stupid player moves on his own.

They had a chance to keep Larry as their coach a few years ago, but Larry likes to make decisions. I don't think they were going to give him that kind of power.

Things are so bad with the Clippers that Fitch asked a new newspaper beat reporter, "Wow, what did you do so bad to deserve this assignment?"

Meanwhile, across town, you've got the Lakers, who might be the surprise team of the season. They have a lot of young talent, but nobody expected them to get out of the blocks like this. Cedric Ceballos is playing great, and he only cost the Lakers a first-round pick, which, if L.A. keeps playing the way they are, will be a low first-round selection for the Phoenix Suns. That's a steal—again—for Lakers General Manager Jerry West, who's got an all-star in Ceballos. Ceballos knows how to score on the baseline like nobody else. If you get him away from the baseline, he might kill himself, but the guy definitely knows how to put the ball in the basket.

Nick Van Exel is an up-and-coming point guard, and he has a chip on his shoulder but in a good way. Eddie Jones is going to be a quality two-guard in this league. Anyway, they're playing great.

And I can't help but notice my very special friends, the Knicks. They were struggling early, but coming into our game Tuesday night, they've won six in a row and are 18–12 overall compared to our 19–11. And no matter what, Pat Riley always has them ready to play. That's the key. They don't have a lot of talent, they play real ugly, but they find ways to win. If they don't, the city and the fans will let them know about it real quick.

New York is a great place to play if you're the visiting team. In fact, New York and Chicago are my favorite places to play on the road. I love it that every time you touch the ball, the focus is on you. I love when the kids come to boo me. I love being the enemy.

There are so many people out there working nine to five. The boss gets on them; the wife screams at them for not being affectionate enough, for not bringing flowers. So they come to a game to get away from all that. Then that's my job, to give them a show, to make them forget for two hours. Let them take their frustrations out on me. The NBA is the entertainment business. That's me: I entertain.

Hey, I'm not as ruthless as Bill Laimbeer was. That's borderline dirty. I'm not a dirty player, but I like to ruffle some feathers, to see how people react. The bad guys are supposed to wear black. That's okay, I'll be the bad guy.

I love playing at the Garden, but I don't think I could play for the Knicks. Nothing against the Knicks (okay, a little something against the Knicks), but I just don't like the city. I like the laid-back life of Indianapolis. In New York, there's almost too much going on.

Monday, January 9
New York

In 1994, after we beat number-one-seeded Atlanta in the second round of the playoffs, people asked, "Who do you want to play next?" I said, "I want to play New York. We don't want to dodge anybody. We want to play who we consider the best team."

We had beaten Orlando. We had beaten the Hawks. We wanted the Knicks next. We thought they were the best team even though they didn't have the top seed in the conference. The way we figured it, we had a lot of unfinished business because they had beaten us 3–1 in the playoffs the year before.

So we got to New York today, and I was watching one of the

TV stations there, and Charles Smith was talking, saying, "Reggie Miller wanted the Knicks, now he's got the Knicks."

We were playing cards, and I was thinking, "Look at this clown." Now, if this were Patrick Ewing or Anthony Mason talking, I could respect that. But this kid, with all that size and talent, averaging 14.8 points and doing all that talking—I don't think so. Hell, the game before ours he scored just 4 points and had 2 rebounds in eighteen minutes against the Minnesota Timberwolves. The Timberwolves! He had more personal fouls than points, 5–4. He doesn't know a thing about talking shit.

People say I'm the best trash-talker in the league, but there are others who are a lot better. Charles Barkley, hands down, is the best talker and entertainer in the NBA. I think Vernon Maxwell is a great talker, a great showman, and won't back down. If there's anyone I respect in that regard, it's Vernon Maxwell. He's just like me: He'll take on a center.

Gary Payton, for a little guy, is cockier. What I do isn't cocky. I don't get down and play defense like Payton does, slapping the court with the palms of my hand. Payton is cockier; I'm more confident. I'll talk when we're up 16 or when we're down 16. A lot of players shut up when they're losing, but to me the mark of a true talker is someone who will pop off no matter what. Doug Collins, who's doing Tuesday night's game for TNT, says I'll talk shit (well, he doesn't use that exact word) regardless of the situation. He's right, too. Anytime, anywhere.

Tuesday, January 10
New York

Met the media after our morning shootaround. Just to look mysterious, I wore a black ski cap and black sunglasses.

"Good to see you guys again," I said.

And I meant it. I love this high-energy stuff. I love coming to

New York for these big games. You can feel the city heating up for this one. It's great.

One guy asked who had the best team. I told him Orlando had the most talent, but that doesn't mean they'll win the championship.

Another guy started asking me why I'm not taking more shots. I'm averaging thirteen shots and 19.8 points, and they want to know why I'm not shooting more. I don't get it.

"I'm not going into every night thinking I have to shoot eighteen to twenty-two times," I said. "I never shoot the ball a lot. I don't need to score for this team to win. There might be nights when I'm on when I'll shoot a lot."

"What about Spike?" asked someone else.

"I ain't going head to head with Spike," I said. "The media made him bigger than life in that series."

"What does it take to beat the Knicks?" asked someone else.

"When you play against them," I said, "you got to play like a dick sometimes."

And then the big question: Did O. J. do it?

"No," I said as if it really matters what I think about O. J., "but I think he knows who did it and he's covering up for somebody. He'll get off, I hope. He's one of my heroes."

I called Macaulay Culkin before the game. I met Macaulay when we were in Chicago in 1994 practicing for Dream Team II. He was there filming *Richie Rich,* and we went to Planet Hollywood as a team. Planet Hollywood was giving us a special dinner ceremony, and he came to the dinner with his brother. We were just messing around and we became friends. I went to New York a few times toward the end of the summer to do a couple of things, and that's where he lives. We hooked up and had some fun.

He's a really great kid. I think a lot of people say he's a brat, he's spoiled. I'm telling you, this kid really has no clue—well, maybe he does now, but when I was talking to him, he really had no clue as to how famous he is or the clout he has. I like that, and I think that's really good parenting. They're not supposed to let him know.

As best as I could tell, he's just a normal kid who likes to play video games. Now maybe hanging out with Michael Jackson and all that might have tainted his image a little bit, but to me he's just a normal kid who knows basketball inside out. He was telling me stats on guys I hardly even knew. I was saying, "Man, Mac, you know what you're talking about a little bit."

So I called him up before the game, and he said, "Oh, yeah, I had my tickets three months ago." He told me he had a bet with a friend that I was going to outscore Starks. I told him that was going to be an easy bet, knowing that Starks has been in a slump for the last month.

It felt like a playoff game tonight. Cold outside Madison Square Garden, but steamy and intense inside. Going in you could see the ticket scalpers doing their business. Someone made some serious money, because this game was sold out for months.

I was psyched. We were coming off our huge win at Houston and had been playing a little better. We trailed Cleveland by one and a half games in the Central Division.

Meanwhile, New York had won six in a row, which was the longest streak in the NBA at the time. After suffering through a five-game losing streak a few weeks earlier—the most consecutive losses ever for a Riley-coached team—the Knicks seemed to have their act together. Plus, there would be another sellout crowd at the Garden, their ninety-sixth straight. I wouldn't want it any other way.

I was nervous as usual. Anytime I come into the Garden, I get nervous right before the game, but once the game starts, the nervousness disappears. Broadway, baby. The stars come out. The atmosphere is electric. New York has so much flavor and style. You'd have to be comatose not to get pumped up to play in those surroundings.

The Garden is one of the few places where I don't shoot before games. I know those rims like they were related to me. I feel the same way about the rims at The Forum and the Sports Arena in Los Angeles and, of course, the rims at Market Square. Anyway, tonight I was so focused on the game I didn't feel the need to go out there and shoot. I just stretched, watched some game tape of the Knicks, and counted the minutes until tipoff. I couldn't wait, especially since we had lost four consecutive regular season games to these guys and ten of eleven overall, and eight in a row at the Garden.

While I was stretching, some cute little kid wearing glasses stood up behind the baseline and started yelling something at me. Maybe he wanted an autograph or something. I leaned forward.

"You're a scrub, Reggie!" said the kid.

So much for a personalized photo for him.

Big night on Celebrity Row, which is where the heavyweight entertainer types usually sit at courtside. The Knicks' public relations department even put out a list of the VIPs in attendance. Tonight it was Alec Baldwin and Kim Basinger, Robin Leach, Maury Povich and Connie Chung, Tom Brokaw (must have been a slow news day), and that guy from "Saturday Night Live," Kevin Nealon.

And, oh yeah, Spike.

Let me set some folks straight on Spike and me. People make such a big hoopdy-do about this thing between Spike and myself because of what happened in the 1994 conference finals. Yeah, Spike yelled "Miss!" when I'd go to shoot. Who cares? I've been yelled worse.

And, yeah, Riley got all pissed at Spike for pumping me up during game five with his heckling. But the New York newspapers shouldn't have blamed Spike for the loss. Spike isn't what cost them the game, and I wish the focus had been on the players and the coaches rather than a celebrity fan. Spike shouldn't have needed police protection to get out of Indianapolis during a playoff game.

Spike is just a die-hard Knicks fan. He bought his season tickets the day after New York got Patrick Ewing in the 1985 NBA lottery. He yells at everybody. He yelled at Scottie Pippen during the playoffs, and Pippen got right in Spike's face. And a couple of weeks ago against Cleveland, Spike started chirping at Mark Price, reminding the guy of his five first-half turnovers. Price got hot in the fourth quarter, and after the game was over, he pulled Spike's cap down over the filmmaker's head. Price was just kidding around, but you see what I'm saying? Spike is an equal-opportunity heckler.

Spike and I have always been friends. The media has blown that other thing out of proportion. Before our game tonight, Spike sent a bag to me in the locker room. It was a jacket from his store in Brooklyn, Spike Lee's Joint. I thought that was nice of him. We've got a friendly rivalry. People on the surface might think we're at odds, but behind the scenes we're all right. Spike's a good guy.

So there are all these celebrity people in the front row, and I'm thinking, "This is going to be a show tonight."

And it was. I made sure of it.

During the game, after I made a nice little jumper, I kind of made a detour and ran past Alec Baldwin. Remember that movie *Malice* where Baldwin plays a power-ego surgeon who has to appear on the witness stand during a trial? There's a scene where he's being questioned by one of the attorneys, and Baldwin, his hair slicked back like Riley, his eyes cold and dark, leans forward and answers, "Do I feel like I have a God-like complex? I *am* God."

So after I made the shot, I ran past Baldwin and paused just long enough to look at him and say, "Yes, I *am* God!"

I don't know if he heard me, but Kim started to laugh. It was a wild night, a crazy night. I mean, I was even running past

Maury Povich, yelling, "*This* is 'A Current Affair.'" He must have thought I was nuts.

But I love doing that kind of thing. Those celebs pay big money to be in the front row. I knew what they were coming to see and hear, so I was going to give them a show. It's not very often that you go to New York and play like that.

By the way, just for old times' sake, I glared at Spike after making a jumper. Even pretended to put the guns back in the holster after making the shot. Spike turned away. He knew better.

It was supposed to be a defensive battle. We entered the game holding opponents to 45.1 percent field goal shooting—which is very good—and New York was holding teams to 44.2 percent. Opponents averaged 96.5 points against us, while Knick opponents averaged 97.4. Anything under 100 in our league is damn good.

So what happens? They beat us, 117–105.

They shot 61.8 percent from the floor; we shot 61.5 percent. They hit 11 of 17 three-pointers; we hit 6 of 9. Starks, that bitch, had 31 points (can you believe it—10 of 16 from the floor, 8 of 11 from the three-point line?), and I had 28.

The thing is, we wanted them to take outside shots because they hadn't been hitting them coming into our game. I don't like doing it, but I've got to give credit where credit's due: Starks played great. He hit big shots, shots he hadn't been hitting lately. Too bad he hit them against us.

We shot lights out and we lost. Damn.

It was a physical game, but you expect that from the Knicks, who lead the league in cheap shots. One of their guys, Anthony Bonner, got hit in the first half and took six stitches above his right eye. He came back. Dale Davis got hit in the chin and took three stitches in the second quarter.

I got banged around. Nothing new about that. It seems more and more defenders are trying to body up on me before I get the ball. Don't matter. I'm used to it. And I'll still hit the shot.

It wouldn't have been a Knicks game without getting into it with somebody. This time it was Charles Smith, who talks shit about as well as he shot against the Bulls in the 1993 Eastern finals. You remember: He got his shot blocked three times in that Chicago series. Now he wants to dunk everything. Hey, he should have dunked it back then.

You know me, I'll talk shit the entire game, whether we're up or down. Smith, you hadn't said a word the whole game, got real brave with about twenty seconds left and the Knicks ahead by 12 points. Anybody can talk shit then, but it means nothing. Talk it when the game is still up in the air, not when everyone knows you've won it.

With about three or four seconds left, we ran an inbounds play where I come around, get the ball, and try to drive in and make a layup. But when I came underneath, the ball kind of slipped out of my hands. Smith was standing right there and deliberately came down on my head. The ball was already loose, and everybody was moving toward the other end of the court. So I let him know I didn't appreciate him popping me with an elbow, and I pushed him. Then Anthony Mason stepped in, and I told Smith, "You ain't nothin' but a big pussy. You're the biggest pussy on the team."

After the game I waited for him in the tunnel. I shoved him a little. He shoved back. Then some of our guys and their guys separated us. The reporters poured into our locker room a few minutes later and wanted to know what I had said to Smith. I told them I was congratulating him on a good game.

As usual, Starks didn't say a word to me before, during, or after the game. He almost never does, even if he has a big game, like he did tonight. Ever since he got kicked out of the head-butt game, he keeps quiet. I think he's learned, but it took him a while.

I saw a quote from Starks in one of the New York papers about our relationship. Starks said, "His whole objective is to get inside your mind and distract you from what you are sup-posed to be doing. I hadn't learned that over the years. Now I don't do it as much. There is a respect factor between us. He doesn't get to me anymore."

I remember when we came out on the court for game four of that series in 1993. I walked toward him at center court to shake his hand, but he wouldn't shake it. All the Pacer fans saw him do it, and they started booing him. So I looked straight at him, pumped my fist, and said, "Yes! Yes! I got him! I got him!" He just looked at me.

From that point on we never said a word to each other (not counting talking shit) or shook hands.

Then came the 1994 Eastern Conference Finals. Game seven. It was late in the game. They were up by about 4 points with only a couple of seconds left. Starks got intentionally fouled, made the free throws, and we called time-out. After our huddle, I went out on the court early. I was standing near the Knicks bench, and he was standing nearby at the three-point line with his hands on his knees. I mean, he was right in front of me. Out of the blue he turned to me and said, "Great series. You're a hell of a ballplayer."

I told him, "Thanks. Keep it in the East. Good luck to you guys."

And that was the only time we've spoken to each other.

By the way, I know I told Starks to keep the trophy in the Eastern Conference, but I was just being a gentleman. I guess when it came right down to it, I couldn't root for the Knicks. I had to root for Vernon and the Rockets. Like I said, I can't stand those Knicks.

We came out for tonight's game and, bam, no handshakes or anything from Starks. Back to the same old thing. We don't talk. I don't even try anymore. I shake the captains' hands, Patrick Ewing and Charles Oakley. I also shake Derek Harper's hand.

Harper. Now there's a guy who's undergone some kind of media transformation. It kills me that everybody thinks Harper is some kind of a big tough guy now. Since he's with New York he wants to be tough.

In the 1994 series, he was another person I was talking shit to. What I didn't direct toward John I directed toward Harper. Derek and I were so funny. In game four of '94 we were on a roll, and we were kicking the shit out of him and the Knicks. I went in for a layup, and he hard-fouled me. We're talking back and forth. I said, "Is that the hardest you can foul me, you little bitch?"

I was at the free throw line, and I said, "Derek, now you think you're a tough guy. But when you were down in Dallas, you weren't shit."

He said, "Fuck you, Reggie. Fuck you."

"You want a piece of me?" I said.

He said, "I better not catch you out nowhere alone."

"You ain't gonna catch me nowhere alone," I said. "Little Jo Jo English whipped your ass on national television in front of the commissioner. What the fuck are you gonna do fucking around with a heavyweight?"

The whole time I talked shit to him, Haywoode was just looking at me like he didn't know what was going on. I wasn't about to stop.

"Jo Jo threw you into the stands," I said. "What do you think I'm gonna do to you?"

I was just egging him on. You could see steam just rising from him.

Almost forgot one last thing.

Sorry, Mac, you lost your bet. You need to pay the five dollars to your friend. Starks was on fire tonight.

Wednesday, January 11
Boston

We've got the Celtics tonight. A back-to-back, which is a bitch.

Boston's been up and down, but this is a must-win game for

us. Charlotte beat Cleveland last night to move into a second-place tie with us for the division lead. It's going to be like this all season. It's going to be a tight race, and it's going to be interesting. We've got to win our share of road games.

This is a winnable game for us, and then we go to Washington, so this is really going to test the character of this team. We played well against New York, so if we shoot the way we shot last night, I don't see why we can't beat this team by ten-plus.

Unbelievable. You'd think after playing a great game like we played against New York, we would come out with some type of fire against the Boston Celtics tonight. It didn't happen. Instead, the Celtics showed up to play and beat us, 100–97.

Seems like every time I watch TV and I watch other teams play New Jersey and Boston and Washington—the teams that suck—they've got no problems. But when we play them they get pumped up.

Now I finally understand: We are the hunted.

Too often we get this mentality where we think we can just show up and the game is automatically ours. Instead, teams are coming out to kick our Pacer asses.

That's exactly what Boston came out to do. I think we had a good game plan from the start. We got into the game okay, but for some reason—the road trip, the emotions from New York, fatigue—we couldn't get a lead and keep it.

I'll take my share of blame. I missed a free throw that could have tied the game with 16 seconds left to play. We had two other chances to tie in the last 13.8 seconds, but we missed both shots.

Dominique has lost a lot on his first and second steps, but he can still put the ball in the hoop. He scored 20 tonight, which isn't bad for somebody who turns thirty-five tomorrow. I got 23 tonight, but it doesn't matter. We lost.

I've even got Jess Kersey, who's one of the best officials in the league, on my ass these days. During the game against the

Celtics he told Larry, "I know he thinks he's Mr. Perfect, but I *will* throw his ass [out], and I really don't care."

Man, this sucks, I'm telling you. We keep giving games away. We're getting outrebounded. We're getting outplayed. And it's happening on both ends. Things like that can't happen, especially when we're playing teams like the Celtics, who came into the game 13–19, twelve and a half games behind the Magic. It's unbelievable. We've got to get some better play all around, from one through twelve. Things just aren't going right at the moment. We've got one more game on this trip. We go to Washington. We'll see how that turns out.

Thursday, January 12
Washington

For some reason we practiced at the Naval Academy today. What a trip, man. We've got a practice going on, and a few yards away there's all these midshipmen on artificial turf, surrounded by netting, practicing their golf swings. Turns out they have a golf class scheduled the same time as our practice in their big field house.

I'm thinking, "What kind of place is this?" I wonder if Pat Riley would have a shootaround when midshipmen are out there golfing and hanging around the court.

Most of the time that doesn't happen. Larry's really strict about shootarounds, about letting media and folks watch. But I guess since it was the historic Naval Academy, home of David Robinson, he kind of let his guard down a little bit.

I don't think I would have been Naval Academy material. They make freshmen (they're called plebes, I think) stand on dinner plates in the hallways of the dorm and yell out what's on the menu that day. And during the nonstop chatter, they've got to tell everybody how many more days until they play Army, their big rival. Crazy shit like that.

As we were leaving the academy, we saw all these pizza delivery cars parked just inside the gate. Sure enough, you could see a trail of midshipmen coming from the dorm to pick up lunch. Guess the menu wasn't too good today.

Scottie Pippen is at it again. I just read where he said no place could be worse than playing for the Bulls. He said the Bulls should trade him or Jerry Krause, their general manager. That's *not* going to happen.

Scottie's pissed that Krause didn't re-sign Horace Grant and that Scottie's salary isn't among the top forty in the league. Hell, he's the fourth-highest paid player on the Bulls. He doesn't become a free agent until the 1997–98 season. He'll be thirty-two by then.

These two guys are worse than Webber and Nellie. Krause had Scottie's agent kicked out of a restricted area near the locker room Tuesday night because the agent didn't have the right credentials. And two weeks ago Scottie called Krause a liar.

All I've got to say is thank goodness for Donnie Walsh, our team president. Donnie's fair, he's honest, and he doesn't get caught up in petty stuff.

**Friday, January 13
Washington**

Before the game tonight, one of the radio reporters wanted to know what I thought about my five thousand dollar fine for fighting with Charles Smith.

"You're shitting me," I said.

"No, man, you got fined five thousand dollars."

"You're kidding me. How much did Smith get fined?"

"Nothing."

"Nothing?"

"Nothing."

"Well, ain't that a bitch. But it's not the first time I've been fined, and it won't be the last."

My teammates were laughing about it. Hey, it's not their money, right?

I'm shocked by the fine, but I can understand why the NBA did it. You can't slap someone on national TV and get away with it.

I was just letting Smith know I didn't appreciate that shit. If you're going to talk shit and do all that stuff, then do it during the course of the game. That's why I can respect Anthony Mason on that team. That bitch does all his crazy stuff during the mix of the game. I respect that. I don't like guys who talk shit when the game is won. Do it all when the game is on the line. I talk all my shit before the outcome. If we lose, then, hey, y'all were the better team. But don't do something when the game is over. Nuh-uh, I don't think so.

It's a five thousand dollar fine. I'll pay it. Anyway, that will go a long ways—me, six seven, 185 pounds, taking on six ten, 250 . . . and winning. Plus, he didn't even get fined a penny.

Very nice. Very nice. We beat Washington, 113–99. Everyone came out and played hard, played the way we're supposed to play.

We knew Washington was hurting. Chris Webber was out with a dislocated left shoulder. Kevin Duckworth was in street clothes because of a left Achilles injury and, if you believe the Bullets management, because he's too fat. And Don MacLean, a UCLA guy, was out because of tendinitis in his knees.

Still, they're a scary team. Everyone's a scary team for us these days because everyone's getting pumped up for us. We don't know what team is going to show up against us.

Finally we got a chance to play our game. We got some great

bench help from Tank Thompson and Sam Mitchell. Everyone played great. It was a chance for us to finally get a taste of a road victory. We've been playing well at home but playing like shit on the road. Road life is hard, but you have to be able to play through it. Tonight we did.

Got another look at Bullets center Gheorghe Muresan, who is the biggest son of a bitch I have ever seen. The guy is seven-seven, weighs 303 (they say; he looks bigger), played at Cluj University—wherever the hell that is—and is a sight to behold. This is his second year in the league, and tonight he scored 8 points and had 5 rebounds and 3 blocks in twenty-eight minutes. Not bad. It's a bitch to shoot over him. It's like trying to shoot over the Empire State Building. You know what's really funny? Someone told me his nickname in the French league was "Ghita," which means "tiny." And his parents were only five nine and five seven.

Muresan plays hard, but, damn, it feels like he's going to fall down any minute. I think Rik has his way with him most of the time, but because the guy is so damn clumsy and unorthodox, he's always hitting you in the face with his elbows. He must have gotten Rik four times tonight. You don't know whether to punch the guy or feel sorry for him. One thing you can't take away from him, he does play hard. I've got to give him credit. And that rookie from Michigan, Juwan Howard, is going to be a damn good player. Hit eleven of thirteen tonight against us.

As for that guy behind our bench, Robin Ficker, he and Larry went at each other the whole night. Ficker is an attorney and a longtime Bullets season ticket holder whose hobby is heckling. I mean, get a life. Tonight he was yelling at us during our huddles. We could hear him perfectly because he was seated right behind our bench.

"Don't listen to Larry!" he was shrieking. "And don't listen to that hippie next to him [George Irvine, one of our assistant coaches]."

Larry got tired of that real fast.

"Hey, Ficker," Larry said. "You're nothing but a schmuck. You've always been a schmuck."

People sitting around Ficker were going "Wooo," getting all agitated. That's because Larry and Ficker were going at it. Ficker looked at him, like, "How dare you come back at me. This is my forum." Everyone was laughing. It was crazy. But face it: Ficker is one crazy man.

I think he's funny. A few years ago, when he was reading passages to Michael from that book *The Jordan Rules*, I thought that was pretty funny. He never says anything foul, but he's just so damn loud.

Some things are original, other things you've heard for the last five or six years. But it's not so much what he says but how loud he says it. His voice is so obnoxious and continuous, especially during the time-outs. Here you are, wanting to relax and get your thoughts together, and he's shrieking at you. He doesn't care if the Bullets are up by 20 or down by 20. He just likes to talk and talk and talk.

Tonight he had on a purple T-shirt and was carrying around a black megaphone. When we made our way to the court for the start of the second half, Ficker was bowing to me and saying, "Oh, it's Reggie Miller, the great Reggie Miller. Welcome."

Sometimes I feel sorry for his kids, because he brings them to the game. I'm thinking, "How does it feel to have a loud-mouthed dad like that?" I mean, that would be something, to go to a PTA meeting and hear your dad yelling, "Johnny deserved an A for that!" That would be as funny as hell. I guess fans get their kicks whatever way they can.

I remember a couple of years ago—his wife was taking him to court or something like that—and another fan came to the bench and gave us copies of what had been in the newspapers about Ficker. So after we got done drilling Washington, we turned around and started reading this stuff to him. I've never seen Robin Ficker turn so red in my life. It was as funny as hell. We finally got him back.

Saw Don MacLean, who was two years behind me at UCLA, tonight at the game—or should I say Rocky MacLean? Can you believe this guy goes out and gets in a fight and breaks his hand? I was watching ESPN, and they were talking about Don and what had happened in the fight. Craig Kilbourne, the ESPN guy, said something like, "Yes, ladies and gentlemen, it was the first time Don had defended anyone all year." That is some cold shit. I must have laughed for about five minutes on that one.

I know a few guys on that Bullets team. Rex Chapman and I have been good friends the last three or four years. I think he's one of the most respected two-guards in the league. He plays hard. When he gets hot, like a John Starks, he can shoot any kind of shot and it will go. That's one player you need to get on early before he gets his rhythm, because if he gets hot, it's lights out. He's an explosive leaper as well as a quick shooter. If he gets it going, it's over. Lights out. You can't stop him.

Fortunately for us, he didn't get it going tonight. He had only 12 points and needed 11 shots and 6 free throw attempts to do it.

A lot of times when I was making shots, I was looking at the crowd. One funny moment: I was taking a shot, and there was this guy who was heckling, being a real dick. I hit a shot, turned around to the guy, and said, "Take that, bitch." The referee was Luis Grillo, and he said, "Hey, watch it. That can be taunting."

Taunting? *The crowd?* C'mon. In the first half, when I took a shot and looked at the crowd, Ronnie Garretson came up to me and said, "Just be sure you're directing that all toward the crowd and not the players." He knew I was directing it to the crowd.

Luis was upset because I said, "Take that, bitch," but you

can't be sensitive out there. Everyone's too damn sensitive nowadays.

After the game, one of our beat reporters—I think it was Conrad—started asking me about the All-Star Game. According to the latest fan voting, I'm third among the Eastern Conference guards, behind Anfernee Hardaway and Joe Dumars.

"You think you'll make it?" he asked.

"Nah," I told him. "I'll be in Jamaica getting a tan."

"What about being picked by the coaches?"

"Hell, no. Think about this shit. We're Indiana."

Then I started politicking for Dale Davis. Dale's been playing great. He got 25 points and 10 rebounds tonight, has started all 33 games, is averaging 12.1 points, is shooting 58 percent from the field, leads the team in blocks and rebounding, and plays his ass off every night.

"He should make it," I said. "Something's wrong if he doesn't."

"What about Larry Johnson?" someone asked.

"Larry Johnson ain't having that good a year," I said.

"Kevin Willis?"

"You've got to be shitting me. He's a good rebounder, but he's not having an All-Star year."

By the way, I got 4 rebounds tonight. I was pretty proud of that until Byron or Vern or somebody started giving me shit about it.

"He got four?" they said. "How'd that happen? He can't jump that high."

Then they started calling me "Reggie Olajuwon."

We have a nice little home stand coming up. This is a chance for us to get back in the race. We're in third place, one game behind Charlotte and two games behind Cleveland. We play tomorrow at home against Milwaukee.

A friend of mine sat next to the Bucks' advance scout tonight. Caught a look at his notes, too. According to the Milwaukee scout, the "book" on me says I'm a poor defender, that I can shoot over any big guard in the league, that I'll play mind games with a defender, that I love to shoot off screens, that Rik and I are the go-to guys, that you shouldn't let me get untracked early, that I'm better going to my right than my left, that I'm a trash-talker.

Interesting. Very interesting. I'd probably agree with everything he said except the poor defending thing. That's always been the perception of me, that I'm not a good defensive player because I'm such a great scorer, and I have to admit when I first came into the league I was a very average defender.

But Coach Brown has made me a better defender, and it's something I work hard on and really have a lot of pride in. What you have to understand is that after my third or fourth year in the league, the points didn't mean very much to me. You can score all the points you want, but wins mean more than anything, and the way you win is by playing good defense.

Anyway, I'd like to prove that scout wrong about the poor defender stuff and prove him right about everything else. But for some reason we always get Milwaukee after a long road trip. To me, they're one of the hardest teams for us to play. We don't match up with them very well. We only beat them by 5 points the last time we played back in November.

Saturday, January 14
Indianapolis

I told you we match up bad with those guys. Milwaukee's Todd Day beat us with a tip-in with 1.2 seconds left to play. They won, 97–95.

I'm telling you, the emotions that go into basketball, well, people don't understand the ups and downs of this game. You can go from such an emotional high—like it was at Washington, feeling good about the road trip and finally coming home—and then return to Market Square and suck. We led, 15–2, then trailed, got back into it, tied it (I hit a pair of threes in the last fifty-four seconds to make it 95–95), and then lost when Day tipped it in.

If there's one thing people need to know about an NBA season, it's what we go through as players. The emotions—it's like a roller-coaster ride. Everything's great one day, the next it's not. I was talking to my wife, and she said, "If you didn't feel that way, you'd be like some of those other players in the league, the ones who don't care."

Maybe that's true and all, but people don't understand the hurt. It seems like we always get Milwaukee after a long road trip. This was our fourth game in five nights, and those bitches were rested, ready and willing to go. Man. They played better than we did, that's all I can say. We had a chance to get back into the goddamn race, and man, we blew it.

We've got Utah coming in here, and they've won thirteen consecutive road games. The good thing about this is that I feel we're going to stop their streak even though they've been playing well.

Home-court advantage, right?

Monday, January 16
Indianapolis

Whoa, a lot has happened in one day.

The preliminary stuff: We came in and were getting ready for the game. Usually Larry puts the lineups on the board and details what the matchups are going to be. But this time we looked on the board, and the starting point guard was Haywoode, who was running third on the depth chart a couple of weeks ago.

Larry took Mark out of the lineup. Mark hasn't been playing particularly well so far. He's been in all thirty-two games but is only shooting 44 percent from the floor, averaging 8.4 points. He's also averaging 7.9 assists, but 3.3 turnovers. Plus, Larry doesn't like the way he's playing on defense, doesn't like his lack of aggressiveness.

I don't know if it's the new system or what. He's played for Larry before, so he knows what Larry expects out of his point guards. But he hasn't been playing like people expect or like the Mark Jackson of old.

Larry put Haywoode in there to spark the fire like last year, when we went 34–18 with him at the point. It was a surprise to all of us because we had no idea at the shootaround, and then to come in and see that. It's just a question of how Mark is going to take it. He's a pretty religious guy and may see this as another obstacle. But it isn't life and death with Mark.

"My faith isn't in man," he told Dan Dunkin of the *Star*. "This isn't any competition [between Mark and Haywoode]. This is about winning."

To make matters worse, we lost another game at home. I'm telling you, it almost makes you wonder why you play basketball.

We had Utah on the ropes in overtime, we had them beat. But we couldn't make free throws down the stretch, me in particular. Geez, I think I was 3 of 6 for the game, and I'm an 89.6 percent free throw shooter. No excuse for that.

I had a potential three-point play in overtime that would have put us up by 3. I made the bucket, got Karl Malone to commit his sixth foul, but missed the free throw. That's big in the NBA: a three-point lead. That's two possessions or a three-point try.

All together, we missed 4 of 5 free throws during the last 1:37 of the game, and 16 overall.

Malone went to work on us. We fouled him out in the overtime, but by then he had scored 42 points in forty-one minutes. I'll tell you what, if any one team is playing great, it's

Utah. Stockton . . . no wonder he's great. He sets up those guys perfectly. He had 19 assists tonight.

Magic Johnson was a great setup guy, too, but this guy sets those guys up perfectly. Everyone on Utah ought to give Stockton a bonus at the end of the year. I mean it. He puts the ball in their lap every time. He sees things that I don't see, that no one else in basketball sees. Geezus, the guy has it all.

Larry wasn't happy we lost, but we did play harder if that's any consolation. He told the media after the game: "Everybody's been talking about how good we are, but I haven't felt that way since we left training camp. I told the guys I didn't like what I saw."

I'll vouch for that.

Now we have the Lakers in two days. They're another team that's playing well on the road. Utah, Phoenix, the Lakers are teams with some of the best road records in the league.

So much for this home stand. We've gotten beat by Milwaukee and Utah, and we still have L.A., Atlanta, and San Antonio. Then we go on the road to Miami for a game and then come back to Market Square for Phoenix, Philadelphia, Cleveland, and Orlando.

We'd better get our act together, or we'll have wasted our longest home stand of the season. Last year at this time we were beginning to make our big run. Now we're just trying to survive.

Tuesday, January 17
Indianapolis

Well, this is really wild. Coming into today's practice, I would have bet some serious money that after a few losses like we've been having, Larry would be like Geronimo or Cochese and go for everybody's head. Instead, he's kind of lightened up.

Larry changes like the weather. When you think it's going to be the worst, it's not. When you think it's not, he snaps. This is one coach who is hard to figure out. It's just wild. It's different.

Wednesday, January 18
Indianapolis

So we're playing the Lakers, who are probably the surprise team from the West. Del Harris really has that ball club playing well. They're back to the fast-breaking, Showtime, open-court style.

I think Cedric Ceballos and Nick Van Exel are playing at All-Star levels. That's really funny with Nick, in a way. I was watching ESPN's "Up Close" show about a month ago, and they had a special on him. He was talking about teams that had overlooked him in the 1993–94 draft. He said he was going to pay them back.

Hey, we were one of those teams. He said that Indiana would have been an ideal place for him to play. Instead, we took Scott Haskin, a six-eleven forward from Oregon State.

Van Exel said he wasn't sure if Haskin had played twenty games for us, which is almost true; he's played twenty-seven, but a lot of that has to do with the back surgery he had this year. He said it was Indiana's loss, and it was going to be payback time. You know what that means: I'm going to have to get into a verbal confrontation with this young buck. But he does play hard, and he can shoot his ass off from threes.

Aw, I'm only kidding about getting into it with Van Exel. But I'm not kidding about the importance of tonight's game. We need a victory—bad.

Well, the game we needed to get, we got. That Van Exel put on a show. He came in to prove a point, and he did. He played at the University of Cincinnati, which is only about an hour and a half from here, so no wonder he wanted us to draft him so bad. (It's also why he needed thirty tickets tonight.) You look back at that draft, and we had our shots to take him. Hell, he didn't go until the second round, so everybody had their shots to take him. But he's really proven himself to the league.

The game came down to the final shot. Tony Smith had a chance to win it for the Lakers, but he missed an open fourteen-footer. Tough. It's about time we got a break.

Smith took the last shot because Haywoode did a great job of shutting down Van Exel on a drive in the last few seconds of the game. Van Exel had to pass the ball to Smith.

This Laker team is looking good. They play hard and play together—Vlade Divac, Ceballos, and Van Exel. Man, that little bitch can play. I wanted to start talking shit to him, but I decided to let sleeping dogs lie. He was on fire, especially in the second half when he scored 25 of his 30 points.

We were up by 10 with five minutes to go. Next thing I knew we were down by 1 after he hit a three-pointer with fifty-something seconds left. We had to come down and make a shot to take a lead. Then we had the big stop at the end. It was a good win.

Hopefully we can keep it going against Atlanta. Even though they don't have the team they had a year ago with Kevin Willis and Danny Manning, they can upset you. Mookie Blaylock is still a very capable point guard. Kenny Norman has been playing well for them, which doesn't totally surprise me, but he's also been putting up numbers for them, which does surprise me a little bit.

Playing Little League, at age eight. Baseball was my first sports love, but by high school I realized it was too quiet and slow for me.

Me and Cheryl, my Hall of Fame sister, at Poly High. Since I'm taller, this is after she stopped playing one-on-one with me.

With two proud parents, my mom, Carrie, and my dad, Saul, at my UCLA graduation in 1987.

Dancing with Marita on our wedding day—the happiest day of my life.

The full Miller family: (top row) Darrell, me, dad, and Saul Jr. (bottom row) Tammy, mom, and Cheryl.

(Clockwise from top) The highs and lows of the 1994 Eastern Conference finals against the Knicks: Torching John Starks for three of my 25 fourth-quarter points in game five; glumly walking off the floor after our game seven loss as Derek Harper and the Knicks fans celebrated; Spike Lee, off the hook after his Knicks got by us.

Kevin Johnson, my old high school rival, has his own way of congratulating me as we accepted our medals for winning the World Championship of Basketball in Toronto.

Larry Brown and I don't always see eye to eye, but I think there's no question he's one of the top two or three coaches in the game.

(CREDIT: INDIANA PACERS)

The biggest event of the regular season was M.J.'s return against us in March. I was so glad to see him, even after he took me down in the final seconds. (CREDIT: AP/WIDE WORLD PHOTOS)

Dale Davis, dunking over Patrick Ewing in the Eastern semifinals, is a true warrior, something he showed by coming right back from his separated shoulder in the semifinals. (CREDIT: AP/WIDE WORLD PHOTOS)

Shooting over Greg Anthony—which I knew was no problem—for three of my eight points in 8.9 seconds in our huge game one comeback against the Knicks. (CREDIT: AP/WIDE WORLD PHOTOS)

My pal Mark Jackson—who hates the Knicks as much as I do—tries to keep me from running at Spike Lee in the emotional wake of that game one win. (CREDIT: AP/WIDE WORLD PHOTOS)

Yes, yes, yes! Mark exults, and I was just worn out, as we finally got past the Knicks when Ewing's finger-roll went long and out.

Does Rik look happy? He just hit the biggest shot of his life, the fifteen-footer that beat Orlando in the Miracle at Market Square, in game four. (CREDIT: BETTMANN ARCHIVES)

At the celebration and rally in Indianapolis after Orlando knocked us out. As Byron Scott said, with the way the fans supported and lifted us all season, we should have thrown them a rally, not the other way around. (CREDIT: © TONY VALAINIS)

Thursday, January 19
Atlanta

Reporters keep coming up to me and asking, "What's the deal in the fourth quarter?" Just because I haven't been scoring in the fourth quarter as much, people are going nuts on me.

I don't know what's going on. I think after the fourth quarter I had against New York in the 1993–94 playoffs, people expect me to score 20-plus points when the final period comes around. Sometimes that's just not the case. Sometimes you're the decoy, sometimes you just don't have it going.

But I do need to be more assertive in the fourth quarter. We've been up by 10 points or so recently heading into that quarter, so when I come back in, I'm more coasting than anything. But then a team comes back on us, and since I haven't been shooting it, it's tough for me to turn it on. I need to be more aggressive.

Friday, January 20
Atlanta

Hey, I told you—those Hawks, it's always a close one for us with them. We won, 99–89, but we didn't start to pull away until early in the fourth quarter.

Craig Ehlo, who doesn't score on anyone but us, had 22 points on 9 of 11 shooting. He plays good defense, I'll give him that, but any other time I see him shoot, he's bricking it.

It was a close game until the third quarter. Something we really needed was for our subs to make a move. At the start of the fourth quarter we had Haywoode, Byron, Dale Davis, LaSalle Thompson, and John Williams on the floor. They played the fourth quarter and played great.

It was tied, 71–71, heading into the fourth, and that's when the bench bailed us out. Byron has been great. He's been the biggest lift this year and last. He's the reason we went to the Eastern Conference Finals during the 1993–94 season. No question. He gives us leadership. People really underestimated his talent in Los Angeles. You look at the great Laker teams—with Magic, Kareem Abdul-Jabbar, Michael Cooper, James Worthy—he might have been the fifth or sixth guy mentioned on that team. But he's much more valuable to us. He's been places where guys on our team, including myself, wish and dream they could go. Without his leadership and court savvy and his knowledge of the game, we wouldn't be as successful as we've been.

This is a guy who says he's thirty-three but looks twenty-eight or twenty-nine. It was a steal for us. I can't believe nobody picked him up off waivers last year. How could the Lakers let him go? That was the stupidest thing they could have done. Sorry, Jerry West, but I don't buy the youth-movement logic.

Anyway, it was great scouting on our organization's part, because Byron was a steal. He signed for the minimum last year, but I know Donnie Walsh did a good job rewarding him and he deserves it. We don't look at him as a third or fourth option; he's the man here. He's been carrying us as of late. He's the best backup two-guard in the league. I learn from him.

When I was at UCLA, Magic, Cooper, and Byron were the main ones who helped me make it to this level today. Those three guys took me under their wings and said, "Look, if you want to make it to the next level and be successful in the NBA, this is what you're going to have to do." I listened and learned and asked questions. They helped me out tremendously. I've always respected Byron, and I always thought he was one of the top shooting guards when he was with the Lakers.

Saturday, January 21
Indianapolis

There'll be lots of familiar faces when we play San Antonio tomorrow afternoon. First of all, we've got Bob Hill (we've called him Bo ever since he coached here) coming back to Indianapolis. Bo was my coach for nearly three seasons. Good coach, too. He had a 113–108 record here, but we never finished higher than fourth in the Central Division and never won a first-round playoff series in three tries.

Bo used to be on Larry's staff at Kansas. He was an assistant last year with Orlando, and we ran them out of town during the playoffs, so I know he has a little vengeance on his mind. As it turned out, he and Gar Heard were the finalists for the Spurs job.

I don't know if Bo really got a fair shake here. He's a great guy, don't get me wrong, but I think the organization was really looking for something else. I think Bo tried to make too many friends on the team, and sometimes you have to separate that. Friends and ballplayers, that's tough to do in this league.

Then there's Chuck Person, the Rifleman. Chuck and I played together for four years. Chuck is one of those players who isn't afraid to take a big shot in the big game. Not many of those guys in the league.

When I was a rookie in 1987, Chuck took me under his wing. He was my vet, and I did things for him. I think he took a lot of criticism here because people really misunderstood him in Indiana. People thought I was the reason he was traded, but that wasn't the case and Chuck knows that.

Chuck is a great guy and has a great family. His brother Wesley is in the NBA now, playing for Phoenix. I remember when we used to call Wesley "Sticks." He used to come here and shoot around with us when he was, what, a senior in high school? He was just a scrawny kid.

"Chuck, *this* is your brother?" I'd say. Chuck is maybe 240 pounds, and Wesley is my size—skinny. Man, someone's been doing steroids—I'm just kidding—or eating a lot of greens and meat loaf.

This will be our first afternoon game of the year. What's been nice is the attendance. A lot of the games have been sold out. If you build it, they will come. That's exactly what's been happening here at Indiana.

Oh, I forgot. They've got the "Admiral," David Robinson, and the "Wild Thing," Dennis Rodman. They also have Sean Elliott. This is a character game with that wild bunch coming in. Yeah, this will be a good little reunion.

Sunday, January 22
Indianapolis

Yes, baby. Three in a row.

This game was wild. A little bit of everything, from pushing and shoving to takedowns, to Sam Mitchell taking Rodman over the seats, to comebacks. What an exciting game.

We knew they were going to come fired up, because this is Bo's first stint as a head coach since the Pacers replaced him. I knew he was coming back to try to make a point. We knew that, and this was one game where we controlled the tempo until about the last two or three minutes. For us the best tempo is to get into a half-court game and run on opportunity breaks. We're a half-court team.

Again, we really had trouble scoring points in the fourth quarter, including myself. I haven't been able to score those points in the fourth, which is why everyone's been on my ass lately. I had 14 points tonight but none in the last quarter, which is the third consecutive time that's happened.

We were up by 7 points with seventeen seconds left to play when they made the strangest run I've ever seen. Here's what happened:

- They came down, took a shot, and missed. Rodman got the rebound—one of his twenty-five in thirty-five minutes—and dished it back out to Elliott. Elliott took a three, made it, and they were down by 4.
- Rodman and Sam got tangled up on the play. Well, more than tangled. Rodman had him in a headlock, hit him, baited him—which was pretty sweet and smart if you think about it.

Now, Sam Mitchell is a nice guy. Believe me, we're not going to do anything foolish with 16.6 seconds left in the game. But Rodman kind of hit him, and that set Sam off. Sam already was mad because Rodman pushed all game. That's how he gets a lot of his rebounds, by pushing. He gets good position, but he pushes a lot, too.

So Sam got fed up and threw him over the first row of seats, where the people sit on the floor. Great takedown.

Unfortunately for us, the only thing the referees saw was Sam throwing Rodman. They didn't see anything Rodman had done to start the whole thing. So Sam got ejected on a Type II flagrant foul. Larry almost had to be restrained after that call.

- After the ejection, Rodman got two free throws. He made the first one and then went to the line for the second. Fans were going crazy, throwing things on the floor. Larry was going ballistic, and I was standing there thinking, "This can't be happening. They've got a chance to win the game. We've led the whole game, controlled the tempo, and they've got a chance to win this bitch."
- Rodman missed, but they got the ball on the side because of the flagrant foul. They called a time-out and set up a play. They were down, 96–93, with a chance to tie. I mean, this could be a 7-point possession if they make the three.

Lucky for us the play was dumb. Elliott came out and tried to shoot a quick three over me, which was really wild because they had plenty of time to try something else. They missed, we got the ball, they fouled, and Haywoode made two. It was a free throw game from then on. But can you imagine if they had gotten to overtime and won that game? Shows you how quickly a game can change. It also shows you how smart Rodman was to do something like that.

People always get on him, thinking he's stupid because of all the crazy things he does. But after the game, I went to talk to Bo, and he said, "Hey, you'd love this kid. He has a lot of problems off the court, but he's working through them. He plays hard, and that's all you can ask for."

Rodman is a trip, isn't he? Wow. The word *confused* comes to mind when I think of him.

You ask twenty-seven coaches in the league if they'd like to have Dennis Rodman on their team, and I think twenty-seven would say yes. But it's the things that he does away from the court—not showing up for shootarounds and practices—that causes everybody to have doubts about this guy.

I like Dennis Rodman because I like the bad guy. I like guys who wear black hats. I like different kinds of guys. The earrings, the tattoos, that's flavor. I like that. But I'm not sure he makes a full commitment to the team.

This guy really has a big following. When I was over there tonight talking to Bo and Jack Haley, Rodman came out and people went crazy. So his image isn't as tarnished as people perceive it to be. He's kind of like an NBA cult figure, bigger than life.

He's very smart, a very smart ballplayer. Like that thing he did with Sam—very smart. I'd want him as my teammate, but only if he were on time and responsible and came to workouts and practices. Hell, yes, I'd want him on my team. But what's tough is that you never know what Dennis will do. Or won't do.

Dennis plays great defense. He gets his hands on every rebound and loose ball. He can see the floor. He's a good passing big man. People don't understand: When Detroit was winning those back-to-back NBA championships, he and Joe Dumars were the ones who were keeping Jordan down.

But even though he can do all those things, I think he'd be too disruptive to a team. I want teammates I can depend on. I don't think I could depend on Dennis every day to do what was best for the team.

Rodman doesn't usually talk on the court, but he talked tonight after Sam threw him over the chair. I went up to him and said, "How you gonna let my man take you down like that?"

He said, "I baited him into it. Watch. He's gonna get thrown out."

I said, "But you're gonna get thrown out, too."

"Hey, it ain't gonna be the first," he said.

"Yeah, that's true," I said.

So guess what happens? Sam gets thrown out because it was a flagrant foul on Sam. The referee didn't see Dennis give him the first push. Smart guy to do some stuff like that.

But let's face it, Rodman is out there, way out there. I saw those *GQ* magazine pictures with him standing naked in some field somewhere. The man has more tattoos than the Illustrated Man, he's dated Madonna, he's got rings through his belly button, he's got orange-dyed hair—I'm telling you, the man is out there.

But the man has had a tough life. He's been without a dad since he was three. He got cut from his high school team (and don't you think that coach is feeling pretty stupid these days). He grew something like eight or nine inches during the summer after high school. He flunked out of junior college. He was a janitor at the Dallas–Fort Worth airport but got caught stealing stuff from one of the gift shops. When he was twenty-two, he got kicked out of his mother's house, which is some cold shit. He played for some little NAIA school in Oklahoma and kicked everybody's ass. He made it to the NBA in 1986 with the Pistons, won two championships, but had to deal with his marriage breaking up and losing his kid in the custody battle. The Pistons broke up, and Rodman ended up in San Antonio.

As a player, there isn't anybody better rebounding the ball. The thing is, he makes you put up with all the other shit. Like last year—a lot of things he did I felt were unacceptable: not traveling with the team, going with Madonna in the limousine. When he gets on the court, he plays his ass off, but you have to remember, it's twelve guys on a team, not eleven, plus one, plus Madonna and her entourage and her dancers and her choreographer and her stylist. You can't have all that. It's got to be twelve guys playing as a team.

I'll give him credit, though: The man is not afraid to speak his mind. He ripped Shaq ("You call that entertainment?" he said. "They've promoted him like he's God, but all he does is dunk the damn ball"). Someone asked Shaq to respond, but the big guy wasn't in a commenting mood. "My responding to Rodman is like talking to a Bugs Bunny doll. I don't like to talk to Looney Tunes."

Not bad, Shaqster.

Rodman ripped the officials not long ago ("I'm a marked man no matter what I do. They are trying to teach Dennis Rodman a lesson"). Maybe he's right. He got thrown out of a game against Houston last week for staring at referee Gary Benson. Didn't say a word and still got chucked.

I wish he had gotten thrown out tonight. It would have saved us a lot of trouble.

Now we go to Miami looking for a fourth straight win. I think we can get that as long as the guys stay focused. If we can get that one, we'll be all right.

News item: If you want Scottie Pippen in a trade, it's going to cost you your two best players and some high draft choices. Scottie's damn good but ain't nobody gonna pay that much for him. Also, the Bulls' owner, Jerry Reinsdorf, said he isn't going to redo Scottie's contract.

Gonna be a long year for Scottie.

Monday, January 23
Miami

Going down to Miami, I say to myself, "This is just like the Boston, New Jersey, Milwaukee thing. Which team is going to show up? The real Pacers? The real Heat?"

Miami's been struggling as of late, but, damn, I hate teams like this. They're 12–26, but they have some players who can score. Of course, against everybody else they suck. But against us they're probably world beaters.

You think I have a defeatist attitude?

Practice was kind of light, nothing heavy. When you win three in a row, that helps.

Larry's been okay lately, nothing too tough. He told Dan Dunkin that we're starting to play the way we did before when we were hard to score against.

Haywoode's playing well, too. He's averaging 13 points, 5.3 assists, and 2 steals since replacing Mark as a starter 4 games ago. Even John Williams is showing signs of maybe being able to help us. In the last two games he's played a total of thirty minutes and scored 15 points and had 5 rebounds.

Tuesday, January 24
Miami

Why did I have to be right about Miami?

This might have been the worst game of the year for us: Miami 107, Pacers 96.

No effort at all. No intensity. No nothing. It was like we were in quicksand all night. I think we got caught up in Super Bowl weekend down there, which doesn't say much for us.

Damn, we got beat by the Miami Heat. That team can't play dead, and they come out and outrun us. It's disappointing because we're right there. We get to a game out of first, and now this. I'm telling you, this shit sucks. We're not playing very well, and it's showing. We got outrebounded by nineteen tonight. Not having Antonio Davis is catching up with us. We win three games in a row, and then we take a gigantic step backward. Gigantic.

Larry was cussing everybody out, including me. He said I didn't want the ball because I took only twelve shots. Actually, he said, "Our fucking star doesn't want the ball."

I didn't say anything. I pretty much sat there and took it. No sense escalating the problem, not after getting beat like we did.

Wednesday, January 25
Indianapolis

We've got Phoenix on the 26th. Geezus, it just gets harder and harder.

The Suns are 31–8, have the second-best record in the league, have seven players averaging in double figures, and have won seven straight road games. Great.

Plus, Larry blasted us in the papers today. We probably had it coming. He said we weren't doing the "manly" things, that we weren't hustling or communicating enough. "The bottom line," he said, "is we're not a team."

Just got back from shootaround and nearly two hours of watching film (Larry rarely makes us do that), where they told me I had just been named to the starting team of the East NBA All-Stars. It's the first time ever that any Indiana Pacer has been selected as a starter. Back in 1990 I made the team, but only as a reserve.

To tell you the truth, if I hadn't been voted on as a starter, I don't think I would have made the team. I don't think the coaches would have put me on. Other years when I had great statistics I never made it, so I didn't think I'd do it this time around.

If I hadn't made it, that would have been okay. I was on the team in 1990. Once an All-Star, always an All-Star is what I say. It's just like being a president. They don't say, "How you doin', Mr. Reagan? How you doin', Mr. Bush?" They say, "How you doin', Mr. President?" In boxing they still call Mike Tyson and Muhammad Ali "Champ."

David Benner, our P.R. guy, set up a press conference. You'd think I'd be ecstatic, you know, jumping up and down, but I'm not. If the team were playing a lot better, I'd be more excited. Don't get me wrong, I am excited about being selected as a starter, but if my own team isn't playing well, that reflects on Reggie Miller. My main objective right now is to get the team playing well.

So I was at the press conference, and Conrad Brunner asked if I deserved to be on the team. Now what kind of stupid question is that? Granted, I'm not having one of my better years statistically, but look at my last three years when I didn't make the team. Look at who they picked ahead of me those years. Look at their horseshit numbers and ask them if they deserved to be picked. I had ten times better numbers than they did, but my team wasn't winning. That was always the excuse: My team wasn't winning. Now that my team's winning, I make it.

So what happens: They come up with some stupid question about whether I deserved to make it. I just went ahead and said, "Yes," but I can't believe he asked that question. Do I have the highest scoring average in the league? No, but that's not what my game's about. I thought he knew that.

Anyway, Penny Hardaway of Orlando is the other guard. Shaq's in the middle, and Grant Hill and Scottie Pippen are the forwards. Reserves will be named later.

I had more than nine hundred thousand votes. That really surprises me. I didn't know I had nine hundred thousand fans, to tell you the truth. Geezus, that scares the hell out of me.

I was watching SportsCenter—this is so funny—and they were naming the starters for the All-Star team. They went through the West: Dan Majerle, Latrell Sprewell, Hakeem, Shawn Kemp—this was Craig Kilbourne from ESPN talking, by the way—and then he gets to the East: Grant Hill, who was the leading vote getter out of everybody; Scottie; Shaqster; Penny; and then he could have said anything, but instead of saying, "Reggie," he said, "Cheryl's brother, Reggie."

Just lets you know that no matter what I do, I'll always be Cheryl's little brother. That's not a knock. I could win ten titles, lead the league in scoring, but I'll always be known as Cheryl's little brother. I don't know where he got that from.

I've been thinking more about the media. You know the guy I really like? Charlie Rose.

When I was in New York, I got to do his show, which is one of the best programs on PBS—hell, on any network. I've always been a big fan of Charlie Rose. He doesn't have a lot of pro athletes on his show. Instead, he usually does a lot of politically oriented interviews on issues of the day. The format is simple: a round wooden table, a couple of glasses of water, Charlie and his notes. Good questions, good talk.

I've done hundreds and hundreds of interviews, but this one was different. That's because on the show I did, William F. Buckley, Jr., one of the great conservatives, was there doing a segment with Arthur Schlesinger Jr., who is a world-famous author and staunch liberal. These guys are huge in the political world.

I was in the green room with them before the show, and they

were talking about the Knicks and the great series last year. I thought, "I cannot believe I'm talking to these guys." David Benner was in there with me.

Arthur Schlesinger came in and was talking to Mr. Buckley. He said, "So what did you for the holidays, William?" I was kind of talking to Benner but also half-listening to their conversation. That's when Mr. Buckley said, "Oh, as customary, we were out on the boat."

That's when I knew I wasn't in Indianapolis anymore.

Anyway, he said, "We were out on the boat in the Caribbean for a couple of weeks."

I was thinking, "Oh, my God, these guys are huge."

They went on the first segment, and they were on for twenty to twenty-five minutes. I watched the interview in the green room, and they talked about liberalism, Bill Clinton, John Kenneth Galbraith, Milton Friedman, Newt Gingrich, the Contract with America, and I was thinking, "How am I going to follow these guys?" It was like following Pavarotti with a kazoo.

But Charlie's a big basketball guy—he's from North Carolina, I think—and we had a great time. We just talked about everything, from basketball to politics. It was a great interview and really enjoyable. I'm always excited about doing his show.

I also like doing David Letterman's show. Jay Leno is great. Those kinds of guys are funny and witty. Roy Firestone is good, too, a great interviewer. Those guys make it fun.

Then there's someone like Jim Rome, who does a talk show on ESPN2 and whose whole deal is confrontation and controversy. The guy is a terrible interviewer. I've never done his show, but after I saw what he did to New Orleans Saints quarterback Jim Everett—he kept baiting Everett by calling him "Chrissie"—I knew I'd never do his show. They've asked me to do it four or five times, but I'll never do it. When he becomes a better interviewer, then maybe I'll come on; he has to improve on his skills a little bit. He's not all that hot.

When it comes to the Indianapolis media, everybody's been pretty fair. It's nothing like New York or Philadelphia or Boston. That's really helped me out, too.

I've had a few problems with the Indianapolis writers. During Dan Dunkin's rookie year (hey, they can be rookies, too), he gave ratings of everybody on the team; A, B, C, D, F. He gave me a C or a C+. At the time I was averaging something like 23 points, and the whole thing really busted my ass. So I went up to him and said, "Where the hell did you get that from? What was your basis for that?"

We had a problem for a little while where I didn't talk to the media, but finally I realized it wasn't worth it. These guys are trying to get inside your head. For the most part, Dan and Conrad are really good guys, and I can't let something like that get me off my game.

I try not to read the sports pages, but somebody's always going to have a paper in the locker room. Or somebody will come in and say, "Did you see what so-and-so wrote?" I try to read *USA Today,* something that's objective and neutral, as opposed to, say, our local columnists.

I admit it, though: I read the New York papers when I was there. I had to, because Santa was coming to town. I wanted to see what they were saying. But no matter what they write, good or bad, it can change in an instant. It's the law of the jungle: The media will turn on you in a minute.

And while I'm thinking about it, I hope players have finally gotten over this thing about women reporters in the locker room. I don't mind women reporters in the locker room at all. They have just as much right to be there as anybody else. They've seen it all, and we've seen it all. So what's the big deal?

My only personal rule is that I like to get dressed before I start talking to the media. I don't want some old woman in Sioux City, Iowa, seeing me half-naked on ESPN.

Thursday, January 26
Indianapolis

Well, it's really going to be a long year now.

Dale went down during the Phoenix game and dislocated his right shoulder with 10:27 left in the second quarter. He had surgery on his left shoulder two years ago and popped his right one out during the game against the Suns. He's going to be out two to three weeks. We're really in trouble now. No Antonio for another two to four weeks. No Dale. No rebounding.

They're calling the Suns the Dream Team of the NBA, and I can see why. They've got Danny Majerle, Danny Ainge, Dan Manning, Charles Barkley, and Kevin Johnson (who was hurt). They also have this kid Elliot Perry. Geezus, what a find. This guy does all the little things for them. K. J. had better not slip up, because he might not have a spot when he gets back. Well, maybe I'm exaggerating, but I'm telling you, this Perry kid is something else.

I know K. J. will always start for this team, because K. J.'s one of the top two or three point guards in the league. But this kid plays hard. He can't do all the things K. J. can do, but, man, they wouldn't be 32–8 or 9 without him.

As usual, we blew another game. Even without Dale we had our chances to win, but we didn't. We held the Suns to 92 points, which is 20 points below their league-leading average, and we still lost by 6. About the only guy who stood out for us was Rik, who is playing really well these days.

Now everybody has to step up. With Antonio out with a bad back and Dale out with a bad shoulder, the firm of Davis & Davis is on disability right now. We're not going to get back to the level we want with these guys hurt and us not stepping up.

Note to Conrad: Just saw the stats for the starters on the Eastern and Western Conference teams. I'm averaging 19.8 points, which is better than Majerle, who doesn't even start for the

Suns, and Hill and Kemp. Maybe Conrad ought to ask them if they deserved to be picked.

Ah, shit, I'm just in a bad mood.

Even though they beat us, it was good to see Charles Barkley. I'll never forget what Charles did for me when I was back at UCLA. He probably doesn't remember it, but I do.

Magic Johnson used to have his annual Midsummer Night's Magic charity game, which benefited the United Negro College Fund. People usually don't remember that the first one of those games was at UCLA's Pauley Pavilion. That was also the first and only time Larry Bird played. Boston had won the championship that year, and I remember my eyes were this big when I saw him there.

I had played with Magic at UCLA during pickup games, but here was Barkley, Dominique, Bird, Kevin Willis, Spud Webb . . . everybody who was anybody. All these players were at Pauley, and all these Hollywood stars were there, too. It was unreal seeing all these famous people.

I was sitting right behind one of the benches before the game, and Charles Barkley was out there warming up. This was back before he lost some weight. This is when he was huge, when they called him the "Round Mound of Rebound."

So I was watching him warm up, and all of a sudden he stops shooting, squirms through the crowd, and starts walking toward me. I'm thinking, "Oh, my God, what's he going to do, hit me or something?" I mean, I didn't know Charles Barkley, and he sure as hell didn't know me.

Instead, he says, "Hey, I like your game. Don't change anything."

I was like, "Whoa, Charles Barkley. Cool."

I had all my homeboys around me, and I was soaking it in. I don't know where he got his information from, but I did a lot of bad things in college—just like Charles. I guess that's why he told me not to change.

Looking back, I'm not real proud of some of the stuff I did, but when you're young, you do things you wouldn't do later.

One time, during my sophomore year at UCLA, we were playing Brigham Young. They had a guy named Devin Durrant who was a dirty player. All that stuff about those Mormon boys being upstanding young men? Forget it.

We were getting beat by 10 points or so when Corey Gaines, one of my teammates, tried to take a charge from Durrant. Both of them fell, and Corey was called for the block. As Durrant got up, he spit on Corey. Durrant was from Europe, and I guess that's what they do over there. None of the refs saw him do it, but I wasn't going to let Durrant get away with that. I was going to stick up for my buddy.

Well, I was sick. I mean, like sneezy-cough-flu sick. When I saw what Durrant did, I summoned up one of those disgusting yellow mothball-sized loogies that you get when you're sick. As soon as Durrant got up, I spit that slimy thing right in his face.

Technicals. Thrown out. Suspended for the first half of our next game.

We went from there to St. John's. I had a consecutive games-played streak going, but I also had heard rumblings from Walt Hazzard, who was our coach, that he was going to replace me in the starting lineup with Craig Jackson. He was our big blue-chip recruit, so I figured this was a great opportunity for Hazzard to do this.

So I sat for the first half and went in after halftime. It didn't matter. This was when St. John's had Chris Mullin and Walter Berry and Mark Jackson. They beat us by 19.

Another time we were playing at Arizona and getting the shit drilled out of us. Booker Turner was the referee. Booker is a very fair referee, but I had had so much bad history with Arizona coach Lute Olson that it wouldn't have mattered who was officiating that day.

If there was one coach I could not stand, it was Lute Olson.

To this day we don't get along. I think he's a dick, and I feel the same way about his teams. I always thought his players were a bunch of wimps. They played too structured, too girlylike. Me and my boys never got along with the Arizona boys. I hated the Arizona Wildcats. I remember elbowing one of his players once, and Lute told the player to press charges against me. Can you believe that? Hey, I just wanted them to know that this brother is not gonna take too much shit.

Anyway, this was my junior year, and I went up to Booker after he made a call and said, "Booker, you know what?"

Now Booker and I usually got along, so he said, "No, what, Reg?"

I said, "This is the worst game I've ever seen you officiate in my life. You know what it seems like to me? Seems that all these motherfuckers in here paid you to referee a game like this."

Booker nearly fell to the floor in shock.

"I can't believe you said that, Reggie."

"Booker, I don't want to hear it. You got paid off."

Then I turned to the crowd and started pinching my thumb and forefinger together, like I was feeling dollar bills.

"You were paid off, Booker."

Technical. Hazzard ran out, grabbed me, and said, "What the hell are you doing out here?"

"Coach, that motherfucker was paid off!"

Hey, I was a psycho in college, I'm telling you. I had a very bad temper. No excuse. But I've learned—the hard way.

I think when you're growing up and playing street ball, you pick up a kind of language that only you and the other players understand. You trash-talk, but when I say trash-talk, I don't mean your mama this, your mama that. It's nothing like that.

Today's game is more mental. Everybody in the NBA knows how to play basketball or else they wouldn't be there. But what separates the good players from the great players is their mental capacity, not only to overcome their opponent but to get through tough spots.

I think that's one thing I really thrive on. I always feel mentally stronger than any opponent I step on the same floor with. He might have more talent than I do, but I don't think anybody is mentally stronger than I am. I'll match wills with anybody.

Probably the greatest player, both physically and mentally, was Michael. No question. On occasion I tried to break him, tried talking shit to him, but it never worked.

Man, I was stupid back then. It was during my second year in the league, and we were playing an exhibition game in Cincinnati against the Bulls. We were kicking the shit out of them, and Michael was just going through the motions. You know, exhibition game, big deal.

Then Chuck Person, who always talked shit to people, started egging me on during one of the time-outs.

"Talk shit to Michael," he said. "He ain't any good."

I was hitting shots all night, thinking I was hot shit, so I said, "Yeah, okay, I will."

We got back out on the court, and I started talking. I'd make a shot and yell at him, "Take this, bitch." I'd make a driving layup and say, "Don't get me started, bitch." Or if he hit a jumper or something, I'd say, "Is that your best shot?"

The next thing I knew it was like, ding-dong, Michael's home. We were up something like 12 points with five minutes to go. That's when Michael scored the next 20 points—on me. They won the game with ease.

As we were walking off the court, Michael came up behind me and said, "Don't you *ever* talk shit to me again." And then he was gone.

Two things: I never talked shit to Michael again. And I never listened to Chuck Person again.

Michael could talk some shit, too. He was also one of the most physical players I ever faced.

Remember that fight we had a few years back in Indiana? Here's how it really started:

It was a fast break, and we were coming back on defense. I was trying to catch B. J. Armstrong, who had gotten ahead of me on the break. I accidentally got tangled up with Michael; we both tripped, and he fell on his wrist. B. J. missed the layup, and I caught the rebound on the floor and threw it to one of our guys on the outlet.

We both got up, and he went over and talked to Phil Jackson, their coach. I went over to him and said, "Yo, Dog, you all right?" He looked at me all crazylike. I think he thought I purposely tried to trip him.

I said, "Mike, you all right?"

He kept looking at me crazy. So I said, "Fuck you, then."

The next play they started running that motion offense of theirs, that 1932 offense that they think is so mysterious, and Michael began giving me elbows and shots. I thought, "This guy is really tripping out," but the referees weren't doing anything about it. Now I'm thinking, "Damn, these guys are going to let him get away with this shit, too."

A shot went up, and I went to box him out. I tried to give him a good pop, but he moved out of the way. We got the rebound, had a fast break, and Vern went in for the layup. But Vern missed it because Michael ran right in front of him at the last moment. I was trailing the play, tipped it in, and then saw Michael's momentum sort of carry him out of bounds.

After I tipped it in, I purposely went out of bounds and gave him a shot. And that's when it started. I got in his face, and he started grabbing and took a swing at me.

Said and done, I got thrown out, got fined ten thousand dollars and I'm thinking, "You got to be kidding me." No foul, no T, nothing on Michael (though he did later get suspended for one game for the fight). I had scratches and blood coming down, and I told the refs, "Look at me. And I get thrown out, and there wasn't a scratch on him."

The refs said I got thrown out because I went out of my way to throw a little elbow. And then one of the refs came up to me and said, "You should have come to me when he first threw the elbow."

What?

"Fuck that shit," I said. "You saw it happen right in front of you. Y'all didn't do nothing about it. I'm not gonna sit there and take that shit. I gotta protect myself out here."

That's when all the media was talking about preferential treatment to superstars. Well, I saw it. It's true.

At that time our games weren't selling out. The only time we sold out was when Michael or Shaq came and the Lakers came. So maybe they had a point there; Michael was a money-maker, so maybe they shouldn't be in such a hurry to throw him out. The fans didn't come to see Reggie play, they came to see Michael.

In the heat of the moment, you don't understand it, but later you do. Jess Kersey was the lead official that night. I thought Jess should have handled it a little differently. That's because I think Jess, Earl Strom—when he was alive—Jack Madden, Eddie T. Rush, and Jake O'Donnel are probably the best officials I've seen in the league. But I think he handled that situation wrong.

You try to get in people's minds as much as possible, but you also have to find out who you can and can't mess with.

My rookie year, when I was young and gung ho, we were playing the Pistons in Detroit. That's when they had the Microwave, Vinnie Johnson. I remember I blocked his shot out of bounds and started talking shit to him. Then Vern came up and said, "Don't talk shit to that motherfucker because he's crazy."

When Vern says that, you listen. The Microwave might go off and score 50.

Another guy you never said a word to was Larry Bird. People said this white boy didn't know how to talk shit. Believe me, this guy knew how to talk shit, all right, and could back it up, too.

My rookie year, we played the Celtics at Market Square. It was a close game, but we could never beat them. It came down to free throws. There were about twenty seconds left, and we fouled Bird. We were down by 3 points. Bird went to the line to shoot two.

I was standing on the line—and being a rookie dumbass and not realizing this was one of the best free throw shooters ever to play the game, I tried to throw off his timing. As he went to shoot, I kind of said out of the side of my mouth, "Hey! Hey!"

He stopped right before he shot, looked at me, and said, "You got to be kidding me. Rook, you got to be kidding me."

He shot one. Boom. We were down by 4 now.

Bird got the ball again, and before he shot, he said, "Rook, I'm the best shooter in the league right now. In the league. Understand? And you're up here trying to say something?"

Boom. We were down by 5.

What made it worse was that Kevin McHale and Danny Ainge were laughing their asses off. I was thinking, "What a dumbass I am. You're up here talking shit to Larry Bird. He's at the free throw line." I felt so stupid.

The one boost of confidence I got was after my second game in the league, which was at the Boston Garden. The Celtics were about ready to beat us—there was maybe a minute or so left—and I was standing back there as someone was shooting a free throw. Standing nearby was Bird, but I wasn't saying a thing. I mean, this was Larry Bird, and I was playing in only my second game. But he took a couple of steps over and said, "Reggie, keep working on your game. You're gonna be a great player."

I didn't know Larry from Adam, but that meant a lot to me. I had played decently that night, scored 10 or 12 points. But for him to come up and say something to me ... he didn't have to say anything. I was just another snot-nosed rookie. But something must have caught his eye.

Of course, Chuck Person tried to talk shit to Larry all the time, but it didn't work too often.

In my fourth year in the league, we were playing at the Boston Garden. It was close to Christmas, I think. Chuck was all psyched up to face Larry. I think Chuck envied Larry, especially when Boston came to Indianapolis. Chuck played for the Pacers, but Larry was born and raised in Indiana. He played at Indiana State. He lived in French Lick during the off-season. Chuck resented Larry's coming to Market Square and having the place sell out, with everybody wearing Celtic green in Bird's honor.

Hey, the man's from Indiana, right? So you got to give the man his props. He's one of the greatest players of all time. I think Chuck envied that.

So we were playing in the Garden, and Larry was taking the ball out in front of our bench. He had been on a roll, and I think Mike Sanders was guarding him at the time. Chuck was on the bench, and he said to Larry, "You wouldn't be doing that shit if I was out there."

Larry turned to Bob Hill, our coach, and said, "Bo, put this clown in."

Bo started laughing, but Larry said, "No, Bo, I'm serious."

Then Larry turned to the scorer's table and yelled, "Sub!"

Man, the ref was starting to do the five-second count, and Larry was doing this shit. Chuck wouldn't get up, so Larry said, "I thought so," and then threw the ball in just in time. I was thinking, "This guy is crazy."

Later in the same game they were coming down on the fast break. Their point guard threw the ball to Bird, and he got it at the three-point line, in front of our bench again. Mike Sanders was on him. Larry turned around, found Chuck on the bench, and said, "Chuck, this is for you: Merry Christmas."

He turned and shot a fallaway three. Boom. Nothing but net.

It was hard not to laugh, but this was Larry Bird serving our ass up. Damn, this guy was talking some shit, some of the best ever.

Very few players can get to me, but the all-time best was Drazen Petrovic, who used to play for Portland and then New Jersey before he was killed in an automobile accident in Germany in June 1993. I loved him as a player but hated him as a person. He got under my skin. Maybe it was because I was jealous of the way he shot the ball. Quickest release in the game. One shooter to the other, I envied his ability. But, man, that Yugoslavian shit used to eat me up. I'd be talking shit to him, and he'd still come off screens. I'd be dead on him, and he'd make the shot in my face. Just like I do to other guys.

One time in New Jersey, we had a lead, and I was talking constant shit to him. They started to make a comeback, mostly because of Petrovic's shooting. He came off a screen, made the shot, and all the way down the court he was pointing in my face, saying shit. He was the Yugoslavian version of me—except I was easier to understand.

People didn't think he talked shit. They figured he was a foreign player, what did he know about the game? Trust me, he knew the game from A to Z. I think playing with Clyde and those guys in Portland for two or three years really helped him out.

Saturday, January 28
Indianapolis

Something wild is happening. Just came from the shoot-around. We're very shorthanded right now because of the injuries to Dale and Antonio. Derrick McKey is banged up, but he's going to play tonight against Philadelphia.

The coaches were telling everyone they have to step it up

while Dale and Antonio are out. Then they went to John Williams as he was coming out of the locker room and told him he's going to have to step up and play some minutes. John couldn't handle it. It freaked him out.

John has been going through a lot this year. They keep calling him "Hot Plate," and I kind of think he likes the name. As you know, John is more than three hundred pounds.

This guy has skills. If he got down to 280, even 290, he'd be a force in this league. He can do amazing things with the basketball and he knows the game, but I think his weight is keeping him from playing the way he wants to play. I also think he has all this aggression and frustration built up. They have him on about ten different diets and are always giving him all sorts of advice.

Well, I think the pressure just got to him. He snapped and said he couldn't handle it and left practice and quit. Hard to believe. This isn't like an elementary school game where you can quit and go home. Someone has to step up and play. We're going up against a pretty big front line with Shawn Bradley, Scott Williams, Clarence Weatherspoon, and Sharone Wright.

Now this. What's going to happen next with this team?

At least we aren't the only team with problems. Pippen got fined six thousand dollars for throwing a chair on the court during Tuesday night's game at Orlando. He got suspended for one game, which cost him another twenty-six thousand dollars. That's one expensive chair.

This thing with the chair: Was it because of what happened during that game, or was it something else? He wants out. Maybe he's doing theatrics so he can get out. Maybe this was one of those tactics.

If you ask me, he might be going at it the wrong way. People look up to him. Fans and kids look up to him. Barkley says we're no role models, but Scottie has a big following. You have to remember that the Bulls were the kings: the merchandising, the Nike ads, Scottie and Air. You know they're going to be hounding Scottie at the All-Star game. That's why I'm glad I'm going to be part of it, so I can see what's going on. It's going to be interesting.

Also saw something in the paper today about John Nash, the general manager of the Bullets. They had a game canceled because it was too wet on the court from the hockey rink underneath. It was the second time it happened this season.

Nash said, "We lead the league in something now."

Yes, baby. Yes. Yes. Byron Scott hit a three-pointer at the buzzer in overtime to beat the Sixers, 106–103. Finally, a win.

Man, what a tough game. Those bitches would not go away. We were shorthanded, but we did it. John Lucas has those Sixers playing hard. We watched Phoenix in Philadelphia the night before, and they blew that game, so this was a back-to-back for Philly. We knew they could do one of two things: fold or play the game hard. They played hard.

As I said, we are the hunted this year, and they came out and played extremely tough. Dana Barros might make the All-Star team. He's having a good year. He's always been a dagger in our heart. Tonight he hit a three-pointer with 5.6 seconds left to send the game into overtime. And there I was thinking we had it won.

I finally scored some points in the fourth quarter, pulled out of a slump, and then, bam, Barros hit that three. But thank goodness for Byron. As soon as he released it, I said, "Like the ball had eyes."

Byron saved us—again.

Sunday, January 29
Indianapolis

Why does Bobby Knight have to say what he says?

He did an interview with *Inside Sports* not long ago and said he got less out of Damon Bailey than any player he's ever coached. Now that's some silly shit to say.

Damon has been on the injury list since September because of surgery on both knees. You think the kid hurt them playing at Bedford–North Lawrence High? He hurt them at Indiana, hurt them playing his ass off for Bobby Knight.

Dunkin did a column on Damon. Damon could have ripped into Knight, but he didn't. Damon's a good guy, had a great career at Indiana, and deserved better than that from Knight.

Monday, January 30
Indianapolis

Forty-one games down, forty-one to go.

We're 24–17, compared to 18–23 at the same time a season ago. January didn't help. We went 7–8, which is the first losing month we've had since December 1993.

Maybe we can recapture some of our magic of last season. That's when we were hot in the second half, going 29–12. I don't know if we can do that this time around, not with Dale and Antonio hurt.

We're not in much of a position to look ahead. We did that earlier in the year, and it got us nowhere.

Had to give Antonio a little shit today at practice. He's still recovering from back surgery, but he was on the court doing a little shooting and stuff.

"Remember Antonio Davis?" I said as everybody was shooting around. "Whatever happened to him? He used to run up and down the court and dunk and growl on people. What happened to that man?"

Antonio didn't say anything. He just kept shooting. But he was smiling, I think.

Mel Daniels was at practice, too. Mel was a star in the old ABA and had his jersey retired by the Pacers. He's now a scout for the organization, and a damn good one.

We were sitting in the weight room after practice, and everybody started asking Mel about some of the college players he's seen lately. I hadn't heard of some of the guys, like Keith Van Horn of Utah. Mel loves the way he plays.

Mel has a very simple way of scouting. He always says, "Either the motherfucker can play, or the motherfucker can't play."

By the way, I just learned I made the All-NBA Whine Team. A writer in Portland did a poll with the league's refs and had them pick an all-whine team. It was me, Dennis Rodman, Gary Payton, Clyde Drexler, Charles Barkley, Alonzo Mourning, Dikembe Mutombo, and Vernon Maxwell.

Thank you very much.

Whiner Coach of the Year honors were split between Miami's Kevin Loughery and Larry.

Tuesday, January 31
Indianapolis

Just heard who made the All-Star team as reserves, and I'm telling you, there's going to be some controversy over the coaches' picks.

No Clyde Drexler. No Jimmy Jackson. No Jamal Mashburn. Jimmy's the fourth-leading scorer in the league, and he couldn't get in. Mashburn's the sixth-leading scorer, and he couldn't get in. Man, very tough.

The thing is, if you had taken Jimmy, then who would you keep out? Mitch Richmond? John Stockton? Gary Payton? See what I mean? It's tough to choose.

And if you pick Mash, do you ignore the Mailman? Hell, no. Same thing goes for Detlef Schrempf and Cedric Ceballos, who made it over Mash.

A big turnover in the Eastern Conference, though. None of the guards from the 1994 game made it this year. It went from B. J. Armstrong, Mookie Blaylock, John Starks, Mark Price, and Kenny Anderson, to me, Penny Hardaway, Dana Barros (I told you he should have been picked), and Joe Dumars.

February 1995

Wednesday, February 1
Indianapolis

We've got Cleveland tonight, and I'll give them credit for proving a lot of people wrong, including myself. They're one and a half games ahead of us in the standings—they're in second, we're in third—and they don't have Brad Daugherty, Gerald Wilkins, or Mark Price. Daugherty has a bad back, Wilkins is gone for the rest of the season because of an Achilles injury, and Price has a broken bone in his right wrist.

Mike Fratello has gone in there and done a great job with this team. They get all over you on defense and play the slowest offensive tempo in the league.

I say all these nice things about the Cavs, and then we drill them, 101–82. Cleveland works hard, but you can't have all those guys out with injuries and not expect it to catch up with you.

I only had 12 points tonight, but who cares? I didn't need to shoot.

The best moment of the night? Vern got a standing ovation when Larry put him in early in the fourth quarter. If anyone deserves applause, it's Vern.

And speaking of cheers, I heard that Stockton passed Magic Johnson tonight as the NBA career assists leader. I'll bet you a year's salary that the Mailman got the pass that broke the record.

Friday, February 3
Indianapolis

The Magic are in town, and everybody's talking about their 35–9 record and Shaq and Penny and how they're running away with the Atlantic Division lead. Hey, let 'em go. They can be caught.

This is the first time we've played Orlando since we swept them in the playoffs last year. But they're a different team from a year ago. They added Horace Grant, who really helps them on the boards, and Brian Shaw, who gives them some outside shooting off the bench. They've got a lot of talent, but let's see what happens when they face some adversity. They lost to Seattle last night and get us tonight. Let's see how they handle a back-to-back against two good teams.

Told you. We won, 118–106, and it seemed like more.

Horace and Nick Anderson didn't play because they were hurt, but it evened out because we didn't have Dale or Antonio. So call the injury thing a draw.

Rik was great tonight. He had 27 points and 10 rebounds and got the best of Shaq. Plus, our fans were pumped up. We had our eleventh sellout of the season, which is the first time that's happened since 1972.

Here's another first: We just gave the Magic their first two-game losing streak of the season.

Saturday, February 4
Cleveland

I can't figure this shit out. We drill Cleveland and Orlando, and then go on the road and do this: get beat by the Cavaliers, 82–73, in the ugliest game I've seen in a long time. We scored only 35 points in the second half. We missed dunks. We didn't work worth a damn.

I had 10 points in the first quarter and finished with 19. And I was our leading scorer, which tells you what kind of job we did offensively.

Larry was so pissed that he replaced me with Vern with two minutes left in the game. And, oh yeah, Byron had to leave the game with back spasms. Just what we need, another injury.

Monday, February 6
Charlotte

Big day for the Miller family today. Cheryl just found out she's going to be inducted into the Basketball Hall of Fame.

Cheryl's so crazy. When she first got the call from the Hall of Fame people, she thought it was me pulling a practical joke. Said I had a warped sense of humor. Me? But once she knew it was for real, she dropped the phone and started shaking.

If anybody deserves to be in there, it's Cheryl. She revolutionized women's basketball, not to mention all the Happy Meals she helped pay for when we were kids.

Back in the fifth and sixth grades, we'd go to the courts at John Adams Elementary or Hunt Park and hustle two-on-two games. We had it down to a science. It was the best hustle scam in Riverside, California.

There were two scams. In the first one, I'd tell Cheryl to hide in the bushes, and then I'd go up to a couple of older kids and arrange a game.

"You guys want to play?" I said. "I'm by myself . . . unless you count my sister."

Then I'd whistle, and Cheryl would come out from behind the bushes looking like she didn't know a thing about basketball. You could see the two other guys looking at each other like, "Oh, my God, this is going to be so easy."

I couldn't blame them. She'd walk on the court wearing those cheap Trax shoes, the kind you get at Kmart. She'd have on those real high tube socks, the ones with all the different colors. Her hair would be in pigtails or braids. She looked like she didn't know if a basketball was round or square.

Then there was the one where I'd bring Cheryl on the court in full view of the other kids and pretend like I was teaching her the game.

"Okay, Cheryl," I'd say, "now just put your hands on the ball like this and try to shoot it at the basket."

Cheryl would nod her head enthusiastically and then heave it over the backboard or ram it into the rim or not even reach the net. What an actress.

After a while, I'd yell over to one of the other kids, "Hey, you guys want to play?"

"Who you running with?"

"Well, my regular partner isn't here, but my sister is. I guess we could play you."

They'd almost fall over themselves trying to get to our court.

We'd play for ten dollars; the first team to 10 by ones would win the money. Then we'd get down, 5–0, double the bet, and then take care of business. I'd look at Cheryl, she'd look at me, we'd wink, and then . . . 10–5 us, and on our way to McDonald's for a Happy Meal. Or if we were tired of Micky D's, we'd go over to Dairy Queen.

We ran that scam for months at all the local elementary schools and junior highs. Easy money.

Cheryl and I have always been close. It's almost like we're twins. I don't know how to explain it, but we're connected on a level that I don't think Cheryl and I even understand. Even when I had to wear those braces on my legs as a kid, Cheryl never felt sorry for me. She was my best friend, my protector. Still is.

Believe it or not, I was a chubby kid until I was five or six. And unlike everybody else in my family, my ears stuck out. My mom says it was because the doctors told her to quit pushing during the delivery, and, well, my ears got caught.

When we were growing up, it was always Cheryl and me against my older two brothers. Darrell and Saul Jr. didn't want us hanging around them. Only if they needed a couple of extra bodies to fill out a team would they let us play with them. In fact, for about five years they had us convinced that we were adopted.

In our house there were two constants: discipline and sports. Out of sheer fear we listened to our parents. Either that or we had to choose between the belt or the switch. There weren't any "Go to your room" or—what do they call them now?—"time-outs." We would have killed for a time-out.

But there was also a lot of love in our family. Things were tight financially, but we never seemed to lack anything. Anyway, sports kept us busy. It wasn't just basketball, either. It was corkball, skateboarding, football. It wasn't anything for us to play basketball in the morning and then roller derby in the afternoon.

For the longest time Cheryl could always beat me up. She was a good three or four inches taller than me. We'd play two-on-two—it would be Saul Jr. and me against Cheryl and Darrell—and Cheryl would knock me down or block my shot. Saul would get all mad at me and say, "You're such a girl." Meanwhile, Darrell would be high-fiving Cheryl. I hated that.

Later, when Darrell and Saul moved on, Cheryl and I would go at it. It was fierce. If I got the best of her in a game, she'd throw an elbow and then run. I'd have to chase her around the block on my skateboard.

Cheryl was amazing. I still remember the night I came home from a Poly Tech game after scoring 39 points. I mean, I was feeling good about myself. Then Cheryl came home.

"Cheryl, I got 39."

"Reggie, that's great."

"Yeah, so how'd you do?"

"Uh, I got 105."

The thing was, Cheryl didn't say it to be mean. But damn, 105 points in one game?

I got my revenge. At the time we both had short afros. One day she was walking out of the house when some of my friends were driving by. They started yelling, "Hey, Reg!"

They thought it was me, which was like the ultimate insult to Cheryl.

"It's Cheryl!" she said. "I'm Cheryl!"

And then there was the day Cheryl quit playing me one-on-one.

It was her freshman year at USC, and she came home for Christmas break. I was crashed out in my room, lying in bed, when she came looking for me.

"C'mon, let's play," she said.

So I got up, and for the first time ever I was taller than her. I had grown while she was away at school. I was about six five or so.

"Reg, it looks like you shot up," she said.

"Yeah," I said. "I'm always tired and hungry."

We got out to the court and she said, "Your ball." I told her she could have it first. So she kind of crouched down, made her usual strong first move, got right past me and put up the shot.

I pinned it against the backboard.

"Foul!" she said.

"Foul? What are you talking about?"

"Foul," she said.

"No, it wasn't."

Cheryl paused for a moment and then said, in a real serious tone, "We're going to play Horse from now on."

And that was the last one-on-one game we ever played. Even Horse wasn't much fun for her once my dad extended the court. I just kept hitting those twenty- to twenty-five-footers. After a while I'd call swishes from twenty-five feet. You couldn't hit the rim or else you'd get a letter.

Cheryl and I are alike in so many ways. We both have jump shots that aren't exactly in the classic style. My wrists knock when I shoot. In fact, that's how you can tell if I'm going to hit a shot—my wrists click together. Sometimes I shoot and the ball has backspin, or forward spin, or has no spin at all. But it gets there, and that's all that matters.

Cheryl shoots from the top of her head. She had to when we were kids or else my brothers would have blocked her shot.

We always had a rule at our house: Don't mess with perfection. Nobody was allowed to tinker with our shooting styles. My dad even used to tell the coaches to leave our shots alone.

What's weird is that if I'm giving a clinic to kids, my shooting form is exactly how coaches teach it—elbow tucked in, that sort of stuff. But once I get in a game, it goes back to my usual style.

The other thing Cheryl and I have in common is our emotions. When I did that choke sign during the Knicks playoff game in 1994, Cheryl said she couldn't wait to get to her office the next day and brag to everyone. Said she was full of pride.

Hey, Cheryl would know about this stuff. She got so mad one time that she pushed an official and got thrown out of a game. Another time she head-butted another player. You didn't want to mess with Cheryl.

Like sister, like brother.

Her full name is Cheryl DeAnn Miller, but I call her "CD" or "Cheryl Dean" because she's such a rebel. I'm telling you, I don't know what I'd do without her. She's the best.

Tuesday, February 7
Charlotte

Man, we needed this one. After losing to Cleveland, we needed to make a statement. We made one, beating Grandmama and Zo and the Hornets, 95–92, in overtime.

Dell Curry missed a free throw that would have tied the game with 8.2 seconds, and we held on for the win. After losing 10 of our last 13 on the road, we'll take a victory any way we can.

Not only did we pick up a game on Charlotte (we're only two games back now), but we got Dale Davis back in the lineup. Just in time for the Knicks tomorrow night.

Wednesday, February 8
Indianapolis

I don't feel like talking about this one.

We had a sellout for the Knicks tonight, and we got beat by 19 points, 96–77. That's 6 in a row we've lost to these clowns, and 12 of the last 13. And they didn't even have Oakley in the lineup this time.

We were hurting, too. Dale couldn't play because of a sore back. Same with Byron. Tank is still out with a bad shoulder, and Antonio can't play because of his bad back. That means we had nine guys available tonight.

New York just manhandled us. We didn't have any big bodies, and they took advantage of it. You need big bodies against the Knicks or else you're doomed. That's what happened to us.

Win one, lose one. Win one, lose one. That ain't going to cut it.

Now I have to get on a plane and go to Phoenix for the All-Star Game. I'd feel a lot better about it if we were playing better.

Friday, February 10
Phoenix

Man, you should see the security at this place. We're staying at the Hilton Squaw Peak Valley, and it's like the president is staying here. Security people. Cameras. They're taking this stuff seriously. Nice resort, though.

I'm going to do what I always do on the road: I'm going to have fun and make the best of it without being a prisoner in my home, so to speak.

Today is media day. That's where you go from interview to interview to interview to interview, and you keep going until all the questions sound the same. After a while, so do all the answers.

First up was NBC's Bob Costas. This guy is good. He's prepared. He asks good questions. Sometimes he asks tough questions, but he never tries to embarrass you. He's fair. I respect that.

We talked about Cheryl making it into the Basketball Hall of Fame. We talked about game five of the Knicks series last year. Everybody wants to talk about game five.

"Has your life changed?" he asks.

I told him it had changed a little, but mostly what's changed is how people look at the Indiana Pacers. That game was on national TV. We were playing against supposedly the best team in the Eastern Conference. No one gave us a shot. But because of that game, people have started to pay attention to us. What they don't understand is that we played hard-nosed basketball in the earlier series against Atlanta and Orlando. Because we were hardly ever on TV, people didn't know that I played with a lot of emotion. Now all of a sudden we're in the media mecca of the world, playing the Knicks in the conference finals, and people notice.

We talked about trash-talking. We talked about the *Sports Illustrated* cover story on the NBA, the one with Derrick Coleman on the front of the magazine and the headline that said, "Waaaaaaaaa!" In a way, Costas was asking me if I thought NBA players had a bad attitude.

I told him it was unfortunate about Vern Maxwell going into the stands to confront a heckler who had crossed the line with verbal abuse. I told him it was unfortunate about Derrick's attitude toward his coaches. I told him it was too bad about the *Sports Illustrated* story, because I didn't think it represented what really was going on with the league.

I don't think my messing with a player, talking a little trash, demeans the game. I don't go after a player's race, religion, or family. Those things are off limits. Hell, half the time when I'm talking on the court, I'm talking to myself. I'm trying to get myself pumped up, to get a mental edge. But people see it and say, "Oh, there he is again, talking trash." But that's not always what I'm doing.

No matter what, I'm not going to quit talking on the court. That's part of my style, part of who I am as a player. All my life I've been put on my butt by bigger, stronger players. But I always get back up. I don't back down from anybody. That's why they call it the NBA: "No Babies Allowed."

Also, I'm not condoning what Vern Maxwell did—you shouldn't run ten rows into the stands after a fan; that's wrong. But I can see how it happens. Fans cross that line all the time, and players have to sit there and take it. You talk about some of the players having bad attitudes; well, some of the fans have bad attitudes, too. But just like the players, we're talking about a very low percentage.

There have been times during games that I've gone up to a referee and said, "Look, there's a guy sitting over there who's taking it way over the top. Can you go over there and tell him to cool out?" The ref says, "Okay, we'll look into it." Nine out of ten times they never do anything. Referees need to start us-

ing their judgment and power out there; so do ushers and op-
erators of arenas.

We also talked about the new three-point line. You know
that answer by heart now, too. We're getting beat by guys who
have no business shooting threes, guys like Charles Smith and
Vin Baker and Zo Mourning and Larry Johnson. Last year we
were begging Larry Johnson to take a three-point shot. Normally, those are two-pointers or bricks. But now they can cost
you a victory.

The rule is supposed to open up the game, but what it really
does is cheapen it. Guys like myself, Danny Ainge, Dan Majerle, Michael Adams—guys who aren't afraid to take and
make twenty-five-, twenty-six-footers—are becoming extinct.
Shooting the true long jumper is becoming a lost art.

Bob also wanted to know about the so-called Golden Era in
the NBA when Larry Bird, Michael, and Magic were in the
league at the same time. Did I think the game was going from a
beautiful, sweet jazz riff to a hip-hop, rap thing?

Good question. I said that it was unfair to judge this new era
just yet. I mean, you've got to give us time. You can't expect
Shaq or Grant Hill or Jason Kidd to be Larry, Michael, and
Magic overnight. It took Michael seven years before he won
his first championship. There are some good teams coming
up—Phoenix and Orlando, for example—but to compare us to
Larry, Michael, and Magic, who are like the founding fathers of
the Golden Era, is unfair because we haven't won a championship yet.

Also, I said, you have to understand that there's more parity
in the league now than back then. Back then it was Boston, Los
Angeles, and then Chicago. Now you've got Charlotte, Cleveland, Orlando, Phoenix, Seattle, Utah, Indiana. There are more
teams in the hunt these days.

After I finished up with Mr. Costas, it was on to ESPN and
more questions about the league's image. Everybody's jumping
on that topic, but I think people are going a little overboard on

this thing. There were a few bad incidents, but overall the league is in good hands.

By the way, I let the tape recorder run the whole time I was doing these interviews. One TV guy from Indianapolis saw it and asked why I needed a tape recorder. I told him I was keeping a journal.

"What, you writing a book?"

"Yeah, right," I said.

"No, I'm serious, man. I don't know."

"Yeah, right."

Hey, no use divulging any state secrets just yet.

We did the interview, and at the end of it the guy turns to the camera and says, "By the way, he's keeping a journal of all his activities this weekend, so I'm sure it's going to be loaded."

On to the print reporters. You sit at a table, and reporters gather around, ask a question or two or three, and then move on to the next player.

Someone asked about the book, so I told them I was writing a trashy novel, kind of like a Harlequin Romance thing. That ended that conversation.

More talk about the NBA's image. About the difference between the Pacers of '94 and '95. About Cheryl. About being an All-Star. About the three-point contest. About fan abuse. About the rule changes. About my favorite midnight snack (peanut butter-and-jelly sandwich with cheese-flavored Pringles). About my toughest opponents (teams: Knicks and Magic; players: Dumars). About the stupidest questions asked. (Usually, it's this one: "What's the stupidest question you've been asked?" But today someone asked me about the color of my underwear and if I wore my underwear when I played. And then there was a TV crew that asked every All-Star, "If you were a sound, what sound would you be?" Or "If you were an animal, which animal would you be?" I'll tell you what I'd like to be. I'd like to be a gazelle so I can get the hell away from that TV crew.)

Bill Bellamy of MTV came by. He's a lot of fun. He doesn't take everything so seriously. In the middle of our interview I saw Grandmama, and I started telling him I was going after his boy Scotty Burrell in the three-point contest. I told him Burrell wouldn't even be in the contest if they hadn't moved the line in. I was just messing with him, though. We were laughing and stuff.

Someone asked me about baseball. Hey, what baseball? They're on strike. Next question.

Wait a second. I've got a solution to the baseball strike. Here's what you do: Put the players association people and the owners in a boxing ring with gloves on, Mills Lane as the referee, and Don King as the promoter, and then just go for it. Whoever is standing at the end of twelve rounds, that's who gets to make the terms for the new agreement. Hey, it's worth a try. The other way isn't working.

By the time the media session was through, I had done about an hour and a half's worth of interviews. I didn't mind. Those people help make the NBA what it is, so I can try to help them with their jobs, right?

Big rumor going around. Word is that Nellie's through at Golden State. Wonder how Chris Webber feels now.

Saturday, February 11
Phoenix

My All-Star competition officially starts tonight with the three-point contest. This is the fourth time I've been in the shootout. I finished fourth in '89, second in '90, and fifth in '93.

I should have won it in '90, but being a dumbass, I won the coin toss for the final round but decided to shoot second instead of first. What I should have done was shoot first and put the pressure on Craig Hodges. Instead, he went out and put 19 on the board, and I could only come up with 18. I might have pressed a little because of that.

This time I like my chances. First of all, Mark Price, who's won the last two of these things, is hurt and can't defend the title. I feel bad for Mark, but that's how it goes.

My original plan was to come in and talk some serious mess with everybody, but then I found out Chuck Person was taking Price's place in the competition. That messes up everything, because Chuck is the guy who taught me how to talk shit in the first place. For me to talk shit to him would be like the pupil going against the teacher. I don't know if I can do that.

Mostly I'm just worried about getting past the first round. That's when you're the most nervous. If I get past the first round, I'll be okay.

Before I left for the arena, I ran into Richard Lewis the comedian out near the hotel pool. He wished me good luck and started talking about how I killed his Knicks in last year's series. He's funny, that guy. He started doing all that nervous gesturing and getting all upset over the Knicks. So I told him, "Hey, I didn't kill your Knicks. Your Knicks beat us, if you remember right."

Well, I lost. I just didn't hit the damn shots at the end.

The way it works is simple: eight players, three rounds, one minute to shoot five balls from five different spots around the three-point line. The last ball in each rack is worth two points. The top four guys advance to the second round, the top two to the finals. Winner gets a trophy and twenty thousand dollars.

I figured I'd need between 17 and 19 points to make it through the first round. I got 17 and made it to the semifinals with Miami's Glen Rice, Charlotte's Scott Burrell, and Chuck, who plays for San Antonio.

Rice went first and scored 19. Then Chuck got 16. I was next, and if I wanted a guaranteed spot in the final I needed to score 20 or more. I got 19 and had to hit my last two shots and 12 of my last 14 to do it. On my last shot—a two-pointer from the right baseline spot—I kept my right hand raised up in the follow-through, just like Dad taught me. That shot fell so pure when it left my hands, I knew it was in.

After it snapped the net, I just put my head down and walked toward the bench. People told me later that Zo Mourning was sitting on the sidelines just shaking his head and going, "Damn." That's because his man Burrell would have to come up with some big numbers.

It didn't happen. Burrell got 17, which meant I was in the final with Rice.

So I got to the final, but that coin toss killed me again. If I just could have won that coin toss and shot first. Instead, I called tails, as in, "Tails never fails." But it did fail. I got heads. As it turned out, I got my head beat in.

Rice went first and scored 17 points. That's not bad, but it's beatable. I got 16. Sixteen? I couldn't believe it. I had my shots but couldn't make them. Very disappointing.

I hugged Glen, told him congratulations, but I wanted that trophy. It would have looked good in my trophy room. I didn't care about the money, about the twenty thousand dollars. I wanted that trophy. It's a great-looking trophy. In fact, when I got to the top of the key and knew it was slipping away, all I could think was, "Damn, I'm not going to get that trophy." I wanted to show my kids, show the kids around the neighborhood. Had I won that thing, I would have acted the fool. I would have gone back and thanked everyone. I would have thanked my third-grade teacher and stuff.

The thing is, I saw Rice earlier in the day at the hotel, and he was practically giving me the trophy, like I already had it won.

Man, if only they knew I was just as nervous as they were. To me, that's the toughest thing, to shoot by yourself in that setting. If you go out on the court, and it's just you and the court, man, you can clear a rack of balls easy. But put twenty thousand fans in the stands, and you hear that weird-ass music they play, well, you start shooting differently. Your heart starts pounding against your chest, and you start shooting differently.

It could have been worse for me: I could have been Dallas's Tony Dumas. That poor kid missed all three of his slam dunk attempts. How embarrassing.

Sunday, February 12
Phoenix

It's about an hour before the All-Star Game, and NBC is doing its pregame show. We're watching the interviews, and as we're getting dressed and taped, Bob Costas and the fellas on NBC start talking about the Charlotte Hornets and how well they're doing this season.

Well, Grandmama and Zo perk up and start saying, "Y'all check that shit out. Y'all see: We're in first."

"Ah, y'all are just renting that spot until we take care of it," I tell them.

That's when Scottie says, "Hey, we got a little surprise for y'all."

We're looking at Scottie, and we have no clue what he's talking about.

"What kind of surprise you got?" I say. "You gonna throw another chair across the floor?"

We're all laughing, but Scottie says, "All right, but don't y'all fall asleep."

Wonder what he means by that?

Going into the All-Star Game, the one thing I was really excited about was being able to play with Pip. People can talk all they want about him off the court, but on the court this kid does everything. He leads the Bulls in five offensive categories, so he must be doing something right. I'm real proud to be able to play with him today and be able to start beside him. To me, that's the highlight of this whole All-Star gig.

Okay, it wasn't the best All-Star Game of all time, I'll admit that. The West team really kicked the shit out of us, 139–112. But they had a squad out there. Those voters really knew what they were doing when they put that West team together. The West had Barkley, Kemp, Olajuwon, Majerle, and Sprewell. Plus, they had Payton, Richmond, The Admiral, Detlef, Mutombo, the Mailman, and Stockton coming off the bench. That's strong.

We had a lot of first-time guys on our team, and we were small, too. Me and Penny at guards, Grant and Scottie at forwards, and Shaq in the middle. That's not very big. We had Dumars, Ewing, Barros, Grandmama, Zo, Vin Baker, and Tyrone Hill as backups, but the West just had too much experience and too much talent. All twelve of their guys had played in an All-Star Game. We had five newcomers.

We had a chance to move ahead in the third quarter, but then Mitch, who was the game MVP, scored 10 points in the last 5:09. He was—how does Dan Patrick say it on ESPN—*en fuego.*"

I did hear a few jeers from the crowd late in the fourth quarter—the game was a rout by then. But, c'mon, it's an All-Star Game. If you're a fan, you should be coming just to have a good time. If you're coming to see a playoff-intensity-type game, forget it. Ain't going to happen. I know what they're saying about the quality of play at times, but it's not like we weren't trying out there.

I had fun. Played twenty-three minutes. Scored 9 points. Had a block and a couple of assists. But stats don't really matter in these games. Some reporter asked me about my three-of-nine shooting, and I said, "Who cares about this?" Seriously, do you think anybody is going to remember what someone scored in an All-Star Game?

One of the best things about the whole experience is to see the guys in a different kind of setting. In an All-Star Game, you put all your differences with the other guys aside. You just try to enjoy yourself, to enjoy the moment.

Monday, February 13
Orlando

Flew straight to Orlando after the game yesterday. Looking at this team, it's time for us to start kicking it in gear. We're only a few games out of first in the Central Division, but we've got to pass Cleveland and Charlotte.

I'm not worried about Cleveland. They have too many injuries to keep playing as well as they have. Charlotte is another story. They're good, but we always seem to have their number. We beat them at our place already, so that might help us down the road.

We need to turn it on like '94 when we had the second-best record in the second half. I hope we can do that again, but we need everybody healthy to do it. We need the two Davis boys back. And we need Byron at full strength. Right now we're getting killed on the boards. Usually, that's where we dominate games. Also, we're not playing the same kind of team defense that we need to. But if we get healthy and step up our defense, I think we have a legitimate chance at the NBA Finals.

We're 27–19 at the break, three games behind Charlotte. We've got Orlando tomorrow night, but our next 10 games are against sub-.500 teams. In early March we've got a four-game road trip out West and then play 15 of our last 21 games at Market Square. So everything is set up in our favor if we can take advantage of it.

Larry is still on me to be more aggressive, to look for my shot more. It seems to be the theme of the season with him and me.

I'm trying to get everybody involved, and Larry's telling me to take more control offensively.

If you look at my numbers, they're the lowest I've had in six years. I'm averaging 19.7 points, which is respectable, but my field goal percentage is .467, which is a career low. I'm getting to the line about five times a game, which is also low for me.

I know my numbers aren't among the league's best, but for us to do some damage this year, everybody on this team has to be involved. Yeah, there's going to be some times when I have to carry the team. But there are also going to be times when someone else has to step up and carry us.

I never make excuses, but facts are facts. I'm one of the hunted. I've got guys trailing me on picks. I've even had Shaq come out and guard me on a switch. I can deal with it. people have got to understand that I'm doing what I think will help this team win. And isn't that what's important, the team?

Update on Tony Dumas: His teammates bought him a three-foot-high basket and put it in the middle of the Reunion Arena floor.

That's cold . . . so I'll have to remember that one.

Tuesday, February 14
Orlando

Well, it was a close game for a half. Then they blew us out in the third quarter and killed us in the fourth. Final score: Magic 111, Us 92.

This time Orlando had Horace Grant and Nick Anderson back, and it showed. Horace got 16 rebounds, and Nick hit a couple of big threes.

•   •   •

I'm telling you, things are happening in this league. Clyde Drexler got traded today from Portland to Houston. Now he's reunited with his old Phi Slamma Jamma fraternity brother Hakeem. The Rockets gave up Otis Thorpe and a UCLA kid, Tracy Murray, and a conditional first-round draft pick, but I think this helps Houston. Clyde needed a change of scenery, and Hakeem will get him excited about the game again.

Houston needed him, too. My man Vernon Maxwell is serving a ten-game suspension for going after a fan, so the Rockets can use a shooting guard. Clyde's one of the best.

I also saw where Miami fired Kevin Loughery. The day before, Nellie resigned at Golden State. Crazy business.

Wednesday, February 15
Indianapolis

We drilled Detroit, 114–88, but that's not the big news. Before we played the Pistons, Larry dropped Haywoode to third team, moved Vern up to second string, and put Mark back as our starting point guard. It worked. I got 31, and we buried Detroit in the fourth quarter, outscoring them 28–12.

Thursday, February 16
Indianapolis

Antonio practiced with us for the first time in two months. And Damon finally got to practice for the first time as a pro. Remember, he had surgery on his knees right before training camp.

I'm happy for us, because we really need Antonio. I'm happy for Antonio, because I'm sure he was frustrated with the back injury. And I'm really happy for Damon, who is a good kid and loves the game.

• • •

Thank you, Clyde. The Rockets beat Charlotte tonight, which means we're only two games back. I told you Clyde would make a difference.

Friday, February 17
Minneapolis

I've got mixed feelings about tonight's game, because the coach of the Timberwolves is Bill Blair, who used to be Larry's top assistant with us. I think a lot of the guys were devastated when Bill left, because he's such a good guy and a good coach, too. But when we step on the court, it has to be business first and feelings second. That's the way it goes.

We beat the crap out of Bill's team, 110–78. You know, there's some talent on that roster, but, man, I have some doubts about Isaiah Rider, who has some big-time potential. At the All-Star Game he came late for the photo session for the players in the dunk contest, and the NBA fined him ten thousand dollars. He competed in the dunk contest, but whatever he made for dunking, the league basically took back because he didn't show for the photo thing.

Anyway, I saw him tonight, and I thought, "This kid has unbelievable talent, but does he really want it? How can someone with this much talent not want it, not want to be one of the best?" This kid could be one of the best. But right now he's just wasting that talent. Just wasting it.

Blair is such a great guy, it's too bad he has to go through all that stuff with Rider. Rider misses practices and gets fined, then calls a press conference to rip Blair. That's way over the line. Bill deserves better.

More good news: We're activating Antonio off the injured list tomorrow. Also, Mark's playing great. Larry told him the starting job is his no matter what, and it's really made a difference. He's much more aggressive, and he's helped my game, too.

Mark has been under a lot of pressure since we traded for him. The media has been on him. The fans have been on him. Larry's been on him. But he's really coming on. In these last four games he's had 28 assists and only 5 turnovers. That's All-Star stuff.

Thursday, February 23
Milwaukee

We're beating the teams we need to beat. Went home to Market Square and drilled Miami, 106–87. Then we won at New Jersey, 113–94, and tonight beat the Bucks, 98–86. Dale had a huge game, 21 points and 14 rebounds.

By the way, I hope Tony Dumas didn't see any highlights of me in that New Jersey game. I fell on my ass after missing a dunk.

The trading deadline came and went today. We didn't do anything, which is fine with me. I like our team, and I don't see how we could have improved ourselves without giving up something good in return.

Everyone was talking about Pippen being traded by the Bulls, but it didn't happen. In fact, things were kind of quiet. Pip stayed put, which probably doesn't make him very happy. Majerle, who was supposed to go to the Bulls in a trade for Scottie, didn't get traded. Derrick Coleman and Latrell Sprewell aren't going anywhere, either.

I have no idea if I've been put on the trading block this year or any year. There are rumors all the time, not so much about me, but rumors about players all the time. But if they do trade me, please send me someplace warm—Orlando, Miami, Phoenix. I think I've paid my dues in cold weather.

But please, no Clippers. If someone gets traded there, you

send them a condolence card. Cleveland? I would not want to go to Cleveland. Cleveland and Milwaukee. Now watch, I'll probably get traded to one of those places. There's nothing wrong with management there, but it's a terrible climate.

Granted, Indiana is no warm-weather mecca, but at least we've got something happening there. You never see Pan Am Games in Cleveland or Milwaukee. You never see Final Fours. We even have Mike Tyson. We've got Black Fest. More things happen in Indiana than those other two places. We got the Indy 500, c'mon.

Trade rumors don't usually cause much tension between teammates. That's because we know it's a business, so we treat it that way. Nothing is permanent. Donnie could pick up the phone tomorrow, make a deal, and, poof, I'm playing for somebody else. That's how it is. Trades happen.

In a way, it's not a whole lot different from working for a Fortune 500 company and getting transferred to another city. People get transferred all the time.

I've been lucky. Vern, who is probably my best friend in the league, has been a Pacer ever since I came to Indiana. Mark Jackson and I have always been pretty good friends, but we've gotten to know each other a lot better since we became teammates. Even though we play on different teams, Kevin Johnson and I are still good friends. Same with B. J. Armstrong and Stacey Augmon.

You can build friendships with other players in the league. In fact, it's a lot easier than you think. The tough part is trying to help relationships grow between the families of teammates.

I remember Vern Fleming's wife, Michelle, was real distant to Marita when Marita first came here. Marita and I were just dating at the time, but later, after we were married, we asked Michelle why she was so hesitant around us. She said, "Because you never know if you're going to be here or not or if Vern's going to be here or not. If you have a great relationship and then someone gets traded, that hurts."

Marita didn't take it personally. She's a model and an actress, so she can relate to some of the things a professional athlete goes through. She understands the sacrifices that have to be made. She understands how hard it is to be on the road all the time. She understands how competitive a profession can be.

I met Marita at a benefit dinner in Los Angeles. A mutual friend, Carra Wallace, introduced us, and it was infatuation at first sight. For me, not her.

Marita didn't want much to do with me at first. She didn't know anything about sports, the NBA, the Pacers . . . nothing. That was fine with me; I wanted her to judge me on my own merits, not because I played pro basketball.

If nothing else, I was persistent. She finally said she'd go out with me but only if Carra came along. We went to dinner, dropped Carra back home, and then went to a movie, *Regarding Henry*, with Harrison Ford and Annette Bening.

Some dates you never forget.

Marita fell asleep at the movie.

We dated off and on, became serious, and got married on August 29, 1992, in Chicago. Happiest day of my life.

Monday, February 27
Boston

Very nice, baby! Very nice!

Seven wins in a row. I like it. I told you we needed to turn it on, and we have.

Detroit. Minnesota. Miami. New Jersey. Milwaukee. We got Dallas last night 100–92. And tonight, in our final appearance ever in the Boston Garden, we beat the Celtics, 108–97, on their parquet floor.

Defense is the key. We're starting to play the same kind of defense we played during our big stretch last year. Everything's starting to click. And didn't I tell you Orlando would come back to the pack? They started out something like 35–8, but going into yesterday's game they'd lost 5 of their last 11.

I'm gonna miss the Boston Garden. I know it has rats. Kevin McHale said he saw a rat here so big that he thought it was a rabbit. I know it has the world's worst visitors' locker room. I know there are dead spots on the parquet. I know it has no air-conditioning. But the place has character. All those banners hanging from the rafters. All the history. All the legends who have gone up and down that court. All those great basketball fans. I love the Boston Garden. It's one of my all-time favorite places.

You know what's really weird? When they tear this place down, the L.A. Sports Arena, which was built in 1959, will be the oldest arena in the NBA.

I have a lot of memories of the Garden, but the one that really sticks out is game five of our playoff series against the Celtics in 1991. Boston won the first game, we won the second, they won the third, we won the fourth, and then we headed back to Boston for the fifth and deciding game.

The game started, and we were killing those kids. This was about the time that Larry Bird started to have back problems. In fact, I remember Chuck Person gave him a good back pick and sent him out of the game. I mean, he was hurt so bad he had to go back to the trainer's room. The Celtics were down by 10 or 11 points with about ten minutes to play.

Boston started to make a little run, but we still felt pretty good. Hey, no Larry.

Someone called a time-out, and as we were sitting in the huddle, the Garden started to erupt with noise. It was deafening. It was like this rumble of voices and cheers all crashing down on the floor. We were looking around, trying to figure out what the hell was going one.

Then I knew.

Larry was back.

The crowd was going nuts, chanting, "Lar-ry! Lar-ry!"

I looked around, thinking, "Oh, shit, we're done now."

The kid came out, hit the next three or four baskets and put on a show. We were done, all right. We lost, 124–121.

Larry Legend.

March 1995

Wednesday, March 1
Detroit

The streak is over. We lost, 92–79, and Grant Hill and Joe Dumars put on a show tonight. We should have paid admission, that's how good those two were.

I was awful. I should have given a refund to anybody who spent good money to see me play. I had 9 rebounds and 9 assists but hit only 3 of 12 shots. You want to blame somebody for this loss? Blame me. The rest of the guys played great and I sucked.

I guess the win streak couldn't last forever, but I could have helped it last at least one more game. Now we've got Washington on Friday night, and we have to play that big front line of theirs without Dale. He dislocated his right shoulder again early in the first quarter.

Friday, March 3
Landover

That big son of a bitch Gheorghe Muresan and the rest of the Bullets surprised us tonight, 111–106.

No way we should have lost to this team, even without Dale. That's two straight losses to sub-.500 teams. What the hell is going on here?

This wasn't a game I'll stick in the time capsule. I finished with 21 points, but I didn't get my first field goal until a couple of minutes left in the first half. Not good.

Larry is getting on our ass because he says we only get pumped up to play the really good teams. He says we have to have that same type of intensity against the sub-.500 teams, such as Detroit and Washington. He's right. We've got Boston at our place tomorrow night. A back-to-back, but we'll be ready.

Saturday, March 4
Indianapolis

We weren't ready.

This is our first three-game losing streak of the year. We made a pact at the beginning of the season that we weren't ever going to lose more than two games in a row. Now look at us: Not only have we lost three straight games, but we've lost them to Detroit, Washington, and Boston, who got us, 107–101, at *our* place.

Now we've got our West Coast trip where we have to play San Antonio and Sacramento (and the Kings are better than anybody thinks) and then Phoenix and the Lakers.

I'm not playing particularly well. I'm struggling. I'm spotting points—25 one day, then 12, then 10. Shooting is all mental, and right now I've got to work through that.

The one bright spot is Rik. He's been the MVP for us all year. I'm happy for Rik but even happier for the team. Now when he gets the ball, he's commanding a double-, even triple-team. Every time he touches the ball that happens. That helps us as a team because it frees up things for us on the perimeter. It gives us more wide-open looks. Right now I need them.

Well, I was wrong about John Williams. I thought he would come in here, get his weight down, and really help this team. Instead, we released him today.

Monday, March 6
Indianapolis

After practice today, Larry, Billy King, and I stayed on the court and worked on my game. It isn't much of a secret that I'm struggling. In the 3 games we lost, I was shooting 31.7 percent from the field (13 of 41) and 15.4 percent from the three-point line (2 of 13) and averaging just 16.7 points. But you don't do anything radical. Everybody struggles. You've just got to work through it and not panic.

If ever we needed to make a move, this is it. We have an outside chance at the number one playoff seed in the Eastern Conference, but a more realistic goal is the second-best record.

Right now we're not going anywhere if we don't start playing some defense. That's the key. I mean, sorry-ass Washington scores 111 points? Boston gets 107? We're feeling the pressure of not having Dale in the lineup, but at least the doctors say he'll be back. When, I don't know. They've got him listed "day-to-day," and he'll be making the road trip with us. But, man, we need him back. Larry says he's the guts of our team, and he's right. Dale does all the dirty work, like getting the tough rebounds, playing physical in the paint. Look at his shoulders. He's got all those vertical stripes on them from all the scratches he gets from playing inside.

Tuesday, March 7
San Antonio

These bitches had won eight in row, and guess what? We beat them by 17 points.

I'll tell you what helped: We had two planeloads of Pacer fans come down and cheer us on. I know it doesn't sound like much, but every little bit helps on the road.

Rik abused David Robinson. Killed him. It wasn't even close. Rik scored 35 and had 10 rebounds. The Admiral had only 19 and 2. I think we all fed off that energy.

They made it a game in the second half, but we took it over in the fourth quarter. Also, I shot a little better: 7 of 13 (3 of 5 from the three-point line) and finished with 22 points.

Dennis Rodman hair update: green.

Wednesday, March 8
Sacramento

I think I know what Scottie was talking about at the All-Star Game.

Remember that stuff about not falling asleep? Well, guess who practiced with the Bulls today and is supposed to practice with them again tomorrow?

Michael.

Man, the rumors are flying about Michael coming back. I saw where someone said Nike shipped the Bulls forty pairs of Air Jordans. The thing is, nobody is denying the rumors—not the Bulls, the Chicago White Sox, Michael's agent . . . nobody.

All I've got to say is I hope the rumors are true.

Thursday, March 9
Sacramento

Two in a row. Two good ones in a row.

Tonight I went against Mitch Richmond, who is one of the top three or four two-guards in the league. He's coming off that high of winning the MVP of the All-Star Game, and I knew he was going to be pumped. But I was pumped, too.

I came out very aggressive. My threes were going in. My off-the-dribble game was working. I scored 13 points in the first eight minutes, hit my first 6 three-point shots, and finished 10 of 16 from the field for 30 points.

Mitch is a great defensive player, but I really wanted to show my stuff. I got my points, and I thought I did a pretty good job on Mitch, who only scored 21.

After we beat the Kings, 109–94, Mitch came up to me and said, "I'm coming back at your place." I just kind of smiled and said, "Okay."

But the two guys who got us over the hump tonight were Dale, who made his return to the lineup as a reserve, and Antonio. They went against Brian Grant and that other kid, Michael Smith, and they controlled the boards. Plus, Rik got double-teamed all night, which really helped open the perimeter game for us.

Grant and Smith are going to be damn good. In fact, that whole team reminds me of our team. They're going to have a good team down the road. I think they need a centerpiece, but once they get that, they're going to be okay. They play hard. They hit the boards. They're tough.

In recognition of our two-game road win streak, Vern and I went to Donnie and made like travel agents. We had a plan.

"Donnie, let's go to Vegas from Phoenix," I said. "We don't play L.A. until Monday, and this can be like a little mini-vacation. The guys can relax. It will be fun."

Donnie thought about it and then gave the okay.

The timing is perfect. We've won two in a row on the road, and we're feeling pretty good about things. I even saw where Phoenix was talking about our being the best team in the East. Barkley and Paul Westphal were saying how much they liked our Davis boys and how, if any one team was complete from one to five, it was the Indiana Pacers. That was nice of them to say, but the last time we played, they beat us at our place by six.

Friday, March 10
Phoenix

Saw K. J. tonight. I know it's been a tough year for him, having to battle through the injuries, but when he's healthy he's one of the best in the league.

Everyone says Kevin Johnson is this nice, kind, Christian kind of guy, and he is—off the court. Really a great guy. But on the court, I'm telling you, some things come out of his mouth that aren't very Christian-like. I heard he called Magic a fag. He's intense.

I've been playing against Kevin since high school. I remember when he was at Cal and they beat us for the first time in like ten years. The game was at Cal, and they went crazy. Players were celebrating on the court, jumping up and down like they'd won a national championship. Some guys were climbing on the backboard.

I was a junior that year, so I went up to K. J. afterward and said, "Look, we are never, ever—while I'm playing at UCLA—going to lose to you guys again."

He said, "Naw, man, the dynasty is over. It's over."

"Okay," I say, "you can believe that if you want, but trust me: I am never going to lose to you guys ever again while I'm at UCLA."

We played them four more times and we beat the crap out of

them almost every time. When we played them in the Pac-10 Tournament, when the conference still had one, I went to center court for the captains' meeting with the refs, and K. J. had a T-shirt from the year before that had the score of Cal's win against us. I looked at the shirt and I said, "That shirt ain't gonna help y'all tonight."

We beat them. I mean, the tournament was at Pauley Pavilion—no way were we going to lose there.

Revenge is sweet.

We beat the Suns bad, 112–97. K. J. got hurt on the second play of the game, and once he went out we jumped all over that. We played their game, and we probably ran them to death. That's surprising for us.

I had only 9 points, and we still beat them by 15. Everybody else stepped up. Mark had 21 and 11 assists. Derrick had 21 points. Rik had 22. And even though I made only 3 of 14 shots, they were aggressive shots. I kept going to the hoop off the dribble, but I just couldn't convert the shots. I'll get there, though.

The important thing is that we won. That's three in a row, on the road, against some tough clubs. I guarantee you that the Knicks and Chicago and Orlando and Charlotte and the rest of them in the East are looking at our box scores these last few days and doing a double take.

Boyz II Men were at the game, and afterward we were talking to them and they were saying, "Man, you guys are coming on."

"Yeah," I said. "You'd better start jumping on our bandwagon and stop jumping on New York's or Chicago's. Just because they're on TV all the time doesn't mean they're the best team."

"Yeah, you're right," they said.

We exchanged numbers, and then it was on to Vegas. We've got our morale back. Everyone's excited.

Sunday, March 12
Las Vegas

Man, what a weekend. Stayed up all Friday night. Stayed up all Saturday night. I'm beat today, but we really needed something like this. The team was able to get away from basketball, to get away from the usual NBA road city, and to have some fun. We needed it.

We acted like all the other tourists who come to Vegas. We went to shows. We watched some of those high rollers. Talked mess with each other. Kind of bonded more as a team. We didn't even think about basketball. Nice R&R.

One of the highlights was when Dale, Sam, Mark, and myself went to a Riddick Bowe fight at the MGM Grand. It was my first championship fight. I wanted to see what the atmosphere would be like, what it was like to see those guys really go at it in person.

We got a real surprise when we got there. In fact, this is how I know things have changed for the Indiana Pacers: When we walked through a hallway and out toward our seats, the crowd just started going crazy over us. I couldn't believe it. The Pacers. We've got a following. The Pacers have a following.

The public address announcer had told the crowd that we were there, and everybody was looking at us and clapping. It was cool, and it made me feel good that people are beginning to recognize that we're one of the better teams in the NBA. Five years ago it would have been, "Indiana who? What the hell is a Pacer?"

Monday, March 13
Los Angeles

While everyone is talking about Michael—will he or won't he?—we're going for our fourth straight road win. We want to be greedy. We want to go 4–0 on this trip. We want to put some pressure on Charlotte, which is ahead of us by one and a half games. We want to send a message to the Knicks that we want that second-best record in the Eastern Conference.

There's a saying about adversity revealing character. Well, we've had injuries. We've had losing streaks. We've had tough road trips. But we've survived. We're showing our character.

Reporters keep asking me about Michael's return, as if Michael calls me up every day and tells me his plans. Hey, I don't know what he's going to do. I hope he comes back. It sure as hell looks like he's coming back. But I haven't talked to him since I saw him in Oakland in December.

Still, if there are rumors, there must be something going on. I can't believe this kid is getting ready to come back. Personally, if I were Michael, I wouldn't come back. There's nothing to come back for.

If he does return, the Bulls become instant contenders. I don't think with twenty or so games left in the season they'll pass us in the standings, but who knows what will happen when the playoffs come around?

Some guys say the Bulls would win the NBA title again with Michael, but I'm not so sure. There are only three guys—Scottie, B. J., and Will Perdue—left from the teams Michael played on. Kukoc has a lot of talent and Michael would help him get tougher, but the Bulls still have some problems at center. And they don't have Horace Grant anymore.

Monday, March 13
Los Angeles

We should have won this game. We were up by 1 point with about a minute to play and then "Sweet Pea"—Lloyd

Daniels—stole Rik's inbounds pass and tipped it in. The Lakers won, 93–91.

If I don't count the game results, it was nice to come home. I saw Mom and Pop. Cheryl didn't come to the game, but Tammy and Darrell did.

I love playing in The Forum. Every time you step on the court, you look up at the walls and see Magic's retired number and Jerry West's and Wilt Chamberlain's. What a feeling that must be. Too bad Magic wasn't here in person tonight. I think he's out touring with his team.

I think it's a shame that my boyhood hero, Magic Johnson, isn't out here playing with the best. I'd have no problem with Magic playing again, and I'm not worried about that HIV stuff. You can't worry about that. I know there are players who are concerned, but if he comes back, he'll have my full support.

Hey, I'm sure there might be somebody else out there in the league who's HIV-positive but who hasn't been tested. You know, not everybody in the league is tested for that. So you never know. I don't think there's any danger, but even if there is, how's it different from the guy you don't know about? You can't start labeling and shunning people that way. I hope he comes back.

Wednesday, March 15
Indianapolis

We were in the second quarter of tonight's game against Milwaukee when some fan near the end of our bench tried to drop his drawers and moon everybody. The arena security guards got to him just in time, but, man, can you imagine that making the ESPN highlights?

Larry saw the whole thing. As they were dragging the guy out, Larry turned to the reporters on press row and said, "March madness." Then he went back to coaching the game.

Wild night. First, we didn't have Antonio because he was with his wife Kendra who had twins tonight, a boy and a girl. Congratulations.

We did have Dale, who made his first start since hurting his shoulder again.

Then we had the wanna-be mooner.

Then we had the Bucks, who were unconscious tonight. Vin Baker was 8 for 13. Big Dog was 10 for 18. Todd Day was 12 for 20. At one point during the second and third quarters, Milwaukee was 23 for 33 from the field.

But even without Antonio and with Milwaukee hitting everything, we were only down 81–80 at the beginning of the fourth quarter. Well, that's when I wanted to take over.

I finished with a season-high 40 tonight, 17 of them coming in the fourth, and we won, 117–108. Not a bad way to begin our stretch run.

I felt so good out there. Took 15 shots and made 12. Hit 10 of 12 from the foul line. Had 6 rebounds. The best thing, though, is that we didn't waste a home game. We've got 20 more regular season games, and 14 of them are at Market Square. We've got to take advantage of that.

I saw where Phil Jackson said Michael is going to announce his decision in the next couple of days. Hurry up, M. J., the suspense is killing me.

Here's what you do, Michael: You practice a few more days, and then you make your triumphant return Sunday, on national television, against me and my boys at Market Square.

I don't know about Michael, but it sounds like heaven to me. Michael and me on the same court again? I'm getting pumped just thinking about it.

Friday, March 17
Indianapolis

There's talk that Michael might wait until next Wednesday's game at Boston or Friday's home game against Orlando to make his debut. Boston is where M. J. scored a playoff-record 63 points against the Celtics back in 1986, so you've got history going there, what with this being the final year of the Boston Garden. And Orlando is Shaq's home, which would mean lots of Michael-versus-Shaq stories. Plus, if he waited until next week, Michael would have more time to practice with the Bulls and get his timing and his conditioning back.

I'm holding out for Sunday for one reason: TV. If Michael comes back next week, he gets TNT. If he comes back Sunday, he gets NBC. Nothing against TNT, but Michael ain't gonna make his debut on cable. He's a network man.

What a mystery this has become. Everyone wants to know what Michael's going to do. A friend of mine told me that all the TV and radio stations in Chicago are going nuts trying to break a story about Michael. Every day there are like fifty reporters camped out at the Bulls' practice facility, all waiting to corner Michael. And every day Michael drives his Range Rover through the gated parking lot and enters through the rear door. One day some TV guy put tape over the slot for Michael's security card, and M. J. had to turn around, park, and go through the front door—all so those media guys could poke boom mikes in his face. Can you believe that shit?

We beat Orlando tonight by 10. It was never much of a game. We were up by 8 after the first quarter, 12 after the second, and were never really threatened. Shaq got 28, but Rik had 21 and forced the Magic to double-team down low, which helped us perimeter guys. I finished with 18.

Orlando just can't beat us here. That's six in a row against them at Market Square. Now we're a half-game ahead of Charlotte. I tried to tell Grandmama and Zo they were just renting first place, but they wouldn't listen.

Saturday, March 18
Indianapolis

It's official: M. J. will be in the building—our building—Sunday, March 19. Yeah!

I'm nervous just talking about it. I'm telling you, this is going to be the most-watched game ever. Holy Moses, the man is back!

My phone hasn't stopped ringing. Friends are calling. Friends of friends are calling. They want tickets. Hell, who wouldn't want tickets to this game? This is like the Second Coming of the basketball god.

Knowing Michael a little bit, I'd have to say he came back for the love of the game. He has a great challenge now, but this is the best position for M. J. to be in. He loves being told he can't do something or his team can't do something. He loves being an underdog.

Sunday, March 19
Indianapolis

I knew it would be crazy today, but I didn't think it would be like this.

I got to Market Square early, about three hours before the game, and scalpers were on the freeway exits trying to buy and sell tickets. On the *freeway.* Someone said the tickets were going for $750 for the courtside seats and between $200 and $400 for everything else.

The place was a zoo. Downtown was already packed with people. It was like a Super Bowl and game seven of the playoffs rolled into one.

The NBC trucks were parked outside, and they had people running around everywhere. Inside the arena they set up a little studio stage for Bob Costas, who will be doing his pregame thing right near the court. I mean, if Bob Costas is here, you know it's big, right?

I came into the locker room, got changed, and then went sightseeing. I wanted to soak in the whole scene.

First of all, there must have been four hundred media people here. I felt sorry for our public relations guy, David Benner. He had to walk around with a bodyguard just in case some photographer or reporter or TV person went nuts about the seating arrangements.

You could feel the intensity in the air. It was wild. I just went out to shoot, and there were media people all around the court. And what really amazed me is that there wasn't an empty seat in the house. I'm not just talking about a sellout—this game had been sold out for a while, even before Michael decided to come back. I'm talking about everybody in their seats thirty or thirty-five minutes before the game started. Usually you have some latecomers, but this time it was packed. It was like they didn't want to miss a thing.

Anyway, I was out there shooting and thinking, "People were saying you were the best two-guard when Michael left, but now the best is back." I was nervous, but mostly I was excited.

After I warmed up, I went back into the locker room, got ready, and then just waited for tip-off. We had our usual team meeting, and Larry said, "It's just another game. Take it for what it's worth."

That's easy to say, but it wasn't just another game. It was Michael. You're out there shooting around, and you can't help but sneak a peak toward the Bulls. You want to see Michael. I know I did. I saw him wearing his warm-ups, and it was like, "He's back." It was really eerie seeing him.

When we're the home team, we always let the visiting team

run out onto the court first. So the Bulls ran out, and I could hear cheers. People were cheering for Michael and the opposing team.

It could have been worse. A couple of years ago, before we started making a move in the league, the Bulls would run out, get cheered at Market Square, and we'd get booed. In our own arena, we'd get booed.

This time we ran out, and the noise was deafening. Our fans were going crazy over us. I was thinking, "All right. Finally. We are for real."

During the national anthem I did what I always do: I prayed, then sang, then looked across the court and started staring at the guy who would be guarding me. This time it was Michael. Just like old times. Except he was wearing number 45, which was his junior high school jersey number, instead of his customary number 23. I guess he didn't want to unretire his original number.

Before the game started, Vern and I went out toward midcourt to meet with the Bulls' captains and the referees. B.J. and Scottie had been their captains all year, but now Michael was there, too.

"Welcome back," I said after giving him some dap.

"Good to be back," he said.

"Have a good one," I said.

That was that. We started out fast, holding them to 15 points in the first quarter and building a 6-point lead. Then we outscored them by 4 in the second period and had a 10-point lead at halftime.

You could tell Michael was rusty. He missed his first six shots and his first free throw before finally scoring with about four minutes left in the half. The whole time I was thinking, "Thank God," because if he had come in and got 50 on us, I don't know what I would have done. He's already the greatest. But if he had scored 50, I would have had to invent all new compliments for him.

There is one thing M. J. definitely needs to work on: game day dressing. He had his shorts on backwards.

A few minutes before the start of the second half, we were warming up, and the Bulls came out of their locker room and walked past where we were shooting. Michael looked at me and said, "Slow your ass down, Reg."

"I can't, M. J.," I said. "I'm hyped."

We laughed, but I knew I wasn't going to slow down. I was too hyper. When I get hyper, I just keep moving and moving. That's what I wanted to do during the game, just keep moving and try to wear Michael down. After all, he hadn't played in twenty-one months. I don't care who you are, if you haven't played in twenty-one months, you're going to get tired.

Everything was going great for us during the first forty-three minutes of the game. We were playing our tempo. We were controlling Michael. We had a 16-point lead.

Then they made a 25–9 run, and it was a game again. Scottie hit a three-pointer that tied it, 92–92, with nineteen seconds left. I was thinking, "Oh, shit, we're going to blow a 16-point lead with the whole world watching." I mean, this game was being shown in France, Russia, Australia, Singapore . . . everywhere. And we were blowing a big lead at home.

With three seconds left in regulation, I was wide open for a jumper. But just before I could get the shot off, Michael slammed into me. His knee caught my right thigh, and we both went down. Because I wasn't shooting and because the Bulls weren't in the penalty, there were no free throws. So if you think about it, it was a pretty smart play on Michael's part. No free throws, and he gets me out of the game.

My thigh felt like someone had gotten a hammer and started pounding away. I limped back to the bench, but there was no way I was staying out of this game. The thing is, my thigh didn't agree.

We went into overtime, and I convinced Larry to put me back in. As I was waiting for the refs to blow the whistle to start play, Michael came up and said, "You all right? What happened?"

I looked at him—and I was just messing with him—and I said, "You took me out!"

"Yeah, I know," he said.

"Don't worry about it," I told him. "I'm all right."

But I was worthless. I could barely move on the leg, so Larry pulled me less than twenty seconds into overtime. I finished with 28 points.

Byron went in and played great and won the game for us. He scored 5 points in the OT, including a huge three-point play with twenty-nine seconds left. We hung on for a 103–96 win and kept a half-game ahead of Charlotte, 4 ahead of Cleveland, and 7½ ahead of Chicago. But with Michael back, you know the Bulls are going to make a move.

Michael ended up with 19 points, 6 rebounds, 6 assists, and 3 steals. If not for him, the Bulls probably wouldn't have made that big fourth-quarter run at us. But he also missed 21 of 28 shots, didn't have a dunk, and didn't have a three. I haven't taken 28 shots in one game all season, and he takes that many in his first game back. That's amazing. It takes me two or three games to get that many. But that's why he's the man out there. He's never afraid to take responsibility for a game. That's why I admire him so much. I know I'll never be as good or as great as he is, but it gives me something to strive for. I'm always working to reach his level.

Michael looked bigger than I remember. His upper body is more muscular, more developed. I don't know if it was baseball or what, but he was more powerful. He's still just as quick, and once he gets his conditioning back, oh, my God, they're going to be tough.

Afterward, Michael did a big press conference, which meant only a few reporters tried talking to Larry and us. A couple of media people wandered in, and Larry said, "You guys made my day. The Beatles and Elvis are back, and you come to talk to me."

I'm glad Michael's back, feel a little sorry for him. There's so much attention paid to his comeback that he's not even traveling with the team right now. He flew to Indianapolis in a chartered jet, has his own security force, and stayed at a friend's house when he was here instead of staying at the team hotel. He has his own personal entourage.

Tonight when I got home, I saw the evening news and they showed the Bulls boarding the team plane and Michael boarding his own plane. I thought, "This kid is living large," which is nice. It just shows you he is different and needs to be treated as different. He's one of those rare, rare exceptions. Someone told me that Mitch Lawrence of the *New York Daily News* wrote that Jordan had six security people: four to carry his throne and two to spread rose petals.

Not bad.

Wednesday, March 22
Indianapolis

Didn't play at Miami yesterday because of my bruised thigh. That's the first game I've missed all season and only the fourth game I've missed in six years.

We lost, 97–95, and Charlotte moved ahead of us by a half game.

I wasn't going to play tonight against the Clippers, but I got to Market Square, felt pretty good, and decided to give the leg a try. I'm glad I did. I hit 12 of 13 from the field, 9 of 10 from the foul line, finished with 36 points, and we won, 107–103. With Charlotte not playing tonight, we moved into a tie for the division lead.

•   •   •

Get this: NBC said 35 million people watched our game against the Bulls, making it the number-one-watched regular season game in NBA history. I hope we gave those people in Singapore their money's worth.

I know Chicago is going crazy over M. J.'s return. I can't remember where I saw it—ESPN or one of the local stations here—but the day after our game with him, the *Chicago Tribune* had a front-page diagram of Michael's right arm and then had a little story about which muscles he needed to work on. If it wasn't so crazy, it'd be funny. I mean, they had this story about Michael's arm above a story about the poison gas terrorist attack at a Tokyo subway.

Friday, March 24
Indianapolis

Sacramento came to town, and I knew Mitch Richmond would be looking for revenge because of what I did at his place a couple of weeks ago. He got his personal revenge—he had a good game, I had a suck game—but we got the victory, 103–96.

Mitch got me good tonight, though. I only had 16 points on 4-of-16 shooting, but he had 30 points and made 12 of 23.

We signed Greg Kite to a ten-day contract today. He was playing in the CBA when we signed him, but he's spent twelve seasons in the NBA. He might not be the best center I've ever seen, but he has something I don't: two NBA championship rings. He got them when he played for the Celtics.

Saturday, March 25
Philadelphia

Beat the Sixers tonight, 84–75, but the big news is that Mike Tyson got out of the Indiana Youth Center today. He spent—what?—almost three years in prison. From champ to inmate number 922335. Weird, man.

Malik Sealy, Haywoode, and I went to see him this past summer. A deal's a deal. Remember that bet with Spike? If we won that 1994 playoff series, he had to include Marita in one of his movies; if we lost, I had to go see Tyson. We lost, so I went to see Tyson.

Guess what happened: The man would not come out to see us. He looked down, saw our names, and said he didn't want to see us. Can you believe that? We waited an hour and a half because they told us he was coming down. But he never did.

Man, that hurt me. I don't know if it was us or what. We were told he said he didn't want us to see him in that situation. Okay, I can understand that, but he's still the champ to me, still the champ in my mind. What I don't get is that Mark Jackson and Haywoode went to see him two months ago, and he said yes that time. They were talking to him and stuff. Me, he stiffs.

I remember the first time I ever met him. It was about five years ago, and he was the champ. He was at Magic's second Midsummer's Night Magic, and we had this deal at the Century Plaza. We had just finished dinner, and all the players were sitting on the dais. In walked Sugar Ray Leonard, and everybody clapped. In walked Mike Tyson, and everyone clapped. They came up to where we were sitting, and soon all the players were talking shit. The lights were down and the entertainment part of the program was going on, but we didn't care. We were having too much fun talking shit to one another. There was Michael, Mark Aguirre, Dominique, Ron Harper,

Tyson, and me. We had our chairs all pushed together, and were just having fun.

At the time, Detroit was winning championships, and Dominique was saying to Aguirre, "We're going to beat the shit out of you next year."

Hey, I was just happy to be there at the table, but you know me, I have to talk shit, too. So I was ready to say something when somebody said, "Don't you say shit, Reggie, because Indiana ain't shit."

So I said, "Hey, we had our moments this year."

Okay, it wasn't a great comeback, but I'm not used to being told to be quiet.

Tyson decided he wanted to talk some shit. He has that high, squeaky voice that could shatter glass, and he said, "Indiana? Where the fuck is Indiana? There's a ball club in Indiana?"

I mean, he was going off on Indiana. I said, "Yeah, there's a ball club there."

So the next day at the game, he's sitting in the front row. He said, "Yo, Reggie. I kind of know where Indiana is now. I've heard of it. But what the hell's a Pacer, huh?"

It was funny at the time, but then came that rape charge, the trial, the conviction, and then the sentence. That's when I said to myself, "I betcha he knows where Indiana is now. I betcha he knows Indiana now."

See how it comes around? *Where the fuck is Indiana . . .*

Anyway, he ended up talking to Haywoode and Mark in prison. He said, "I'm watching TV, and this Reggie kid has a Wheaties commercial. McDonald's. Nike. Where'd this kid come from?"

From Indiana.

Monday, March 27
Indianapolis

There's no place like home. Beat New Jersey by 10, which means four in a row. I got 25 tonight.

Tuesday, March 28
Indianapolis

Is the kid amazing, or what?

Michael goes out tonight and scores 55. I should have known: M. J., the Knicks, Madison Square Garden. Michael had been struggling a little bit, but tonight he rose to the occasion. He is definitely back.

I watched the game on the big screen down in the basement, and at halftime I called Mark Jackson. Michael already had 30 points, so I wanted to bet that he'd score 60. Just missed.

Wednesday, March 29
Indianapolis

We are on a roll, baby! Beat Cleveland tonight. That makes five wins in a row, eight out of nine, and eleven out of thirteen.

Thursday, March 30
Indianapolis

Better start getting that Central Division Champions banner ready. Charlotte lost tonight to Dallas. Thank you, Jason Kidd.

We're up by three games.

Friday, March 31
Indianapolis

It was "Throwback Night" tonight against the Nuggets. What they should have called it was "Throw-up Night." We got embarrassed, 107–92, in front of a sellout crowd.

It started out fun. We wore replica Pacer uniforms from the 1974–75 season when the team was still in the ABA. In fact, when they first told us about it a couple of days ago, I said to Haywoode and a couple of the fellas that we had to take this throwback stuff a step further.

So Haywoode went to a beauty parlor today and bought a bunch of Afro wigs that looked like 1970s Linc Hayes–"Mod Squad" 'fros. We even tried getting the coaches to wear some 1970s stuff, but they wouldn't go for it. Larry, when he was coaching Denver back then, used to wear bib overalls on the sideline. A lot of other coaches thought they were styling with those leisure suits. There was some scary stuff out there in the '70s.

Right before we went out for final warm-ups, I put the wig on. I've never had that much hair on my head my entire life. It felt so weird, but I wanted to see what I looked like with that much of a 'fro. Thank God I never had one of those when I was younger. I looked so silly.

I wasn't the only one who went with the retro look. Haywoode wore one, and so did Vern and Dale. Let me tell you, there is nothing scarier than seeing a six-foot-ten brother with an Afro. Dale and that scowl and that 'fro—man, very scary.

So we came out of the tunnel, and the public address announcer started with his usual "La-dieeees and gentle-mennnnnn, here are—"

And then he saw us with our 'fros.

"—here are, I think, yourrrrrr Indiana Pacerrrrrsssss!"

We came out, and the crowd was applauding and laughing and pointing. They didn't know what to make of it. I'm telling you, it was really a funny sight, especially with Derrick and me wearing knee-high socks, too.

Then came the game, and that wasn't so funny. Mutombo hit 10 of 11 shots for 22 points, and the Nuggets ended up beating us, 107–92.

Not a bad month—11–6—but it should have been a lot better. We should have gone at least 12–5, maybe 13–4. Then we wouldn't be worrying about Charlotte or the number two playoff seed in the Eastern Conference. But we are, and it's our own fault.

April 1995

Monday, April 3
New York

Look out, New York, we're coming after you. Whipped Portland last night by 11, and now we're here for the big game against the Knicks.

We're up by two and a half games in the Central Division and one and a half games behind the Knicks for the second-best record in the Eastern Conference. If we can get that, then we'll have home-court advantage during the first two rounds of the playoffs. That's huge, especially if you get to game seven. New York had the home court in 1994, and it made a big difference for them.

I'm not saying much this time around. The reporters are looking for some spicy quotes, but this game doesn't need any spice. We've lost twenty-eight of our last thirty at the Garden. We've lost to the Knicks by 12 here this season and by 17 at Market Square. We're playing to keep our lead in the Central, to get the second-best record in the Eastern Conference, and to make a statement to the Knicks. There's nothing I can say that's going to top that.

Larry says it's the biggest game of the year, and he's right. We've got everybody back, and we've got to keep the pressure on New York.

We signed Kite to another ten-day contract. We might need this guy to pound on some folks.

Tuesday, April 4
New York

Damn, too bad we couldn't have done this in game seven of last year's playoffs.

We finally beat them in a regular-season game at their place. I hit an eighteen-footer with 28.7 seconds left that put us ahead, 92–90, and then sank a free throw with 2.3 seconds left to seal a 94–90 win.

Spike and I were going at it a little bit tonight. Nothing serious, but when I hit the jumper at the end, I just turned and glared at him. He was wearing that stupid Knicks jersey with Starks's number on it.

God, I love beating these kids, and I love doing it in front of all those stars on Celebrity Row. This might be the biggest win of the year for us. We played great defense—the kind we used to play all the time last year—and held the Knicks to just 5 points in the last five minutes.

Derrick came up big for us with 18 points, Mark got 11 rebounds, and I finished with 27 points.

Larry said before the game that he wanted to see what kind of team he had. I think we showed him. And it showed us we could win in New York, that we didn't have to be scared of the Garden.

Wednesday, April 5
Indianapolis

About the best thing you can say about this one is that we beat the Bullets, 102–90, and won our forty-eighth game, which is a team record. After being here during those years when we lost that many, this was sweet.

I don't know if it was post-Knicks letdown or what, but I played awful. Didn't even have a field goal. Haywoode, who got cut by the Bullets, played great. So did Rik and Byron and Dale.

I'll take a win over points any day, but I'm really disappointed about the way I played. It's unacceptable.

Friday, April 7
Atlanta

I don't know if I'm getting a little tired, but we lost to the Hawks tonight by 12 and I had trouble finding my shot. I hit 5 of 12 but finished with only 15 points—and I was our leading scorer for the night. Maybe I'm hitting the wall. Maybe the whole team is hitting the wall.

We had beaten these kids three straight times, but tonight they came out and drilled us. We'll probably play the Hawks in the first round of the playoffs, and unless we get our shit together, they'll beat us again.

Steve Smith got me tonight for 26, and Larry was pissed. He was screaming at us during halftime and kept us in the locker room until there were only two minutes left before the third quarter started.

Man, this one hurt. Charlotte won tonight, so they picked up a full game on us and are only two back. The Knicks didn't even play, and they picked up another half-game for the Eastern Conference's second-best record.

After the game we had a twenty-minute meeting just with the players. Larry didn't tell us to have it, we just called it on our own. I think Vern and Byron and Sam are the ones who got it going. In a nutshell we said we weren't playing as a team and that everybody has to make more sacrifices. We had to duplicate the same kind of effort as last year when we won our last eight regular-season games.

It's easy to say, harder to do. But if we want to be in a good position at the end of the regular season, then we'd better start right now. Ain't no team scared of us, and we're sure as hell not going to sneak up on anybody.

Sunday, April 9
Indianapolis

All right, that's more like it. Charlotte came in here thinking we were ripe for another loss, and we stomped them, 97–68, on NBC. We had another sellout crowd, and those fans were all over Zo and Grandmama and everybody else on the team. When it comes right down to it, this game was for the division title.

Charlotte didn't have Burrell, Dell Curry, and Michael Adams today, but I don't think they would have made much of a difference. We had heard about their coach, Allen Bristow, calling their team defense the "Great Wall of China." Big deal, they held Philly to 66 points. Philly sucks this year. Do it against somebody with a winning record, and then I'll notice.

Anyway, if anybody had a great wall of anything, it was us. I was looking at the stat sheet after the game, and we must have set some sort of record for defense. Charlotte had only 22 field goals and shot 33.8 percent. The last time we put the glove on somebody like this was a few years ago against Boston when we held them to 71 points.

Larry was like a proud father. He told us it was the best defensive performance of any of his teams in twenty-three years of coaching. He was very emotional. He said we should be real proud of the effort, and later he told reporters that he'd like to make a highlight film of this one and tell people, "This is the way you're supposed to play."

Not only did we give Charlotte something to think about, but we clinched home-court advantage for the first round of the playoffs. That is huge. We're up by three games on the Hornets in the Central with only six games left to play, so things are looking good. Plus, we're only a game behind the Knicks for the second-best record in the East.

By the way, it's not really a downer or anything, but I only took 7 shots today, hit 4, and finished with 16 points. Who cares, right? We won, we played great defense, and we're back on track.

Tuesday, April 11
Chicago

There are two franchises I could never play for—New York and Chicago—just because of my history with them.

New York you know all about, but I've had my run-ins with the Bulls, too. I had that fight with Michael. I've gotten into it with Scottie. And then there was the bowing incident.

It happened in 1994. I hit a shot to put us ahead with practically no time left, something like 0.8 seconds. So I went to center court and started bowing to the audience, like I was taking a curtain call.

The crowd went nuts. I heard the boos, and it was great. I thought, "Yeah, finally," because we had lost to those bitches five straight times the year before.

The Bulls called time-out, and as I was going back to the huddle, I kept on bowing. The crowd couldn't believe it. The fans started booing even louder, and my teammates were eating it up. We'd won the damn game.

The time-out ended, but the Bulls called another. Then they ran this play—the same one that they ran later in the year when Pippen refused to play in the final 1.8 seconds because he was mad at Phil Jackson. Except this time Pippen was in the game. Toni Kukoc rolled out to the top of the key, and Pippen threw it to Kukoc's left shoulder. (It's hard to defend Kukoc because you're used to defending guys who are right-handed. Kukoc is left-handed, and when he catches it, he's facing the basket, which is a great advantage in that situation.) I was guarding Steve Kerr, and Kerr went toward the corner. They threw it in, and I saw it going to Kukoc. I started running toward the basket just in case the shot came close. I was right underneath the basket, and Kukoc got the ball and turned and shot. I saw it, and thought, "Oh, . . . my . . . God. . . . This . . . shit . . . is . . . going . . . right—"

And just as I was ready to say, "In," there it was: Bam! Snapped the net. *Rrrrrrrr* went the buzzer. Bulls win.

All of a sudden Pippen and Pete Myers came running up to me and they were bowing and stuff. What could I do? I just stood there.

What was so bad about it was that we played them the next night at Market Square, and they just beat the shit out of us. It was terrible. That took all the steam out of us, that loss in Chicago.

Now we've got M. J. & Co. tonight, and I know Michael's going to be pumped for this one. He's had almost a month to get back in playing shape, and I'm sure he remembers I outscored him 28–19 in Indianapolis when we won the game in overtime.

Since Michael's come back, the Bulls are 7–3, and he's averaging almost 28 points and 7 rebounds, which is amazing . . . except for M. J.

I've got a secret weapon, though. The Bulls gave it to me. It's called the United Center. M. J. is only shooting 34 percent there. He said if it was up to him, he'd blow the place up.

That's what I want. I want him thinking about the United Center when he's playing me. I'll take every edge I can get against Michael.

I'm telling you, these Bulls were afraid to play us tonight. We should have jumped on those kids, but we let it slip away and lost, 96–89.

Michael still looks rusty. He shot 8 of 27.

I wasn't any better. I missed 13 of 16 and finished with 12 points. If you're keeping track of this stuff—and they are in Indianapolis—I'm 12 for 39 (30.8 percent) in my last 4 games.

The one thing I noticed tonight is that Michael didn't let me have the open jumper like the last game. He's in better shape, so now he can keep up and get in your face. Just what I needed.

Also, I owe M. J. an apology. It turns out he didn't have his shorts on backwards when he played us. The Champion Company, which does the uniforms for all the NBA teams, screwed up when it sent a rush-order set of custom-made jerseys and shorts to Michael. Champion stitched the NBA logo on the wrong side, which is why it looked like the shorts were on the wrong way.

Thursday, April 13
Indianapolis

The Knicks come to town tomorrow night, and they're hot. Just got done watching them beat Washington for their seventh win in eight games. Patrick is playing really well, but the guy who makes the big difference for them is Oakley. He was out for thirty or so games because of foot surgery, but now he's shooting almost 60 percent from the field and rebounding as well as ever.

We've had two days to get ready for the Knicks, which should help. Wednesday's practice sucked, but today's was better. We're starting to get some energy back.

Byron keeps telling everyone that tomorrow's game is like a game seven. If we win, we still have a chance to get the second-best record in the Eastern Conference and guarantee ourselves the home-court advantage for two rounds. If we don't, then New York has all but clinched it.

No matter what happens with that seeding stuff, I definitely want that Central Division banner. Since I've been here, we haven't won a thing. If we could win tomorrow night, that would give us fifty victories and, at the very worst, keep us one and a half games ahead of Charlotte with just four games left.

Friday, April 14
Indianapolis

This one was a killer. We had these clowns, and then Starks—and I was covering him like the morning dew—finds Harper in the corner with 4 seconds left on the shot clock and less than 10 seconds in the game. Harper hits the three with 7.5 seconds left, and the Knicks move ahead, 87–84. We come down, miss, and then have to foul Starks, who makes one of two. We lose, 88–84.

I got to the line 9 times tonight and made all 9, but I also shot just 4 of 12 from the field.

Still, we should have won this game. We had an 8-point lead at the end of the third quarter, and we had Starks completely bottled up on that last play to Harper. I guess I've got to give both of those guys credit, but I don't want to. Starks made a nice midair pass, and Harper knocked down the shot when he absolutely had to.

Charlotte won again—its third in a row—and the Hornets

are only a half game back. Man, I can't believe we might blow this thing.

Just saw on ESPN that Glen Rice scored 56 against Orlando. Maybe I shouldn't feel so bad about his beating me in the three-point contest after all.

Sunday, April 16
Indianapolis

Thank God for the Minnesota Timberwolves.

We finally got our fiftieth win, and Charlotte lost today. That means we're up by one and a half games with only three games left for us and four for them.

Bill Blair has a bad back, so he didn't even make the trip here today to coach. It wouldn't have mattered. They could have had Red Auerbach on the sidelines and we still would have beaten them by 39. We had built up a lot of frustration, so somebody had to pay. Unfortunately for Minnesota, they were the ones in town today.

I know fifty is just a number, but for us, it means a lot of things. They haven't had fifty wins here since the 1972–73 season. You can't really consider yourself an elite team in this league until you reach that fifty-win mark.

I'm happy for myself, but I'm really happy for guys like Vern, who's been here for eleven seasons, and for Donnie and Mel and George Irvine, guys who have been around this franchise for a long time.

Wednesday, April 19
Indianapolis

Dunkin and Conrad keep asking me what's wrong with my shooting touch. I keep telling them there's nothing wrong, that

I'm just not shooting the ball very well right now. I'm also not getting as many touches as I usually get.

Everybody has their little struggles, and this is mine. But slump? The word isn't in my vocabulary. I'm too good a shooter to get in a slump. I might have some off games, like I'm going through right now, but I'll never be in a slump.

I wish I had some great answer for the media and the fans, but the truth is I'm sort of struggling and I'm sort of saving myself for the playoffs when the points really count. That might sound like I'm trying to cover my ass or make excuses, but I don't know how else to explain it.

Yes, I'm not shooting as well as I usually do. No, I'm not worried. I worked out an extra half-hour after yesterday's practice with Billy and felt better. He told me to quit relying so much on jumpers and put the ball on the floor more.

Thursday, April 20
Indianapolis

Philly played us tough tonight, but we won, 103–91. All we need is one more win or one more Charlotte loss and we're the Central Division champions.

Thursday, April 20
Orlando

I never thought I'd root for the Knicks, but I had to tonight.

I went with Mark and Antonio to a sports bar to watch the Knicks play the Hornets in Charlotte. If the Knicks won, they clinched the second-best record in the Eastern Conference and the home-court advantage through the second round, but we clinched the Central Division title. If Charlotte won, we had to win one of our last two games.

But Patrick came through for us. The Knicks were down by

12 with about nine minutes left, but then Charlotte blew the lead. So thank you, Knicks.

Friday, April 21
Orlando

We were stretching before the game tonight, and everybody was all happy and hyped. We were telling each other, "Central Division champs," and hugging, shaking hands, kind of enjoying the franchise's first-ever NBA division title.

Then we went out for the introductions, and the O-rena public address guy said, "And now, for the Central Division champion Indiana Pacers . . ." We heard this and we were saying, "Yeah, that sounds kind of good!" And then Orlando ran out, and the guy said, "And now, your Atlantic Division champion Orlando Magic."

The place went crazy, but as I was standing there, I thought, "This is nice. This is how it should be for the conference finals. Central versus Atlantic. Number one seed versus number two."

And then they drilled us.

I've got to admit it: We didn't really care. I'm not saying we didn't try, but it was tough to get really pumped up for this game. We had won the division. We couldn't move up in the playoff seeding. The regular season was almost over. We were on the road. Some of our guys were trying to heal up some injuries. See what I mean?

So Orlando killed us, 110–86. I led the team with 14 points, and I can already see the headlines: "Pacers Lose—Miller Goes Eighth Straight Game Without Scoring 20 or More Points."

I guess Dunkin figured out that we were 26–9 when I scored 20 or more. That's fine, but none of that means anything come playoff time. Anyway, we won five games this month when I didn't score 20 or more, so what does that say about the stats?

Sunday, April 23
Indianapolis

Before tip-off today, everybody in Market Square Arena stood, and we had a moment of silence for the victims of the Oklahoma City bomb explosion. Just when you start thinking basketball is a real big deal, something jolts you back to reality.

We came out with a game face today against Atlanta. We had to, since we'll be facing the Hawks in the first round of the playoffs. Plus, we wanted to show them that their win against us earlier this month was a fluke.

I scored 22, and we won, 103–87, but I'm still getting questions about being in a slump. They're saying my shooting eye is gone, that I'm afraid to take a shot.

Me, afraid?

I keep telling people this is where the real season starts anyway. M. J. put it best; he said the regular season is garbage. He said from this point on is how your team will be remembered. Larry made a good point, too; he said the Central Division title means nothing except that we won fifty-two games and someone gave him a baseball cap with "Central Division Champions" on the front.

This is the best part of the year—the playoffs. I just turn into a different person. I get cranky, moody. I get evil. I don't know how I turn it on and off, but it's Reggie Time. This is the time of the season that separates the men from the boys. Don't ask me to explain it because I don't know how.

Here are the final numbers for the regular season:

- We went 52–30, which was the third-best record in the Eastern Conference and seventh best in the NBA. We have the home-court advantage in the best-of-five series against Atlanta, which starts Thursday. When we win that one, we'll play the winner of the New York–Cleveland series. If it's New York, the Knicks get the home-court advantage in the best-of-seven series because they had a better regular-season record than we did.

- I finished the 82-game schedule with a 19.6 scoring average, which is my lowest since the 1988–89 season, my second year in the league. I shot 46.2 percent from the field, made 195 three-pointers, and shot 41.5 percent from the three-point line. I shot 89.7 percent from the foul line.
- We finished 33–8 at home, 19–22 on the road, and 35–21 versus Eastern Conference teams. We beat every team in the league except Utah.

Round One: Atlanta

Monday, April 24
Indianapolis

I've been watching lots of video of the Hawks. I bring it home and keep it on for hours. I take lots of notes. I study my opponent until I build up a dislike for him. It's nothing personal, but come playoff time you can't afford to care about anybody's feelings. Right now I'm getting to dislike Steve Smith a whole lot.

Wednesday, April 26
Indianapolis

Everybody else gets to give postseason awards, so why not me?
Most Valuable Player: The Admiral, David Robinson.
I think he's done everything possible for them to have the best regular season record. He should win the defensive player of the year award, too.
To me, the true indicator of how good he is came when the

Worm, Dennis Rodman, went down. When that happened, David's scoring average went up something like 7 points. He means so much to that team. He might not be the absolute best player in the league this year—that might be Hakeem or Jordan or Pippen or Shaq—but he's the most valuable.

Rookie of the Year: Jason Kidd.

During the first half and maybe even during the first three-quarters of the season, I would have picked Grant Hill. But after looking at Kidd, he's really turning it on. Look at all his triple-doubles. Look at Dallas's record last year without him, and look at their record this year. He's made a huge difference, almost twenty-five games.

If you go by popularity, Grant would win hands down. And talent-wise, Grant is better. But impact-wise, it's Kidd. Remember, Jimmy Jackson has been hurt, and let's face it, they've got some holes in that lineup. But Kidd is so determined and he's so fast. He's probably the fastest person in the league with the ball. The only other guys who are close are K. J. and Mahmoud Abdul-Rauf.

If you ask me who's going to be the best rookie in the long run, I'd say the best franchise player might be Glenn Robinson. He can take over a game with his offense. He has all the tools, but I think he got caught up with the number one draft pick expectations and all the bad pub about the $100 million contract demands. Maybe that did work against him.

Coach of the Year: Bo Hill.

I think everyone's picking Del Harris, but I'd have to go with Bo. I mean, he had to contain and control Dennis Rodman. He got Rodman to show up for practices. And when Dennis did his crazy shit, Bo didn't put up with it—he either suspended him or didn't play him.

And I'm not saying this because he's my coach, but I thought Larry did a great job this year. The thing is, people expected us to win and we did. But when you think about it—with Antonio out for almost forty games, Dale hurt, John Williams not being able to work out his weight problem, all those early road games, and the fact that we were the hunted—Larry did a hell of a job. I think he should have gotten it last year, too.

Most Improved Player: Rik Smits.

I'm biased, but I've seen how far Rik has come not just this year but during his entire career. Being the number two pick, a lot was expected of him. It was tough on him, but as you can see, he's hung in there, become more vocal, and definitely is a big part of our success. In fact, I think he's our team MVP this season.

I know a lot of people will pick Dana Barros. Barros is the underdog. He's five feet ten or so. He plays for a bad team. He made the All-Star team. He had good stats.

But Rik meant more to us as a team. Without him I don't know if we could make a run at the NBA title.

Flop Team of the Year: Golden State.

This is a team in disarray. They traded their franchise center away. Sprewell and Hardaway are fighting. Sprewell called Hardaway "a Nellie brown-noser." Nellie quit. Mullin was hurt.

Talk about a slump. But they still have a lot of talent.

Thursday, April 27
Indianapolis

Playoff time, baby. Atlanta. At our place.

We've taken the mind-set that this is going to be a seven-game series for us, that we have to beat Atlanta four games to advance to the next round. Yeah, I know, it's a best-of-five series, but sometimes you've got to play mind games with yourself and with the other team.

That's what we did in the final regular-season game against the Hawks. We wanted to pound them, and we did. We knew they weren't going to show us their best stuff. They didn't run any plays. They just ran motion and passed a lot. Still, we wanted to send them a message. We wanted them to know we were ready.

All the pressure is on us this time around. Last year we sneaked up on them and knocked them out of the playoffs. Now they want to do the same to us. They want to come into Market Square and steal one.

What they don't realize—what a lot of people don't realize—is that I didn't show my best material to them, either. Come playoff time, with all the video that's available of the regular season, other teams can scout your A, B, and C moves. But once the playoffs begin, it's time to bring out the D, E, and F moves. You can't show those moves during the regular season because there's too much scouting going on. Sometimes, in a big game against, say, the Knicks, Orlando, or Chicago, you use something special. But you don't bring out your best shit and waste it against the Clippers or the Timberwolves. You save it for the playoffs.

If we play like we're capable, we'll beat Atlanta. We won the season series, 4–1, so it's not like we don't know what it takes to beat these guys.

Mookie and Steve Smith are their key players. Three weeks ago when they whipped us by 12, Mookie and Smith both had big games. And they let us know it, too. Smith would do his little antics and stuff, talking shit. I watched and listened and said to myself, "Okay, bitch, you keep on talking."

Whenever he'd make a shot, he'd stand there and kind of pose. When he'd shoot a free throw, if the ball was bouncing on the rim, he'd yell, "Get in there!" Another time he posted me up on the blocks, made the shot, and I fouled him. He started glaring at me, giving me a look like, "You can't check me."

So I've got some business with Mr. Smith.

We did just what we wanted to do tonight: controlled Mookie and Steve. They were 12 of 32 for a combined 34 points and we won, 90–82.

I had 24 points, but Derrick McKey is the reason we won the game. He had 21 points on 8 of 11 shooting, added 9 rebounds and 4 assists, and played his usual great defense. He just destroyed Tyrone Corbin and Stacey Augmon. We really followed Derrick's lead.

People keep talking about how we need another scorer besides myself and Rik. Derrick understands that and stepped up tonight.

To me, the first game of a series is the hardest to win. You want to get into the game quickly and you want to get that first one under your belt. We did that, which should give us a lot of confidence for the next one.

Saturday, April 29
Indianapolis

I got here for tonight's game and everything was wrong. My uniform wasn't straightened out in my locker stall like it usually is. My shots weren't falling when I was warming up. I didn't have any spring in my legs. I didn't feel good about anything.

Then I got in the game and I couldn't miss.

I hit my first three-pointer, and I was thinking, "That felt pretty good." Then I hit my second three, and it was like I was in a mini-zone. I scored 29 in the first half, 39 for the game, and we won, 105–97, to go up 2–0 in the series.

Maybe it's the ginseng I took before the game. Maybe that helped. Man, I'm giving y'all my best secrets, but the stuff really works. I started taking it during the second half of the season, and it helps pep me up. I just feel a lot better when I take it.

People say I could have had 40 points tonight, which would have broken my personal playoff record and tied a Pacers team record. I had 29 at the half, and people were saying, "Did you know?" Yeah, I knew I could get 40, but the game had been decided by then. The way I look at it, I'll need those extra points when we play New York and Orlando or Chicago. You never want to be greedy with the basketball gods. You've got to appease the basketball gods.

I can't remember exactly when I did it, but after one shot I sank, I made sure to stroll past the Atlanta bench and give Steve Smith a look. I was just trying to psych him and the team out. I didn't say anything; I just looked. Looks can convey a lot of thoughts.

Steve didn't like it, though. He got up and started yelling. I have no idea what he was saying. It doesn't matter. Just the fact that he stood up and was upset shows me that I got to him. He's reacting, so that means I'm getting in there.

When things are rolling like this, you've got to let your opposition know what they're in for. It's nothing personal, but I'm going to let Steve know. This is when you put fear in people's hearts.

I had a good game, but it also was nice to see Rik get more involved. He had 27 and 11 rebounds. Also, our defense was solid again.

Afterward, all the reporters wanted to know why I didn't do this all season. As I've tried to explain, this is the playoffs. All the money's on the table now. It's like when you were a little kid and you were playing on the playground. You didn't talk about Magic Johnson beating the Warriors during the regular season. You talked about Magic beating the Celtics in the playoffs. That's when it matters.

Anyway, didn't I tell you about this three months ago?

During the regular season I can do with just taking 13, 14, 15 shots a game. But come playoff time, there's something about wearing the black shoes, taking on a new attitude, the bald heads, the whole psyche of the postseason . . . it just changes me.

Look at my numbers. Hell, everybody knows them by heart around here, what with all the talk about my "slump." Before the playoffs started, I was averaging 19.6. Now I'm averaging 31.5 points. I was taking 13.5 shots. Now I'm taking 18.5. I was going to the free throw line five times a game. Now I'm going eleven. What can I say? It's the real season now.

About the worst thing that happened to me was when Augmon got me good with his elbow as I was going up for a layup. I was bleeding on top of my head and had to come out to get one of those big butterfly bandages put on. Vern and Byron were giving me shit about it, telling me it looked like a yarmulke. I'll admit, it was funny-looking.

Sunday, April 30
Indianapolis

No practice today, but we did have a team meeting.

As I was leaving Market Square, I kept looking at the banner they put up for our winning the Central Division. It's nice and all, but I'd like to put another banner next to it. Something like, "World Champions."

Tuesday, May 2
Atlanta

Tonight I went into the locker room and everyone was telling me about what the Hawks were saying after we killed them in game two—that they lost because they missed defensive assignments and had some missed rotations. They weren't giving us any credit at all, and it pissed us off. I mean, c'mon, how can you say I scored 39 because of "defensive lapses"? A man scores 39 against me, I give him credit, no matter who it is.

So we had a point to prove, not only to the Hawks but to ourselves.

I've been on the wrong end of these series before. One year

we were down to Boston, 0–2, and they jumped on us in game 3 and put us away. The same thing happened with Detroit: Down 0–2, and they stuck it to us early. We were thinking, "Oh, shit," and we folded.

We wanted to make Atlanta feel that way. We wanted them to feel the pressure and just give up. Instead, we went out tonight and got down by 7. We were just going through the motions.

The next time you look up, it's 11–7, and we're right back in it. I remember telling Mark near the end of the second quarter, and I made sure to say it loud enough so Mookie would hear it, "Let's just keep it close, and come the fourth quarter, we'll blow these kids out."

Almost. We buried them in the third period. I hit a three on an assist from Mark, and they called time-out. I was watching Lenny Wilkens on the sideline and saw the way his team was walking, actually moping, to the bench. That's when I knew we had them. We had popped their bubble, just like Boston and Detroit had done to us. You could see the confusion and frustration in their eyes. The final was 105–89.

I was telling Mark during the whole game to shoot, to put some pressure on Mookie. We had to show them that we were the best backcourt on the floor. Mark did it, too. He killed them. He finished with 19 points, 7 rebounds, and 7 assists. I had 32 points and 5 rebounds.

I know we were in Atlanta, but it seemed like a home game. They had an announced crowd of 12,106 at the Omni, but that included two high school bands and a bunch of Turner Broadcasting employees who got free tickets. It also included almost 1,000 of the best fans in the league—Pacer fans. A lot of those folks heard there were tickets available and started booking space on charter flights. They went nuts tonight. Everywhere you looked you could find Pacer fans wearing our jerseys and waving brooms. It was great.

•　　•　　•

Oh, before the game, Augmon, who has the same agent as I do, apologized for the elbow in game two. I got six stitches because of Stacey. Hey, it was an accident. I told him not to worry about it, that his elbows are just as sharp as mine.

Thursday, May 4
Indianapolis

I can't believe what I'm watching. Knicks versus the Cavs at Cleveland. Oh man . . . Harper just banked one in. That kid's *banking* it in. Shit.

New York is going to win this series, but I was hoping the Cavs would at least take it to five games. You know, wear them out a little.

They had their chances in game three, but they screwed that up, too. Danny Ferry had an open shot at the buzzer and missed. Man, don't be bricking the game winner.

However much shit Ferry's been taking ever since he signed that big contract—and done nothing—all that would have been erased if he had made that shot. He would have been the guy who put Cleveland ahead 2–1 in their series. Instead, he's going to be the one who missed the big shot. And so we've got to face our old friends, the Knicks. Seems only right.

Round Two: New York

Saturday, May 6
New York

I almost never read the papers during a series. I'll look at the pictures and ask my teammates, "What are they saying?" and stuff like that, but I don't read the articles. Too distracting. Everything changes from game to game, day to day. I only want to know who is doing all the talking on the other team.

It kills me not to be able to read the papers, especially in New York. But I'll wait until the series is over to look them over. I've got a feeling there will be a whole bunch of articles to read after this series.

Sunday, May 7
New York

Demons time. Time to get rid of some bad memories. Last year we let this series get away. We don't want to make the same mistake.

As for me personally, I have something to prove to myself and to our fans. I felt I really let our fans down last year. After it was all over in '94, the two people I felt really bad for were Vern and LaSalle. They had been there for so many years, especially Vern. And then we blew it.

Vern had been my backcourt mate for a lot of years. He's been there since 1984 when sometimes there were only two thousand or three thousand people in the stands, and the arena workers would put a curtain down before the game so Market Square wouldn't look so empty. If any one person kept going through my mind, it was Vern. I had a hard time holding back tears after that series because I kept thinking of what Vern had been through. I was so disappointed.

So I definitely have something to prove. I want to show everyone that we can beat these guys. That's why we said we wanted to play the Knicks after we beat Atlanta. We have to exorcise those demons of '93 and '94. It's like a little kid getting beat up at the schoolyard; one day the kid has to stand up to the bully. Once he hits the bully and the bully bleeds, he gets confident. We're no different. The Knicks are just bullies who wear jerseys.

I'm confident right now. I know we can win this series. I also know I have to be the most vocal, the one who puts his neck on the line. If my teammates see me put my neck out there and do all sorts of crazy things, then they'll jump on the bandwagon with me. But if they see me being tentative, like I was in '94 during the first two games of that series, then they'll take a step back.

I can't wait for this thing to start. I know these Knicks inside out. Larry keeps telling us to drive to the hoop on them. They defend well, but because of their help defense, because they're taught to help no matter who's driving, someone will be open, someone will get open looks.

After listening to Larry, looking at the tapes, and having firsthand experience, I'm telling you right now we can beat most of their starters off the dribble. Patrick is hurt. Oakley can be beaten off the dribble. Starks is a good one-on-one defender, but I can shoot over him. Harper is fairly decent on the ball. Charles Smith, their worst defender, can be beaten off the dribble. Mason, who's the NBA's sixth man of the year, is a great defender.

Early game. An 11:30 A.M. tip-off Central time; 12:30 in New York. NBC tells us what time to play and we do it.

We had a breakfast meeting to go over the plays and the Knicks personnel, kind of a formal meeting. After that was done, I asked the players to stay and asked if the coaches and trainers could leave so I could talk to the guys for a minute. The talk was short and sweet.

"Look," I said, "I really hate the Knicks. Last year, personally, I didn't think we could win this series. But this year we are clearly the best team. There ain't no way we should give up a great opportunity to win a championship. We should really go after them with all guns blazing. Let's all get on the same page, because I really can't stand this team. They're really overachieving.

"Now, Rik, you've got to put pressure on this clown [and I was talking about Patrick] because he's hurt. Put pressure on Patrick, make him work at the other end, and it will make our jobs on the perimeter much easier."

I said a few other things, but that was the gist of it: Don't let the Knicks ruin our chances for a championship.

Nobody else said anything except Byron, who told us, "We can't let opportunities slip away."

I knew everyone was really focused because they were all looking right at me. Nobody was slouched down or looking bored or looking the other way. We were all on the same page.

In 1994, New York beat us four straight times. But we got our confidence when we went home to Indianapolis and beat them twice in the playoffs. Then there was game five. But even then, with all the confidence we had from moving ahead 3–2 in the series, I still wasn't absolutely convinced we could beat them in the series. We had beaten them three straight, so I knew they were beatable, but there were little doubts way down deep.

All that changed in '95. Talent for talent, and going through what we went through against them in '94, and then watching them in the finals and watching them throughout this year, I know we're a better ball club than the Knicks.

When you think about it, we were the better team last year, but better doesn't necessarily mean you'll win. They beat us in the playoffs because they were more seasoned than we were in '94. They were tougher than we were that year. It was all new to us. They had been in the Eastern Conference Finals two years in a row. That was our first time.

We took the bus over to the Garden. Then we took the freight elevator up to the court. It's the same elevator they use when they take the animals up for the circus.

The Garden smells, but it's a good-bad smell. You come in and smell the elephants and the horses and the tigers. You see the rats running around and the cats chasing them. Just a great atmosphere. It's just an old, dirty gym with great tradition. It's the best place to play: the atmosphere, the stars, the hip clothes, the women. It's great.

You get off the elevator, make a left, and you're right there in the hallways. As usual, I wore sunglasses and was listening to my CD player—Tupac doing "Me Against the World." I don't like people to see the whites of my eyes or anything. Most of the time when I'm at a visiting arena, people are yelling things at me. This way I don't hear what they're yelling. Can't hear a thing.

I got into the locker room, changed, and tried to get out to the court as quickly as possible and shoot with Billy. I don't do interviews before the game during the playoffs, so I didn't have to worry about the media today.

So I went out there to shoot and did my usual routine, getting acclimated with the Garden. Good rims at the Garden. Great floor. I like the Garden and The Forum the best. I think Charlotte and Orlando have nice arenas, too.

Everybody has their routines. When the Knicks come out for their warm-ups, Oakley throws the ball from the tunnel to Spike, who catches it, kisses it, and then throws it back to Oakley, who starts the layup drill. How funny.

Pat Riley is so regimented. They got out there eighteen, nineteen minutes before the game started. We didn't come out until about thirteen, fourteen minutes before. But when we did come out, the place was buzzing. It was crazy. I looked down the star-studded row and saw Matthew Modine, Michael Douglas, Connie Chung, Maury Povich, Lou Gossett Jr., Spike. I was like, "Okay, everybody's in their usual spots, just how I like it." I mean, these people came out not only to see the Knicks but also to see the Indiana Pacers. We have that kind of rivalry now.

I want you to know that I didn't say one bad word about the Knicks before game one. I just said we wanted to play New York and exorcise some demons. But I heard what Derek Harper said, something like, "They want us, so here we are." And Charles Smith said something about our having to come to the Knicks' house if we want to advance to the conference finals.

Hey, that's fine, that's how we want it anyway. We don't want it easy, we want it hard. You've got to be able to win on the road if you want to win a championship.

The game started, and everything felt good. Rik was unbelievable. He took command of the post and made Patrick work. You see, when you play the Knicks, all you want to do is give yourself a chance to win, keep it close to the fourth quarter, and put pressure on them. If they're missing shots, sometimes the crowd turns on them. That's what you want: the Garden crowd to boo them. If they're up by 10 points, that's like 20 points to the Knicks, because they play such great defense. But if you're up and making them take pressure shots, that's what you want. You want them to have to win with their offense.

That's sort of how game one was. We took command early, they came back, but we were right there in the fourth quarter. Actually, we should have been ahead going into those final minutes, but we were pissing away lots of opportunities—again.

The whole thing reminded me of game one from the '94 series when we were going through the motions, not going for the second shots. Oakley and Mason were getting second shots.

But Oakley and Mason and especially Patrick couldn't do anything about Rik. Rik was killing Patrick. He was hitting everything, plus we knew Patrick was hurting. We saw Patrick hurting in the Cleveland series, so we knew we had to attack that weakness. His knees were aching, and he had sore calves. He even wore a protective sleeve on his left calf.

It got so bad that near the end of the game Rik had 25, 26 points, and Patrick had 9. Mark Jackson walked up to Patrick and said, "Look at the scoreboard, Patrick. I have 9 points and you have 9 points. You suck." Mark was just trying to piss him off and get under his skin. I like that. Mark and I, from day one, have been on the same page.

But even with Rik dominating down low, the Knicks came back in the fourth quarter. I wasn't hitting shit, which didn't help, and before we knew it, we were down 105–99 going into the last 18.7 seconds.

Larry called for a time-out. When we were in the huddle, I kept telling the guys, "Look, it's not over. If we get a quick three, then it becomes a free throw game."

It sounded like the right thing to say, but I've got to admit I was just basically talking to talk. I just didn't want a silent huddle. Part of me hoped it would be true, but, c'mon, we were down by 6 points . . . at the Garden . . . not much time left. Face it, it wasn't looking very good for us.

Anyway, the coaches drew an inbounds play for us, and it worked perfectly. I came off a double screen, Mark hit me with a clean pass, and I hit a quick three. We were down by 3 points with 16.4 seconds remaining.

Even at this point I was aware that they had no time-outs left. Oakley had used their last time-out with 1:15 in the game. He did it just before he fell out of bounds after grabbing one of our missed shots. He was hustling—and you've got to give him credit for that—but not having those time-outs at the end of the game was a killer.

So I hit the three, and they had to inbound under their basket. If they had had a time-out left, they could have gotten organized, come up with a play, and taken the ball out at half-court. Instead, they had to make split-second decisions.

Mason had to inbound the ball. Starks came toward the ball, which is what he's supposed to do. He's one of their better free throw shooters, so he was doing the right thing trying to get the ball, figuring he'd get fouled immediately. The guy's a 76.3 percent career foul shooter and 73.7 percent for the season. Greg Anthony also was down there just in case Starks couldn't get the pass.

On defense, it was me, Byron, and Sam Mitchell. Sam denied Starks, and Byron was in front of Anthony. I was going to double-team Anthony and stay behind him.

Well, Mason stumbled and looked like he was going to fall over the line. Everyone was covered, so rather than get called for stepping inbounds before he made the pass, Mason threw it toward Anthony. All I had to do was read Mason's eyes.

Anthony fell and the ball came right to me. Anthony got up real quick, but by that time I had made up my mind: I wasn't going to settle for a layup, I was going to try the three. When you're on the road, you go for the jugular. You don't go for the quick two and then try to foul; you go for the win.

So I scooted a few feet behind the three-point line. By then Anthony was right on me, but that's not much of a problem. He's only about six feet, so I knew he wasn't going to block my shot. I took the shot, and it was good. I mean, everything happened so fast, it was hard for me to think about anything. You don't think about the shot, you just take it.

So it's tied up, and I'm thinking, "Holy shit." They took the ball out again, and that's when we made our mistake—Sam fouled Starks with 13.2 left. But you know what? The more I think about Sam's foul, the more I think it wasn't such a bad move. Instead of holding the ball for a last shot, Sam's foul forced Starks to go to the line and make some pressure free throws. And even if he made them, we'd still get the ball back with a chance to tie or win the game.

Now it was Starks's turn to choke. He took his first shot and missed it. I didn't say anything to Starks while he was on the line, but right before the referee gave him the ball for the second shot, I said, "Hold on, wait a minute. . . . Oh, never mind, I forget." I was just trying to throw off his rhythm, just to make him think about it a little longer.

Starks took the second shot, and it wasn't even close. He almost airballed it. But Patrick somehow got the rebound, took a ten-footer right away, but clanked it off the back. I got the rebound, and Mason fouled me with 7.5 seconds left.

I got to the line, and I'm thinking, "Shit, I've got to make my free throws at least." I was more worried about the first than the second. I knew if I made the first, I'd make the second. So I put the rosin on my hands and made the first shot. Now it was like, "Okay, it's all routine now." So I made the second, giving me 31 for the game and 8 points in 8.9 seconds.

After the second free throw went through, Haywoode told me to pick up Anthony and he'd pick up Starks. So I picked up Anthony, and I was just trying to stay in front of him as he dribbled down the court. I figured he was going to try to get the ball to Starks or Ewing, but those guys didn't come to the ball. They all went south on him.

Time was running out, so Anthony tried to make a move. But he stumbled and fell, and they didn't get a shot off. We won, 107–105, and the Garden was stone silent. I mean, you could hear sweat hit the floor.

Now maybe you're wondering if I hit Anthony on the in- bounds play, the one where Mason threw it to me. Maybe a lit- tle bit, yeah. I nudged him on the first one.

And did I touch him on his final drive? Yeah, but it was in- cidental contact. When you watch the replays, it looks like I pushed him both times, but I didn't do any more than nudge him. Anyway, the refs weren't going to call something like that. Anthony wasn't going aggressively to the hoop, so he can't be expecting to hear any whistle. And if you're not going to call a foul on Michael Jordan when he hacks Hersey Hawkins on the arm in the final seconds of a playoff game— like he did in game four of the Bulls–Hornets series three days ago—then you'd better not call a foul on me when I barely hit Anthony. That's how the playoffs are: no ticky-tack fouls in the final minute.

As I was trying to get off the court, they told me I had to do an NBC interview. Hey, I was just as shocked as everyone about the game, so when they asked me what happened, I told them the truth:

Starks choked. Mason choked. And you can even second- guess Patrick for shooting the ball so fast and not passing it out to someone else so the Knicks could have the last shot in reg- ulation.

I was caught up in the emotion of the moment. I mean, this was an incredible thing. Everybody, including our own coach and team president, thought we had lost this game. Larry told reporters afterward that he thought we had no chance. And Donnie was so sure we were going to lose that he went to the locker room with eighteen seconds left. A few moments later Mel Daniels found him sitting in there, and he said, "Reggie hit two threes and we're tied." Donnie couldn't believe it. He came back out in time to see us win it.

So you can imagine how high we were. I was caught up in the situation, and as I was running back through the tunnel to our locker room, I started yelling, "They don't want it! They're choke artists!"

That's when it all started. You see, I didn't know all the cameras were still on me, picking up every word. That was the beginning of the controversy. But you know what? I don't care. I don't care about that. I love it.

Just to rub it in a little to Donnie, I told him, "Don't you ever give up on us that early."

But to be honest, I almost can't blame him for thinking it was over. We did, too.

Before the media came into the locker room, Larry really let us have it. He was screaming at us, telling us we didn't do the little things that win games, like pick-and-rolls, boxing out, running the right plays, stuff like that. He said that we can't keep blowing leads in the fourth quarter, and we can't wait for Rik to win the game for us.

Sometimes with Larry you're not sure whether you won or lost the game.

I celebrated our win by having a nice quiet dinner. But I think I'll stay close to the hotel tonight. Maybe catch something on Spectravision. I don't want to push my luck in this city. There's probably someone who has a hit out on me. There are snipers everywhere.

Monday, May 8
New York

Everybody in New York—and I mean everybody—is upset about this choke thing. Peter Vecsey, who writes a basketball column in New York and works for NBC, called me up and said that my performance in game one will probably be marred by what I said after the game.

I can't believe that shit. C'mon, why does any of that matter? I told the truth. I said what everybody was thinking in their kitchens and in their living rooms as they watched the Knicks fold. What they were saying to themselves privately, I said publicly.

Hey, the Knicks did choke. Pure and simple. Riley said it, too, after the game. He said the Knicks played their asses off—which they did—but "simply gave it away at the end." Where I come from, that's French for "We choked."

Vecsey said, "But, Reggie, you should have left it up to the sportswriters."

I said, "Y'all were going to write it anyway; just because I say it, it's a big deal?"

Man, the choke thing *has* become a big deal. You walk by a newsstand, and every paper has it on the front page of their sports section. New York has gone crazy. Every headline. Every big picture. These headlines are so big, I can't help but see them.

And while I'm thinking about it, let's get something straight. After the game was over, I told the media, "We got one. We want to get two." I also said that we had a chance to close the series out when we went back home to Indiana. Of course, everybody took that to mean that I was predicting a sweep. Hey, I said we *could* sweep them if we got game two. I never guaranteed it.

If you look at it objectively, we should be down 0–1. But we did what we had to do. We came in and got home-court advantage. We survived an NBA playoff record of 59 fouls—31 on us (including the ejection of Antonio), 28 on them (Derek Harper got tossed). We got a great game from Rik, who outscored Patrick 34–11.

Maybe my choice of words wasn't good. I said in the NBC interview that Starks and Mason choked, but the thing that got everybody going was what I said in the tunnel, that the Knicks were choke artists.

The next day all the papers, all the headlines were about the same: "Reggie Says: Knicks Choke."

I thought, "This is unbelievable."

And let me get rid of another rumor that's been making the rounds. No one read me no riot act after the game. Absolutely not. Larry and Donnie never talked to me about calling the Knicks chokers, and they never told me to tone down my comments. In fact, Donnie was the one who told reporters that the Knicks were always mad, so why would my comments make a difference? Anyway, nobody in the entire Pacers organization told me to tone it down. Clear enough?

After the shootaround today, everybody was asking what I thought about all the controversy with the choke artists comment. I told them I wasn't the one writing the newspaper headlines, that I wasn't the editor. They could write whatever they wanted to—and they usually do, too.

"You ever regret saying something?" someone asked.

"There is nothing I ever wish I didn't say," I said. "If it comes out of my mouth, that means it was meant to be done."

Tuesday, May 9
New York

A couple of the guys said that Starks came out in the papers today and said I was going to have to live with my comments. The quote was something like, "He has to understand what he's putting himself into. He said what he had to say, and now he has to deal with it."

So now I know the Knicks are coming after me and that the Garden is coming after me. But this is what I wanted.

See, I can handle this. I'm not sure everybody else on the team can handle this kind of attention, but if twenty thousand people are focused on me, maybe that allows the other guys to go out and play and not worry about anything. They can relax. I can handle twenty thousand people chanting, "Reg-gie sucks! Reg-gie sucks!" I can handle being called the "Mouth of the Midwest." I can handle the signs that say, "Miller Time Is Over." I love it. In this case, I was trying to be the lightning rod. Let the controversy come my way. I'm used to it.

Okay, we lost the second game tonight, 96–77. They came out and played great, and everybody jumped on my ass, saying that my comments cost us game two. That's bullshit.

What you have to understand is that if it took words from me to get the Knicks motivated to play, then we already have the Knicks beaten. If they needed my words to get them fired up for the second round of the NBA playoffs, then they don't deserve to be here in the first place. My words shouldn't have hurt them that much. They should have already been pumped up and ready to play. That's my whole thinking.

I guess if I had to do it all over again, I wouldn't say they choked. I don't regret saying what I said, but I suppose I could have been more diplomatic. I would have said they gave away one; I would have downplayed it. But would we then have won game two? I don't know. I do know my calling them choke artists wasn't the reason we lost the second game. I mean, I think we're tougher than that. Also, I know my teammates want me to speak my mind. They love it.

Remember, in '94 I took the exact opposite approach going into that seven-game series with the Knicks. After the head-butting and talking shit and all that in the '93 series, I said I was just going to play my game and may the best team win.

Real nice-guy shit. But my teammates jumped on me, saying, "What's wrong with you? You gotta talk shit." So after game two of that '94 series, I said I had to be myself, win or lose. So now I'm myself, no matter who the opponent is.

None of that helped tonight. They drilled us. I only scored 10 points on 3-of-10 shooting, and believe me, the crowd noticed. They were chanting, "Reg-gie sucks!" and "Cher-yl! Cher-yl!" The usual stuff.

I give all the credit to John Starks because he really accepted the challenge. He wasn't going to let me do the things I was used to doing, coming off picks and screens, getting open shots. They did a good job of challenging every shot. Every time I tried to drive, there were three or four Knicks there. They played well, and I didn't.

What I should have done was come out and go crazy with shots and try to go to the hole. So much attention was being put on this game, the referees probably would have called more fouls against the guys guarding me. But I didn't go to the hoop. I kept waiting for the game to come to me. I wasn't aggressive enough. As it turned out, we got killed in the third quarter, mostly because of turnovers (fourteen in the third period, thirty-five all together) and because I didn't look to score.

Wednesday, May 10
Indianapolis

Larry's pissed at me, but I don't care. He's upset that I said what I said after game one. And I'm sure he thinks it's part of the reason we lost game two.

Sorry, but I can't worry about that. I can't worry about what I say or if I'm going to hurt someone's feelings with the choking stuff and all that.

Marv Albert says Larry is only happy when he's unhappy. I'd agree with that.

I respect Larry. You've got to respect a guy who's won one thousand games or so. He's taught me a lot about the game, and I'm a better player because of him. But I'm not afraid to get in his face. Both sides have to be able to take tough talk.

The problem is, you can't have your cake and eat it, too. Tell me which one you want, Larry: Do you want me to be me, or do you want me to pretend to be someone else?

Last year I had coaches and teammates telling me to talk more, to be like the Reggie they knew. So I did, and we came within thirty seconds of the NBA Finals. This year I've got a head coach who's mad at me because I did the same thing this series as I did last year, which is to say what's on my mind.

See what I mean? You can't have it both ways.

Thursday, May 11
Indianapolis

Going into this game, I made up my mind I was going to take the ball to the hoop. In game two I was settling for too many jumpers. I needed to get to the line, to force people to play defense and maybe get some Knicks in foul trouble.

Well, I did all that, but the Knicks also had a plan of their own. They came out today ready to play. They were banging bodies, outhustling us, shooting lights out. Starks was hitting threes. Charles Oakley was hitting shots out his ass. I couldn't believe it was really him.

We were down by 4 at the half, down by 8 at the end of the third quarter, and down by 11 early in the fourth. All I kept thinking was, "We're going to lose home-court advantage just like that."

I was getting a little frustrated, especially with some of the officiating. There were two plays in a row where Rik got hit and I got hit, and there was no whistle. Nothing. This was during the third quarter, and we were down by 9. It was getting close to crunch time, so you needed every call you had coming to you.

Instead, Rik bitched and got a technical. I got a technical when I punched the ball into the crowd after a no-call. I was so pissed.

Our fans started throwing cups and ice on the floor, and it was a little scary for a few minutes. I think Patrick got hit near the eye, and some of the TV-radio guys on press row were ducking for cover.

Larry got on the public address system and told everyone to knock it off. "Hey, somebody's gonna get hurt," he said. "It's not the players' or referees' fault. Let 'em play!"

So we played, and for some unknown reason the Knicks let us back in the game. Instead of burying us, they started to gag again. Patrick got in foul trouble, which isn't anything new. He's been in foul trouble the whole series. This time he got his fifth foul with 8:41 left to play, and Riley had to pull him. Then Charles Smith got his fifth a few seconds later.

We cut the lead to 6, and then Patrick fouled out when he got caught setting a real aggressive high screen with about 3:30 left in the game. It was a gutsy call, but, hey, it was an obvious foul.

I made a shot to get us within 4. Rik hit a free throw to make it 87–84. They hit a free throw, we hit two, and the score was 88–86. Then, with thirty-four seconds left, Rik hit a sweet twelve-footer. We were tied, but I still don't know how we did it.

They called a time-out (I guess they learned their lesson from game one) and set up their play. Oakley had a shot to put them ahead, but he charged into Haywoode. Then we went for the last shot. I went for a stepback three and just missed.

Overtime.

We just dominated them in overtime. Ewing had fouled out. Smith had fouled out. And I'm sure all the Knicks were thinking that they had let another one get away. And they were right, they had.

With no Patrick or Smith in the middle and us up, 94–90, I

made a move toward the basket. Starks was playing me to come off screens and shoot, so as soon as I got the ball, I put my head down, took off from the dotted line in the lane, saw Mason and Oakley waiting for me, and just kept going up. That's when I did that dunk, the Superman dunk.

Back in my younger days I dunked like that. This time I knew someone was going to have to foul me or someone was going to get dunked on. The Knicks never want to give up the easy ones. They've got a saying, "Not in my house, not in the lane." Well, this wasn't their house, it was ours. The dunk put us ahead by 6.

We almost pissed it away at the end, but Derrick blocked Oakley's three-point attempt at the buzzer.

Rik had another good game (21 points), and Haywoode came in and hit a big shot in overtime. I ended up with 26 points and had 11 rebounds, which is a career high for me.

Friday, May 12
Indianapolis

Riley is bitching about the officiating, saying the refs aren't giving Patrick the proper amount of respect.

Is he kidding? If Rik nudges the guy, it's like a traffic cop convention out there. All you hear are whistles.

Believe me, Patrick gets away with a lot. I'm not saying he doesn't deserve the benefit of the doubt, but just because he's a veteran and a good guy doesn't mean the refs should ignore his fouls.

ESPN just had something about Kevin Garnett, the high school kid from Chicago who said he's coming out for the NBA draft. He's a center, and I hear he might go as high as sixth. Toronto is looking hard at him.

All I've got to say is that somebody is giving him some bad

advice. I'd tell him to go to college. I don't care how good he is. If he asked me, I'd tell him he's making a big mistake. He doesn't know how much he'll be missing if he skips college. His social skills will suffer. He won't develop as a person. Even if the kid were physically ready to play in this league—and he isn't—he'd be missing out on a really important and valuable time in his life.

When I was a junior, I thought about coming out early. But I was very content at UCLA. I wanted to play another year. Looking back, I might have gone higher in the draft after my junior year, but I don't ever second-guess the decision. Money isn't everything. I loved being at UCLA.

Saturday, May 13
Indianapolis

We just flat-out beat the Knicks today, 98–94. We had them by 17 in the third and by 13 with 6:22 left to play. After that it was a free throw contest. One more win and we're in the Eastern Conference Finals.

I think game three took a lot out of them. They thought they should have won it. In fact, they were talking about how they should be up 3–0—and they're right. But you know what? I'm not going to give the wins back to them.

I think another reason we're up 3–1 is that we've been playing every other day. For the Knicks, with so many of their starters playing thirty-plus minutes, I think it's taking its toll on them. Patrick's really hurting, and they don't have a deep enough bench to keep up with us.

After the game I was in the interview room, and a reporter said, "John Starks says he only has one comment, 'We're going to win this series.'"

I said, "He has a right to his own opinion."

"Don't you have a rebuttal?"

"He can feel that way."

I didn't feel like getting into a war of words with Starks, but I think there's a double standard going on. Funny, but when Starks guarantees a series victory, there's no big uproar. But if I say we're looking to sweep, everybody goes crazy.

The day wasn't a complete success. Dale separated his right shoulder again. They had to help him off the court, and it looked bad. Now we have to sweat it out and hope he can play Wednesday.

Knowing Dale, I think he'll try to come back. This guy is a warrior, a true warrior. Geronimo.

He and Charles Smith collided in the second quarter, and that's when he hurt it again. Dale grimaced for a moment, but that was it. He doesn't show pain.

Sam came in and, man, this kid played big. He was hitting jumpers. He was rebounding and keeping Mason and Oakley off the boards. He was definitely the game MVP. Without Sam we wouldn't have won. He played twenty-two minutes, scored 11 points, had 5 rebounds, and was the key to our 34–17 run in the third quarter.

Rik had 25 points and I had 21, but believe me, this was Sam's day.

Now we go back to New York with a chance to close the Knicks out. It isn't going to be easy. It never is with the Knicks. We know that from past experience. But they've got some problems, too. Only four teams have ever come back from 3–1 deficits to win a playoff series. We're not going to let them become the fifth team

Monday, May 15
Indianapolis

Cheryl got inducted into the Basketball Hall of Fame tonight. I wish I could have been there, but I know what she would have said if I'd shown up: "I'm gonna kill you. The Knicks series is more important."

Julius Erving was her escort for the induction ceremony. Dr. J. was always one of her idols, and I know it was a big thrill for her to have him there.

In her acceptance speech she thanked me for being her biggest fan and her best friend. She didn't have to do that. All I know is that she's always been there for me, and I'll always be there for her. She's the greatest sister anybody could have. And the best friend, too.

I called her today, and I think I was more excited about the ceremony than she was. Maybe it's because I know I'll never make it to the Hall of Fame. You've got to win a few championships to get in there. But I'm trying.

"Cheryl Dean," I said, "can you believe it? Can you believe it? You're a Famer. You're a legend. Now I can go around and tell people I've got a sister in the Hall of Fame."

"Reggie," she said, "I've always been one."

Tuesday, May 16
New York

I was sound asleep this morning when the phone rang. It was six o'clock, and I thought, "Who the hell could this be?" So I picked up the phone.

"Reggie?"

"Uh . . . no."

"Well, you're a great player."

"I don't know what you're talking about." Then I hung up.

People started calling back an hour later. It was crazy.

Then I went to the shootaround, and when I came back, there were about twenty-five voice messages from people who had called. There were lots of "You suck," "The Knicks are going to beat your ass"—that sort of thing. After that, kids, women, men . . . everybody called me during the day.

Well, here's what happened: One of the New York radio stations found out my road alias and broadcast it. Maybe some Knick fan who's a hotel employee phoned it in, I don't know. Whatever the case, I had to change my alias, which is too bad because I liked my fake name. A hint: The greatest detective of them all.

Sherlock Holmes.

It hasn't been officially announced, but Dale is going to start tomorrow. The three days off have really helped his shoulder heal, but he's still going to have to wear a protective harness. He won't be at 100 percent, but I know this: He'll play hard, and he won't play like someone worried about hurting himself.

Wednesday, May 17
New York

This one really hurts. Now I kind of know how New York felt after game one.

We did exactly what we wanted to do tonight, which was keep it close until the fourth quarter and try to steal the game. We were down 94–87 with fifty-three seconds left and then scored the next 8 points. I hit a three to cut the lead to 2 points, and then we took a 1-point lead with 5.9 seconds when Byron hit a three-pointer from way, way behind the line.

The Knicks called a time-out, and we figured it would go to either Starks or Patrick. We were right. Starks got the ball, passed it to Patrick, who hit a running seven-footer—and I mean running—with 1.8 seconds on the clock.

We should have closed these clowns out tonight, but Patrick came up big. I could have won it. There were those 1.8 seconds left on the clock, and I came off a double screen up high. Sam hit me with a perfect pass as I was going into my shot. I released the ball, and all I kept thinking was, "Man, this shot looks good. If this goes in, they do not know how big a fool I am going to act in here."

But the thirty-footer just missed. It hit a little bit left on the rim and went off. The Knicks won, 96–95. Spike was over there waving his towel at us.

As soon as it was over, Patrick went over to the front row and started hugging John Thompson, his coach at Georgetown. What he should have done was hug the referees. They didn't call him for traveling, which is part of the reason he was able to squeeze into the lane for the shot.

I've seen the replay, and it sure looked to me like he walked. He made a big shot, but he took a couple of big steps to get there. But in a way I can't blame the refs for not making that call. This is game five of the Eastern Conference Semifinals. You can't end a game on a ticky-tack walking call.

I'll say this about Riley and Patrick: They bitched about the officiating the last couple of days, and it worked. Patrick played the last two minutes with five fouls, and I'm telling you, there were times they could have gotten him for his sixth, seventh, and eighth, but they let it go.

I'm not crying about it. That's just the way it goes sometimes in this league. After that call they made on Pippen last year, the refs are more reluctant to make those kinds of last-second calls in the playoffs.

Despite the loss, we were pretty upbeat right after the game. We were thinking, "Okay, we played them well here. Now we'll just dominate them when we get back to Indiana."

Then the media came in. Everyone started asking us about déjà vu, about this being a repeat of the '94 series when we had a 3–2 lead. Were we afraid of those ghosts showing up again?

I said, "No, this isn't like last year. We had won three in a row, and we were going back to close it out. It's tough to beat a team three times in a row, but to beat a team like the New York Knicks four times in a row, well, that's almost impossible. So it's a different scenario."

I don't know if they believed it. I don't care, either.

Rik had another strong game, finishing with 28. He outscored Patrick by 9 points, but Patrick did look good out there tonight. The time off really made a difference in his legs. He moved around a lot better.

I had 23 points but missed 8 of 11 three-pointers.

Thursday, May 18
Indianapolis

I'm in mourning. Orlando just beat M. J. and the Bulls. Damn, I was really looking forward to facing Michael in the conference finals.

I'm shocked about this one. I thought with Michael back that Orlando would fold under the pressure. I thought the Bulls would beat them.

But Michael looked really tired as the series wore on. I was watching the postgame interviews, and he admitted that he didn't give himself enough time to get in shape and work out with the team before he made his comeback.

Some people are already saying that some of the M. J. aura has disappeared because the Bulls lost and because he made a couple of bad plays. Puh-leeaaaasssee. This guy is still the greatest. You watch next year. This is just how Michael loves it, with everybody underestimating him.

It kills me how people are. Everybody was aching for him to come back, and he did. Then, just because he wasn't the Michael of old in a month and a half, everybody starts criticizing him. Unbelievable.

Friday, May 19
Indianapolis

We played not to lose tonight. So, of course, we lost, 92–82. Now we've got to go back to New York for game seven. Geezus, this sucks.

We were scared out there. Scared in our house, in front of our fans. We were thinking about all those comments about last year. It showed, too. We were battling uphill the whole game.

I'll admit it: I was feeling the pressure. I didn't score my first field goal until 9:49 left in the game. Up until then I only had two free throws. All I was thinking was, "Oh, my goodness, this stuff about choking could come back to haunt me for the rest of my career."

Bottom line: I just didn't play well. No excuses.

You can tell Patrick is getting stronger every game. He scored 25 points and had 15 rebounds. I had 18, including 9 straight in the fourth and 15 altogether, but it wasn't enough. We got within 3 late in the game, but then the Knicks pulled away.

During the game Harper came up to me and said, "It's destiny for us to win."

"Maybe so," I said, "but your dream is ready to be shattered. I'll tell you what, Derek. Let's make a bet. You lose this series, then you come down to one of our games against Orlando. If we lose, I'll come to one of yours and watch a game."

I guarantee you he'll never show up.

Saturday, May 20
New York

After practice today, one of the reporters wanted to know who would win game seven.

"We will," I said. "There's no way we can play worse."

I mean, what did he expect me to say, the Knicks?

Then some other guy wanted to know what I thought about the fact that no visiting team has won a game seven since 1982. That's a span of twenty games.

"It's 0 and 20?" I said. 'Man, it would be nice to be the first, wouldn't it? That adds a little incentive right there."

Later we went back to the hotel and watched Houston knock the Suns out of the playoffs at Phoenix. The champs just won't go away, will they?

Barkley said he probably had played his last NBA game, but I don't believe it. As long as Michael is still playing, this kid is going to be playing. Barkley will be back.

Bill Walton, who's a commentator for NBC, was on today's broadcast. He gets on my nerves.

He's been talking about me, about how if I'm going to talk a big game, then I had better play a big game. You should hear this guy. Before the series started, he was destroying us. Then we came back and won that first game, and he was saying something like, "Oh, they were never out of it. Just a diehard team." He changes his tune in eighteen seconds.

Everybody talks about how he talks point-blank, says things straightforward, but I don't see it. He's the same guy who was knocking Jim Harrick the last couple of years, and then UCLA went out and won the national championship. It wasn't until they were on a roll that he started telling people he had apologized to Harrick and made up with the team.

Sometimes I can't believe he's really a Bruin.

Sunday, May 21
New York

I've made a vow to myself. No matter what happens tonight, I'm going to come out aggressive and play that way from start to finish. I haven't done that every game. Some of it was my fault. Some of it was the Knicks' fault. But this time, no matter what they do, I'm going to be aggressive. If my teammates see me do it, then maybe they'll follow.

I came out for warm-ups, and you should have seen the signs—"Miller Time Is Over," that sort of thing. I loved it. It was fantastic. That's the kind of atmosphere I want. I wanted them to take everything out on me.

All the celebrities were in place. Marv Albert and Matt Guokas were at courtside. The world was watching. Game seven. The Knicks. You don't have moments like that in your life very often.

We got off quickly—I had 10 points in the first quarter—and the Knicks weren't playing the same way they played in game six. They didn't play with the same intensity, the same desperation. It was like they almost expected us to fold. And when we didn't, they were thinking, "Oh, shit, we're in a game."

We didn't commit a turnover until 8:54 in the second quarter. Dale started, but this time he didn't wear that protective harness. I know he was in a lot of pain, but he played so much better without that thing. Rik was having a lot of success early, too.

By the time the Knicks woke up, they were 15 points down in the third quarter. I've got to give them credit, though, they didn't fold. They could have easily gone south, but Harper and Starks hit some big threes and got them back into the game. If those are misses, it's a blowout.

I shot my wad in the third quarter when we built up that 15-point lead. I had done so much talking, glaring, and shooting that I had nothing left for the fourth period. I was physically tired from the 18-point first half and the 11-point third quarter and I knew somebody else was going to have to pick it up for me in the last period. In fact, I even said that when I went over to the bench at the end of the third quarter. I was on exhaust fumes by then.

Of course, the Knicks didn't know that. They were all over me in the fourth, thinking I was going to keep taking shots. They were wrong. Only one of my 18 shots came in the last quarter.

Patrick put New York ahead, 84–83, with 6:53 left. I thought the Garden was going to explode.

But we didn't back down. Last year we might have. This year we knew we were a better team. We knew what it took, how to react.

Derrick hit a huge three-pointer with 6:32 in the game. Then Rik hit 3 shots in a row and put us ahead by 5 with 1:18 left to play.

We were ahead, 97–92, when Starks stuck a three—and I still don't know how he made it—from near the corner with 32.3 seconds to go. I was guarding him, and so was Antonio. The thing is, Antonio might have fouled him on the play, too, so that could have been a 4-point play if the refs had called it.

We blew our possession, so now the Knicks had a chance to tie it. We went to our huddle, and I told everybody, "Look, we're five seconds away from going to the Eastern Conference Finals and beating these clowns. One stop defines a season."

Meanwhile, there was some drunk behind our bench who kept yelling, "Hey, Reggie! You had a nice four-game sweep, you punk! You're a punk, Miller. Who's choking now?"

We knew they were going to try to get it to Starks or Ewing for the final shot. They almost always do. So I told Derrick to guard John, and I'd guard Hubert Davis.

As we were setting up to guard the inbounds pass, Larry was on the bench telling everybody to grab their left nut and pray. I guess Frank McGuire, his old coach, used to say the same thing when the game was on the line. Larry called it "The Power."

Hey, I'm for any edge we can get.

Harper got the inbounds pass to Ewing. Antonio was on

him, but there was room for Patrick to make a move. Still, I thought Patrick was going to take one of his running, one-legged shots like he usually does. But then I saw him turn the corner and move past Derrick and then Antonio. I thought, "This kid is going in for a finger roll!"

It was like everything was in slow motion. I just stopped and watched it happen. I couldn't move. I mean, I probably should have gone down low and tried to help, but I just had to stop and watch.

Patrick moved toward the basket, jumped a little too early, and then scooped the ball off his right fingertips. The ball floated toward the rim . . . hit the back of the rim . . . and missed.

Dale got the rebound and the buzzer went off. I'm telling you, it was like a thousand weights had been lifted off my shoulders.

The Knicks had knocked us out of the playoffs twice in a row, had pushed us to game seven last year and won. This year we had them 3–1, and they tied it up and pushed it to another game seven. If they had won this one, I don't know if we would have ever recovered. I don't know if I would have recovered. I know Larry doesn't agree, but this was a huge psychological victory for us. We had to get past the Knicks. It was the biggest mental challenge we faced.

I just ran down the court, fell to the floor, and kissed the ground, saying, "Thank you, Jesus. Thank you. Thank you." Then all my teammates came rushing up. We were hugging, laughing, yelling. All I can remember is Vern and Mark wrapping their arms around me.

Last year when we lost the series to New York, I was the first one to go over to the Knicks and shake their hands. This time it was Patrick who kind of squeezed through the crowd and said, "Congratulations. Good luck."

I've got a lot of respect for Patrick, not only because he came over, not only because he never used his injury as an excuse during the series, but because he was willing to take the shot that won or lost a game. After the game he told the media that's the kind of shot the Knicks pay him to take. He's right. I'd want to take that shot, too.

After Patrick walked over, Spike crossed the floor and gave me a hug and said, "Good luck. You guys were the better team."

Then Jim Gray of NBC came up and wanted to do an interview. I tried to compose myself, but it was hard. I thanked the Lord. I thanked the fans in Indiana. And then I said I was sorry for calling the Knicks chokers—and I meant it.

The Knicks might have choked in that first game, but they're not chokers. There's a difference. They're a classy organization. Pat Riley is a classy coach. I was wrong to say they were chokers in the first place. I'll be the first to say I was wrong.

With Fernando de San Miguel, our strength and conditioning aide–bodyguard, leading the way, I went back into the locker room and began the celebration. I also made sure to hug each one of my teammates and tell them, "Thanks for taking my back." These were the guys who were with me 100 percent when the entire city of New York was coming after my ass— the fans, the media, the Knicks. But through it all, these guys stuck with me. I'll never forget that.

Looking back, if Patrick's shot goes in, we lose the game and the series. We would have gone into overtime, and I think all the momentum and emotion would have been in their favor. But it didn't go in. Maybe one of those demons gave us a break and pushed it out.

I wasn't in the locker room when it happened, but a couple of the guys told me Riley came in looking for Larry. He told Larry congratulations and said, "You're ready." Then he went over and shook Antonio's hand and then Dale's hand. As he was shaking Dale's hand he said, "I should have pulled your shoulder."

So now we're going to Orlando. We're tired. We're banged

up. But we're there. That's the only thing that matters—we're there.

I'm not going to let this ruin my day, but I just heard that be-fore game seven Larry did an interview with Marv Albert and said my comments after game one had hurt the team and that I was feeling the pressure.

Hey, he was crying over spilled milk. This was game seven, a one-game series. He should have come in the locker room and given us a Knute Rockne–type speech, not gone on NBC and second-guessed me. You don't cry about what happened in game one. Hell, we won game one.

You know what I think? I think maybe Larry was feeling the pressure.

Eastern Finals: Orlando

Monday, May 22
Orlando

Got to Orlando today, and an envelope was waiting for me. It was from Spike. He sent a card saying, "Congratulations. You guys deserved it, but please, Reggie, quit cussing me out. I didn't do anything to disrespect you or your wife."

Apparently, after game one, when we pulled that game out in the last thirty seconds, I yelled at Spike. His wife was sitting right next to him, and I guess he got all pissed off. He said I was disrespecting his wife and that I talked shit only when I was ahead.

Well, first of all, everybody knows I talk shit all the time. As for cussing at him and his wife, I really can't remember cussing at him. I think he's more upset because of the looks I gave him after the shots. I really don't remember cussing at him, to tell you the truth. I would never intentionally do anything like that in front of his wife.

Spike, if I did, I apologize.

But Spike owes me an apology, too. He said after game one

that I played up to the New York crowd because I came from a small-market city. Basically he was saying that I did what I did for the publicity.

First of all, I've been doing this stuff since I played in college. Me getting emotional isn't exactly a recent news flash. As for the small-market stuff, I wouldn't change this setting for any big city. I love it in Indiana. I wouldn't trade playing here for New York or Chicago or Los Angeles. I wouldn't mind if the weather was nicer, but as far as a place to live and play, Indiana is the best.

I'll admit it does hurt to get overlooked by the networks all the time. We've got one of the better teams in the league, we've got great fans, and yet we don't get on TV that much. Hey, we've got a following. This is our second straight year in the conference finals. But we only get on NBC and TNT twice each during the regular season? C'mon. You just can't keep putting Chicago, Orlando, New York, Phoenix, and L.A. on TV. You just can't.

A friend back in Indiana told me the TV and radio stations keep playing the last few seconds of game seven. Mark Boyle, the play-by-play guy, had a great call: "Ring the bell! Ding dong, the witch is dead!"

Nice. Very nice.

And one of our team officials told me that about two thousand people showed up at Market Square Arena for the playoff ticket lottery. Only sixty people got tickets, and it only took eighteen minutes for all the tickets to be sold. Pacer-mania.

I'm looking at this Orlando roster, and, man, did they ever hit the draft jackpot or what? They got Shaq three seasons ago, had the draft rights to Chris Webber two seasons ago, and traded them to Golden State for Penny. Now Penny's an All-Star.

This year Golden State got the first pick again. If I were the

Warriors, who won the lottery on Sunday, here's what I'd do: I'd trade the pick.

C'mon, this one's easy. I'd trade down to number eight or nine because you're going to get basically the same thing at number eight or nine as you would with number one. That's because there's no clear number one. Joe Smith, Jerry Stackhouse, Antonio McDyess, Rasheed Wallace—to me, there's not much difference between them. But if you trade down, you get a high pick and you probably get some veteran players in the deal.

Tuesday, May 23
Orlando

I called B. J. Armstrong today.

"How do we play these clowns?" I asked.

B. J. wasn't much help. "I have no idea. I don't know how to play them because they have such great spacing."

Man, was he right.

In case you don't know what spacing is, it's when the players are positioned just far enough apart that you can't double-team a guy and get away with it. With Orlando, if you double-team Shaq low, he passes it out to Dennis Scott. And if you run at Scott, Nick Anderson is one pass away. And if you run at Anderson, he'll pass it to Horace Grant, who can hit the medium-range jumper. And if you rotate to Horace, he'll pass it to Penny for the warm-up jumper.

Another thing B. J. said to watch out for was the third quarter. That's when Orlando did a lot of its damage to the Bulls. He said, "Look, they've got some kind of audiovisual thing, some kind of special camera that lets the coaches look at the game during halftime, and that's when they make all their adjustments. Then they come out and drill you.

"They really don't have an offense," B. J. said. "Their offense is posting up Shaq and Penny. But in the third quarter, that's when we lost the games. There's no way Shaq is that smart a guy to know where we were rotating from. There's no way he could find those cutters unless they had it on video-tape or something. They've got some high-tech scanning thing."

"Interesting," I said.

This Orlando team is a little like us with the Knicks. We owed the Knicks for knocking us out of the playoffs. The Magic think they owe us one for sweeping them in the first round of the playoffs in '94.

Orlando has had four days to rest for the series, and we've had forty-eight hours. But I think we'll be ready. I don't know if we can reach that same level of emotion that we had for game seven against the Knicks, but we'll come close. How can you not be pumped for the first game of the conference finals?

The minute I heard Shaq had finished way behind the Admiral in the MVP voting, I knew we might be in trouble. Someone even heard Shaq tell Nick Anderson, "I'll show them."

But then we went out in the first quarter and took a 23–5 lead, and I thought, "Here we go. Just like last year."

Orlando is not a great defensive team. Compared to the Knicks, the first quarter was so easy for us. I had 17 points in the quarter, and it was like being a kid in a candy store. We took whatever we wanted: open shots, layups, threes. It didn't matter, it was there for us. Plus, we had Shaq on the bench with two quick fouls.

But that's where we blew it. We thought it was going to be that way the whole game. Instead, we got caught up in their style. All of a sudden they were back in the game, and it only took them a couple of minutes. We knew they would make a run, but there's no way you should let a team back in the game that quickly. What killed us was the third quarter . . . and Shaq.

They outscored us 35–21 in the third quarter and moved ahead by 9. B. J. wasn't kidding about that third-quarter stuff, was he?

They had us by 12 late in the fourth quarter, and then we made a run. Too late. We lost, 105–101.

Shaq was incredible. He had 32 points, hit 11 of 16 shots, had 11 rebounds, 2 blocked shots, 2 assists, and stayed out of foul trouble. I really knew it wasn't our night when Shaq, who's a terrible free throw shooter, hit 10 of 10 from the line.

After the fast start, I finished with 26. It should have been more, but I'll give Nick his due. He played me tight in the second half.

Wednesday, May 24
Orlando

I'm telling you right now: San Antonio is going down.

Just watched the Rockets beat them again, at San Antonio, and Hakeem was unbelievable. Forty-one points, 16 rebounds. The Dream is the truth. He is eating David alive.

But Hakeem isn't the only one killing the Spurs. Dennis Rodman has destroyed the San Antonio Spurs. Just when you think you have him under control, he comes out and does some new crazy shit.

Can you believe that *Sports Illustrated* cover? He's wearing hot pants, a leather vest with suspenders, and a studded dog collar, and he's holding some kind of exotic bird.

I love guys who aren't afraid to wear the black hat, but this kid goes way beyond the black hat stage. Bo took him out of the game in the third quarter, and Rodman stood there and pouted. Larry sat my ass down for eight minutes during the second half Tuesday, but you didn't hear me bitch and moan.

I used to think I'd want this kid as a teammate just because he plays so hard, has an attitude, and is the best rebounder in the league. But now? No way. I've seen what he's doing to the Spurs, and there's no way they'll recover.

We don't have that problem. Everybody on this team gets along, and that's one of the reasons I think we'll be fine tomorrow. We just can't let them have another 35-point quarter.

All we want is a split. Get a split, win two back at Market Square, and we'll be in great shape.

Thursday, May 25
Orlando

Came out for tip-off tonight, and Shaq has shaved his head and his Fu Manchu. I kind of smiled at him and rubbed my hand on the top of my bald head, thinking, "Well, well. He's back to his old self." That's because he was bald on Dream Team II.

He smiled back and nodded.

Then everybody went at it again. They were up by 11 at the end of the first period, up by 9 at the half, and up by 6 at the end of the third quarter.

Early in the game, Larry was yelling at Jess Kersey about something. He was looking to get me a call, protecting me, which is what a coach is supposed to do. I was standing near Jess, and I told him, "Don't listen to Larry. Don't worry about all this. I don't care about this. I only care about one quarter, the last six minutes."

"You know, Reg," Jess said, "you're exactly right."

All you want are chances to win the game in the last six minutes. We had our chances to win this game tonight and we didn't do it. If we had made one little jump shot, the series would be tied. Instead we lost, 119–114.

We took everything they threw at us—Shaq's 39 points, Scott's 25, Penny's 19, the Magic's 12 of 29 three-point shooting—and still we could have pulled this one out. Then Nick hit a three with 13.9 left, and that put them ahead 116–111. I hit a three to cut the lead to 2, but then Horace broke free, made the basket, and got the foul with 4.4 seconds left.

What hurts is that we actually had the lead late in the game, but we came down three straight times and didn't score. You can't do that in the Eastern Conference Finals and expect to win.

I had 37 points (12 of 18 from the floor), but it's still gonna be a long flight home. If the Magic win this next one, it's almost academic.

Hubert Davis was at the game tonight. Maybe he was subbing for Harper.

Friday, May 26
Indianapolis

We've got to do something about these Orlando kids. We've gotta take away either their outside game or Shaq down low. Right now they're killing us with both. We need to look at the tape and come up with a better game plan because this one isn't working.

Shaq is averaging 35.5 points and shooting 70 percent from the field. Penny, Nick, and Dennis have hit 23 of 47 three-pointers. The Magic is shooting 54.8 percent from the floor.

Now they come to our place up two-love and there's no pressure on them. All they've got to do is make shots, which they've been doing. We've got to put the pressure on them.

If we can even this bad boy up two-all, with three games left, I think we'll win the series. But if they get out of Indiana up 3–1, it's going to be very difficult. We're gonna have to play like Houston did against Phoenix. But if we even it up, then that three-point line is going to start looking like it's twenty-five or twenty-six feet away for the Magic.

I told Larry we ought to let Shaq get his points and try to

shut down everybody else. The other thing we can't do is play
their style of game. We can't get into a 110–, 115–point game
and win. We've got to win it with defense and make them play
our tempo. Instead, we've been getting caught playing their
style. We can't do that helter-skelter stuff and win this thing.

It's hard not to get caught up in their pace. It's almost like
high school when you're wide open on the break and you keep
taking jumpers. But if you miss a few and they don't, you're
dead.

Even our good-luck charms aren't working. Larry flew his
eleven-month-old son L .J. down for game two. We were 17–3
during the regular season when L. J. was at our games. Maybe
his powers don't work during the playoffs.

Saturday, May 27
Indianapolis

We were only down by one at halftime today, 56–55, but we
still weren't playing our style. They were posting up on us and
killing us. They were hitting their outside shots. So we got into
the locker room, and Larry just said, "Hey, we've got to get better individually, and don't be worrying about help [defense] so
much. Just try to play your own guy a little better."

It worked. We played Shaq and Penny straight up, and it
helped our overall defense. We held Orlando to 44 points in
the second half, finally played some Pacer defense, and won
the game, 105–100.

I had 26, but the guys who really played strong were Derrick
and the Davis boys. Derrick had 14 of his 22 points in the second half and hit a huge jumper from the baseline with 54.2
seconds left.

Antonio did a great job on Shaq when Rik was out with foul
trouble. Antonio scored 9 points and had 10 rebounds. Shaq
had 18 points, which is about half of what he was averaging.

Shaq got frustrated with all the banging and bumping, got in foul trouble, and only played thirty minutes.

Dale scored 12 points and had 7 rebounds. He did it with that bad shoulder, too.

Orlando didn't quit, though. Penny hit a big-time three-pointer with 12.1 seconds to cut our lead to 102–98. They fouled, Mark hit both free throws, and we were up by 5 again. But then we fouled Penny on a three-point attempt with 4.2 seconds. If he made the three free throws, they would be only down by 2, and then anything could happen.

As Penny was going to the line, Mark started talking to him. Penny said, "Yeah, I'm gonna knock these down, right. I'm gonna knock these down."

I looked at him and said, "Penny, I guarantee you will not hit three in a row."

"How much you wanna bet?" he said.

"I'm not going to bet anything, but I guarantee you won't make them. Kid, you shoot seventy-five percent at your best from the line. There ain't no way you're gonna make three in a row, especially here."

Sure enough, he clanked the first one.

"Now look," I told him, "I might guarantee that you miss one of these."

He made the next two, but we ended up winning. That Penny, he's a competitor. I like that.

A crazy thing happened during the first quarter. With 2:26 left in the period, the refs stopped the game, went to the scorers table, and a few moments later the public address announcer said the fans had to quit twirling pinwheel signs behind the Magic's goal. Can you believe that shit?

Larry went nuts. I mean, they were spinning those things in Orlando, and nobody said anything. Now we get to Market Square, and they change the rules.

Turns out that John Gabriel, the Magic's vice president of

basketball operations, complained to the league office about our pinwheels, and that's when the refs were told to do something.

I'm telling you, pretty soon basketball is going to be like tennis or golf. You're gonna shoot a free throw, and everyone's going to have to be quiet. Really, who cares if they spin a wheel or play music or yell or whatever? Players don't pay attention to that. You block that stuff out of your mind when you're playing.

Anyway, the refs changed their minds and let the fans do what they always do. Those fans were great today, especially in the fourth quarter.

Sunday, May 28
Indianapolis

Had a 9:30 media session at Market Square, then had practice until 11, then had to do an interview with Ahmad Rashad for "Inside Stuff."

It's been crazy in Indianapolis this weekend. We beat Orlando Saturday. The Indy 500 is today. We play Orlando tomorrow. We're the center of the sports universe.

I've been thinking about these kids from the Magic. A couple of the reporters today kept asking me about the difference between the Magic and the Knicks, if it was harder to get psyched up against Orlando. Hey, it's two different teams, two different cities, two different attitudes. It's tough building up a healthy hate against the Magic when they keep helping you off the floor. Those guys are so apologetic. Maybe it's a con game.

The Knicks aren't like that. The Knicks never help you up. I'm used to Oakley elbowing me, or Starks trying to step on my fingers when I'm down, or someone kneeing me. You know what to expect with the Knicks. The Magic, they're almost too nice. Maybe I'll have to make up things in my head to get more psyched.

But the Magic have grown up a lot. I thought they'd fold come playoff time, but they haven't. Right now they're like a locomotive gaining speed. They've got a lot of confidence. They're hitting from the inside. They're hitting from the outside.

I think that series with Chicago really toughened them up mentally. That's when they went from boys to men. I know Scottie and Michael tried to play mind games with them. The pressure and mental torture those guys can inflict is amazing. Those two guys are the best at getting into someone's head. They keep coming at you until you're mentally worn down.

But they couldn't do it against the Magic. I'm sure having Horace on the team helped a lot. He's a veteran. He's won world championships. He's played with Michael and Scottie. He was able to tell those young Magic players what to expect and how to deal with it.

Monday, May 29
Indianapolis

Call it "The Miracle at Market Square." Call it "The Memorial Day Magic Massacre." Call it whatever you want, but this was a game that will be remembered a long, long time. I'll never forget it. I'll never want to.

We knew Orlando was going to come in today and try to steal this one. There's no way they wanted to leave here without a split.

As usual, Shaq was Shaq. He got in foul trouble early, only played thirty minutes, and fouled out when his team really needed him at the very end of the game. Horace fouled out, too.

But the guy who really scares me is Penny. He shows no fear

of pressure, which is why I really respect his game. We had a 12-point lead in the third quarter until Penny started taking control. A few minutes later we were down 78–75 with about ten minutes left to play. That kid is something special.

They had us down by 6 with 6:30 left, but then Shaq started clanking free throws. He missed four straight. Everybody keeps talking about Shaq having his own personal shot doctor—that Buzz Bramen guy—but if you ask me, the shot doctor ought to be sued for malpractice. Shaq missed every free throw he tried today. Zero for eight. I saw one of our fans hold up a sign that said, "Shaq Briq."

We moved ahead, 89–87, with 1:11 left, but we couldn't add to the lead. The Magic got the ball with 28.4 seconds, called a time-out, and that's when the craziness began.

We were in our huddle, and Larry said, "If they score, make them score going to the hoop. We don't want to give up the three."

We came out of the time-out, and they had all their shooters on the floor: Penny, Nick, Dennis, and Brian Shaw. The ball came in to Penny, and we knew Penny was going to try to make a play. Penny drove, and Mark went over to help on defense a little bit—you know, where you fake a move and then try to get back to your man. But Mark slipped, and Penny found Brian in rhythm. As soon as Brian got the ball and took the shot, I knew the three-pointer was in. Boom, they were up by one with 13.3 seconds in the game. That was the only shot Brian made all game, too.

We called time-out and went to the bench. I said, "Look, we've got plenty of time left, let's just get a good shot." So the coaches started diagramming a play for us. The play was designed to go to Rik. We were going to have a triangle, with me in the deep corner, Derrick positioned about fifteen feet away, and Rik down low. But coming out of the time-out I kind of said, "Forget that. I'll take a shot, and if I miss we'll go for the rebound."

The play started, and I worked my way toward the corner. Then I nudged Nick, who was guarding me, to get him off balance. Then I saw Rik, and I used him as a screen. Mark got me the ball right at the three-point line, and I was thinking, "I'm going for the home run."

The only problem was that I didn't nudge Nick enough. He was right on me. So when I caught the ball and shot, I knew I had to put a little extra arc on it. He got part of my wrist, but there's no way you expect the refs to call a foul that late in the game.

When the shot first left my hands, it looked like it might be a little left. But then I put one of my "Bewitched" spells on it, and it kind of moved right and went in.

Now we were ahead, 92–90, but there were still 5.2 seconds left. I was thinking, "Oh, shit. There's too much time left." Everyone else was jumping up and down, yelling, "All right! This is it!" Usually I'd be jumping up and down with them, but I said, "Nah, this ain't it." I knew there was too much time. This was just like game five of the Knicks series, when they had 5.9 seconds left and Patrick hit the game winner with 1.8 on the clock.

Orlando called a time-out. This time we were in the huddle, and we were saying, "Derrick, you guard Penny, and the rest of the guys will match up. If the ball goes straight inside, we're going to foul because we're up by two." We wanted our best defensive player to guard their best perimeter guy. Derrick is six ten and Penny is six seven, so we knew Penny would have a harder time getting his shot off.

Dennis took it out, and I was on the ball. Haywoode had Shaw. Derrick had Penny. Antonio had Tree Rollins, who came in for Shaq when he fouled out. Mark had Nick.

We took a delay-of-game call just so we could see what kind of play they were going to run. Then I fell back to try to intercept a pass. Shaw and Penny ran a simple play that forces us to switch men. Now Haywoode was on Penny, and Derrick was on Shaw. That meant Penny had at least four inches on Haywoode for a shot.

Penny got the ball, and I thought, "Oh, shit." Sure enough, he just jumped over Haywoode, got a good look, and made a tough three-pointer with 1.3 seconds. They moved ahead, 93–92. I walked toward our sideline, saying, "Ain't this a bitch."

Another huddle. This time we were going to run a play involving me, Byron, and Rik. I was supposed to set up on one side of the low block, Byron was supposed to set up on the other side, and Rik was supposed to be at the top of the key. If everything went the way it was drawn up, Rik would come down to the free throw line, and Byron would cross over him and cut to my side. I'd do the same thing, except I'd cut to Byron's side. Derrick was supposed to throw the ball to the guy who was open off the screen, either me or Byron.

Right before we broke the huddle, Vern told Rik, "Now, Rik, if the ball comes to you, and Tree is on you, you'll have time to pump fake and get a shot off."

I said, "Look, the ball probably ain't gonna go to him."

I wanted the ball in that situation, where I either win or lose the game.

But Orlando did a good job of switching on our X-cut and we couldn't get open. Derrick did a good job of recognizing that, and that's when everything seemed like it was in slow motion. He saw Rik, and threw him the ball. Rik caught it in rhythm. Pump faked. Tree went flying like a bird. Rik took the shot. Bam, we won, 94–93.

I was so overwhelmed with joy I was speechless. Think about it: four game-winning shots in the last 13.3 seconds— Brian's shot, my shot, Penny's shot, Rik's shot. The whole thing was unbelievable.

When Rik hit that fourteen-footer, I've never heard Market Square Arena that loud. It was deafening. You had to be there to understand how fantastic it was. One of our fans rushed down near the scorers table, took off his T-shirt, and threw it at Rik. I've got to get me one of those T-shirts. It said, "Smits Happens."

Back to the O-rena and game five. We've still got a heartbeat. After today's game, it's beating a little louder.

Tuesday, May 30
Orlando

I believe in destiny. This is the third time during the play-offs we've won games that we should have lost: game one against New York, game seven against New York, and game four against Orlando.

I even brought my Michael Jackson *Destiny* CD on the road with me. Listen to it all the time.

Hey, you need a little luck to win a championship. Maybe this is our turn.

Everybody's confidence is high. We think we can steal game five and go back to Indiana with a chance to win it all. The media is killing Orlando. They've got to be feeling the pressure.

Wednesday, May 31
Orlando

This was the third game in this series we could have, should have won. Instead, we lost tonight, 108–106, when Mark missed a game-tying shot at the buzzer.

You can't blame Mark, though. Rik was out of the game with six fouls, so everybody knew that I was first option on the last play. Orlando did a great job of denying me and Byron the ball, so Mark took the shot, which is what he should have done.

He had a great look at the bucket, and that's all you want, a good look. Unfortunately for us, it just missed.

Shaq was a monster tonight. He had 35 points, 13 rebounds, and played forty-two minutes. You could tell he was trying to make up for his two so-so games at our place.

Even though we lost, I still feel good about our chances. We were down by 14 with less than five minutes left, Rik was on the bench, and we still almost beat these kids.

Thursday, June 1
Indianapolis

I'm getting fired up. This Magic team is talking about looking ahead to the NBA Finals, and they haven't even gotten past us yet. I've heard some of their quotes, and it's unbelievable. They're not giving us any credit. We're playing in our home building, and they're acting like they've got the Eastern Conference Finals all locked up.

Houston is still living the dream. They just beat San Antonio. Told you.

Friday, June 2
Indianapolis

Coming into tonight's game, I had played okay. Twenty-six points in game one, 37 in game two, 26 in game three, 23 in game four, 21 in game five. That's a 27-point average, and I was shooting 50 percent from the field and 45 percent from the three-point line. But I hadn't really had one of those big, big games. I had had some scoring spurts, but nothing consistent.

It was a little frustrating, because Nick Anderson was guarding me most of the time. Nick's an okay defender, but it wasn't like Starks was guarding me. Starks is one of the best one-on-one defenders in the league. With Nick, I felt like I could pretty much do anything I wanted. I was getting the looks I wanted, but I wasn't always making the shots. I figured I was due.

Tonight it happened. I scored 20 points in the first quarter, finished with 36, and we drilled the Magic, 123–96. We basically beat them at their own game, which is transition and getting a lot of open looks at threes.

Everybody played great. Mark had 11 points and 12 assists. Byron scored 9 points off the bench. Rik had 22. Vern made an appearance and had a bucket. Plus, we held Penny to 11 points, and for the first time this series, the Magic shot less than 50 percent from the floor.

Some strange shit happened after the game. The Magic players huddled on the court, but I don't have any idea what that was about, but in the postgame interviews they kept saying that we were taunting them, talking shit to them, trying to embarrass them.

First of all, that's bullshit. We didn't say anything to them. We didn't have to. I think this is something they just dreamed up. It's a young team trying to come up with something. The way I look at it, if a team needs to dream up stuff like that, then we've got them. If they need something to be motivated for game seven at their place, then something's wrong. I could see them doing this if they were coming to Indiana, but they're going home.

When they were up 2–0 in Orlando and hitting all those threes and jumping up and down, we weren't crying and complaining. But now we get a big win at home, tie up the series, and they expect us to be all somber?

We've got a little bit of a mental edge on them now. Hopefully, they'll sit on that plane back to Orlando and think about this game and start getting nervous. With the exception of Horace, none of their guys has ever been in the trenches, which is what I call game seven. That could really help us.

I also was a little surprised when a reporter asked me about Larry's comments in today's *Indianapolis News*. Larry apparently said he didn't know what to expect from me in game six, something like, "I don't know. Who can tell?"

So the reporter asked me if I had read the story.

"No," I said, "but thanks for telling me."

Hey, I've been a little inconsistent, but c'mon.

Got home tonight and Mark called. We had watched Houston clinch on Thursday, and the excitement of watching Clyde and Hakeem embrace and celebrate really got to us. We were getting pumped.

"We're there," I said. "We're one game away from playing those kids."

We talked for almost a half-hour. We went over some plays, but all I could think about was doing what Houston had done the night before.

Sunday, June 4
Orlando

This was going to be our game. This was going to be the win that took us to the next level, to the NBA Finals.

Everybody came into the locker room focused on what we had to do. Everybody understood what it would take, especially after what happened to us last season against the Knicks in game seven.

And then we went out there and played one of our worst games at the most important time. The season's over. The Magic killed us, 105–81.

I know it sounds like a simple explanation, but they made plays and we didn't. You can start with me. I only had 12 points and 13 shots. I've got to give Orlando a lot of credit. Everywhere I went, there was a guy right on me.

I'll take the blame for this one. When you're on TV all the time and you're scoring a lot of points and things are going well, everyone pats you on the back. But when things don't go well and you don't perform, then you should take the blame as well. That's how I feel about this one. Game seven is supposed to be my time, but I didn't do it. It wasn't my teammates' fault, it was my mess. No one played great for us, but I'll take the blame. Going into the game, I wanted to take the pressure off my teammates, but I didn't come through.

We were down early, recovered, and then got killed in the third and fourth quarters. Nick played me tight, and when he was on the bench, Anthony Bowie was on me. They had guys popping out to double me, and their strategy worked.

If I had played halfway decent, we would have been in the game. But I didn't, and we weren't even in the game in the second half. Those are normally my quarters, but not today. I lost this game for us.

The Magic and their fans were really jacked up tonight. I have never heard the O-rena like that before. Usually it's a wine-and-cheese crowd, the kind of crowd that isn't very knowledgeable. Knick crowds are knowledgeable; Magic crowds usually aren't.

But tonight they were really into the game, and the Magic fed off their support. Like I said, the Magic made plays and we didn't. They really played well. They shot 57 percent from the field and hit 13 three-pointers.

I was wrong about the Magic. I thought come playoff time they'd crumble. They proved me wrong against Chicago, and they proved me wrong against us. All I can do is congratulate them and move on.

It hurts, though. One game away from the Finals. One game. Again.

After the game, we dressed, did interviews, got on the charter bus to the airport, and then boarded our charter plane back to Indianapolis.

It was quiet on the plane, but it wasn't like a morgue. Guys were congratulating each other on a great season, but still, we were stunned about the way it ended. None of us expected a blowout.

We landed pretty late, but there were two thousand or so fans waiting for us at the airport. That's another reason I'm really disappointed with the way things turned out: Our fans have been behind us from day one. They've been fantastic. They deserve a championship just as much as Houston or Orlando or all the rest of those teams. I feel bad we weren't able to give it to them.

Monday, June 5
Indianapolis

I can't believe the season is over. You put so much time and effort into a season that starts October 6 and ends June 4. We made a lot of progress.

I'm still having a hard time unwinding. I wake up at 8 A.M., and the first thing I think is, "Do I have to go to practice today?" It's hard just lying in bed doing nothing. I'm trying to find things to do.

Drove down to Market Square Arena and cleaned out my locker today. Then I had a meeting with Larry, then a meeting with Donnie. Then I had a physical with the team doctor. It's the same process for every player.

You do the same thing every year. You take down everybody's summer telephone numbers, and everybody lies and says, "Okay, we'll get together and do something."

I don't know what Donnie and Larry have in mind for the draft or free agents or trades, but I know what we need: We need a backup for Rik. We need a backup for Derrick. We need more scoring off the bench. Otherwise, I think we're in good shape for another run.

Tuesday, June 6
Indianapolis

There can't be better fans than ours. About four thousand people came to a Pacers rally downtown today at the City Market, and it really made us feel good.

A few of us addressed the crowd, and Byron was absolutely right when he said we should have given *them* a rally, not the other way around. And Larry, who's been just about everywhere as a coach, said he's never seen so much enthusiasm and loyalty from fans.

Mark Jackson told everyone that we weren't going to stop until we got it right. My feelings exactly. We've come up one game short in each of these last two seasons. Next year is our turn.

I didn't have a whole lot to say. I just wanted everyone to know that we couldn't have won the Central Division or made it to the brink of the NBA Finals without their support.

"We are here," I said, "because of you guys."

It was sort of a strange feeling walking off the stage and into another off-season. I've been trying to figure out a way to wrap up this year, but I don't think I can. We still have a lot of business left undone. We still have more to accomplish.

I know it's not over for me. Until I get to the Finals and have a shot at winning a championship ring, it's not over. I've got to get to the Finals. I've got to perform in the Finals, where everything is on the line.

Until then, I'll keep wearing those two quarters under my wristband. That's because no matter how many points you score, none of it's worth fifty cents unless you get that ring.

Epilogue

- On Friday, June 9, Reggie appeared on the "Tonight Show with Jay Leno." Val Kilmer of *Batman* fame and *Playboy* model Sandra Taylor, who said she thought the Gulf War was started when the United States bombed Jerusalem, were also guests. The highlight of the evening, as far as Reggie was concerned, came when Cheryl Miller made a surprise appearance.
- On Monday, June 12, Dale Davis underwent surgery to repair his injured right shoulder. Doctors said the operation went as expected, and Davis would be ready in time for the 1995–96 season.
- On Wednesday, June 14, the Houston Rockets completed a 4–0 sweep of the Orlando Magic and won their second consecutive NBA championship.
- On Thursday, June 15, Pat Riley resigned as coach of the New York Knicks. The job was later offered to Chuck Daly, who turned it down, and to Don Nelson, who didn't.
- On Tuesday, June 20, *Indianapolis Star* beat reporter Dan Dunkin told friends he was leaving the paper. His wife had accepted a job in Southern California.

- On Saturday, June 24, Byron Scott was selected in the NBA expansion draft by the Vancouver Grizzlies. It was no coincidence that during Scott's two seasons with the Pacers, Indiana advanced to within one victory of the NBA Finals each year.
- On Wednesday, June 28, the Pacers selected five-foot-eleven Georgia Tech point guard Travis Best with the twenty-third pick in the NBA draft, and six-foot-four Iowa State shooting guard Fred Hoiberg with the fifty-second selection.
- On Friday, June 30, assistant coach George Irvine accepted a similar position with the Golden State Warriors.
- On Sunday, July 30, Reggie was officially selected to play on the 1996 USA men's Olympic basketball team.
- On Friday, October 6, the Pacers were scheduled to depart for Chapel Hill, North Carolina, and the start of training camp. The pursuit of unfinished business would begin anew.

Printed in the United States
By Bookmasters